THE WEATHER FACTOR

ALSO BY ERIK DURSCHMIED

THE HINGE FACTOR

THE
WEATHER
FACTOR

HOW NATURE HAS
CHANGED HISTORY

ERIK DURSCHMIED

ARCADE PUBLISHING · NEW YORK

FIRST U.S. EDITION 2001

ISBN 1-55970-558-2
Library of Congress Control Number 00-135877
Library of Congress Cataloging-in-Publication Data is available.

Published in the United States by Arcade Publishing, Inc.,
New York
Distributed by Time Warner Trade Publishing

Visit our Web site at www.arcadepub.com

10 9 8 7 6 5 4 3 2 1

EB

PRINTED IN THE UNITED STATES OF AMERICA

For William and Alexander

Contents

List of Maps

Acknowledgements

An author, describing real events, does not work in a vacuum. His critique of events that have led to (sometimes avoidable) dramas builds on work that has come before him, from Latin scribes to contemporary reports, though often downplayed or suppressed. And yet, everything has been written up – after the event!

Some of the events, though relatively minor in scale, can compare by their historical impact to the truly massive battles of recent memory. So, for example, while the affair in the Teutoburger Wald of AD 9 saw some 40,000 warriors facing each other, during the Battle of Moscow in 1941, 40,000 cannons thundered, and millions of soldiers died. And yet, big or small, every one of these events produced a pivotal point to history.

I have solicited the advice of eminent present-day historians to guide me in my choice. Other accounts, such as that of the Roman Tacitus, are well recorded and may be found in major libraries. I wish to express my gratitude to the writers whose own efforts provided a valuable foundation and inspiration for my own, in particular the geostrategist Gen. Pierre Gallois (French Airforce, retired) and the West Point historian, Col. Ken Hamburger (US Army, retired), the former German commando leader, Col. Otto Skorzeny (deceased), the expert on Irish history, Robert Kee, the survivor of the terrible typhoon and skipper of the USS Dewey, Capt.

Raymond Calhoun, (US Navy, retired). Their personal accounts were crucial in making this book a reality.

I would also like to thank the many members of the various research institutes I consulted, and without whose help such endeavour would have been impossible: Deutsches Historisches Institut (Paris), Japanese Cultural Institute (Tokyo), Bibliotheque de la Ville de Paris, Institut Neerlandais (Paris), Library of the US Military Academy (West Point), Archives Nationales (Paris), Archives of the Irish College (Paris), Militär-geschichtliche Forschungsabteilung (Vienna), and other research institutions.

THE
WEATHER
FACTOR

Prologue

'. . . winds light to variable . . .'

When it rains, everybody gets wet.
Popular saying.

If you talk about the weather, everyone listens.

'What kind of a day is it?' asks the sweet voice as your alarm goes off. You climb out of bed, grope your way to the window, stare bleary-eyed up at grey clouds and down into puddles, and you groan. 'It's raining.' Many others groan at the same time. The farmer because the rainstorm has flattened his wheatcrop, the young couple about to tie the knot who know that their garden party is off, or the general who's just been told that his tanks are mired in mud. Their day is truly spoiled.

'. . . *winds light to variable* . . .' The weather forecast has become the principal morning information for millions. A nation's humour varies with the weather, especially for those who do not work in a sheltered environment. Fishermen, construction workers and bicycle racers, they all have to suffer the caprice of the weather god. As do soldiers. Not to forget the insurance executive who trembles at the mere thought of a flood. To him, policy-wise, any natural disaster is simply referred to as an 'Act of God'.

Acts of God and the weather have had their profound influence on history. From the destruction of Rome's legions to the first atomic bomb, the list is endless. And will continue to be so in the future.

The old man stared up at the gathering clouds. 'There's only one thing to do now.'

'And what's that?' asked his wife.

'Pray.'

Then the wind came and destroyed all that man had untiringly built.

The Bible tells us so

An Act of God

'And, behold, I do bring a flood of waters upon the Earth, to destroy all flesh, wherein [is] the breath of life, from under Heaven.
Genesis 6:17

The same day were all the fountains of the great deep broken up, and the windows of heaven were opened.
Genesis 7:11

'You must build a boat,' the dog said to his master, *'and put in it all that you would save; for a great rain is coming that will flood the land.'*
A tribal tale from the
Cherokee Indians of America.[1]

One may well imagine the excitement, on that day in Nineveh, in Babylonia, when the spade of an archaeologist struck a solid object and out came the first of a thousand clay tablets, bearing cuneiform writing. It had been lying

[1] Ancient Sumerian, Akkadian and Greek versions all recount the same basic flood story.

undisturbed in the ground for thousands of years.[2] In honour of a mythical Sumerian king who reigned around 3000 BC they bestowed on it the name, the *Gilgamesh Epic*. Could this be part of the original bible? What George Smith translated in 1872 turned out to be the first recorded description of Noah and the Flood:

> ... I caused to embark within the vessel all my family and my relations, the beasts of the field, the cattle of the field, the craftsmen, I made them all embark. I entered the vessel and closed the door ...
>
> From the foundations of heaven a black cloud arose ...
>
> All that is bright turned into darkness ... For six days and nights wind and flood marched on, the storm subdued the land. When the seventh day dawned, the storm was abated, the flood which had waged war like an army, and all mankind was turned into mud ...'[3]

Recent research points to a *biblical flood* as having taken place around 5600 BC, in the Black Sea region. At that time, a solid rock wall, the Bosphorus, blocked off an interior sweet water lake from the Mediterranean. A sudden change in temperature – sudden by the Earth's clock, meaning several millenniums – led to the melting of the Eurasian ice sheet. This brought about a rise in the ocean's water level and the Bosphorus barrier collapsed 7,600 years ago.[4] Without restraint, water poured into the Black Sea at frightening speed. An area of some 155,000 square kilometres became inundated. The deluge forced families of hunters and gatherers to migrate as far south as Egypt and Babylon, and this explains how primitive northern tribes ended up in the

[2] Probably written around 700 BC, but could be considerably older.
[3] Charles Berlitz, *The Search for Noah's Ark*.
[4] The time was established by drilling into the Greenland icecap and studying the layers.

biblical land of the pharaohs. The tale of their miraculous escape (in Noah's ark) was carried over from generation to generation, and eventually written up in *Genesis* and *Gilgamesh*.

Sudden changes in atmospheric conditions will lead to cataclysms; gales and floods, rainstorms and droughts, scorching heat and bitter cold, the list of nature's calamities is endless. Struck by the unexpected, or unpredictable, the impact of violent weather fronts in combination with the colossal forces of nature unleashed against us, leads on to disaster. Suddenly the world we live in changes and man goes down on his knees to pray for divine assistance. Sometimes it is granted, more often not.

Since time immemorial, history has been influenced by nature's elements. The mega-fauna that once covered the globe was extinguished by climatic changes. A sudden drop in temperature killed off the ferocious predators and dinosaurs. Then appeared a creature that managed to walk upright, and who ran around in the nude, suffering from one of two extremes, cold or heat. His initial act was to kill some furry animal and wrap himself in his victim's hide. He ripped a flaming branch from a tree that had been struck by lightning, and carried the torch into his cave to kindle the original campfire. This Age of Fire was followed by the Age of Tools, when man built primitive shelters against sun and snow, wind and rain. It protected him from daily and seasonal weather changes.

The life or death of the people on our planet has always depended on a few degrees up or down. One may well imagine the terror of primitive man, when the days grew shorter and colder and the nights longer. He must have been wondering: will the sun ever return? Is it therefore astounding that man has considered the weather as something supernatural, falling into the realm of a god or a devil? Meteorological phenomena have always been connected with the diabolical or the divine. Our ancestors interrogated the heavens, invoked the saints, and suffered the heaven-made catastrophes. They turned to frogs and almanacs for information about rain and sunshine. They knelt in front of images of patron saints in supplication for the essential gift of life-giving water, or alternatively to stop the water from drowning them. They would go to any lengths to conjure the heavens.

Today we know that spring follows winter as surely as day follows night. We know much more; for instance, that the fertility rate increases during a certain period of the lunar cycle.[5] A scientist will explain that this has to do with gravitation, light, and the variations in the Earth's magnetic fields, which again have an influence on human sexual behaviour. This is a fact that peasants in my village had been aware of long before the age of supercomputers. Does that mean that meteorologists with their eyes riveted on satellite pictures from space, which tell them all about cloud formations over Greenland, anti-cyclones over the Azores and the air humidity in Borneo, are better informed than the peasants in my village? Our farmers listen to the meteorological forecasts then abide by the good sense of their ancestors; they sniff the air, stick up their finger to test the direction of the wind, and study the nervous state of cattle and flies. Only if everything is to their satisfaction do they plant their trees or seed the corn. When sunflowers let their heads hang down in July, they need rain. When it rains in August, it will flatten the wheat harvest, but there will be plenty of truffles in January. Why? Not even our *curé* has an answer to that mystery.

All those who listen attentively to the daily weather prediction will get a general overview for the next hours

[5] The menstrual cycle of a woman is that of the full cycle of the moon, twenty-eight days.

or days. There is one thing neither a scientist nor a farmer can predict – the arrival of a meterological disaster. When it strikes, it does so with the unbridled force of the elements, sudden and deadly whether they be typhoons, avalanches, storm floods, biting frost, hellish forest fires and killer fog, to name but a few. Weather fronts have had their profound and lasting influence on human history. Legions were destroyed in a thunderstorm, armadas sank in a typhoon, tanks got bogged down in mud, an invading army froze to death, and an atomic war ended before it even began.

It is not always foul weather that carries bad news. Good visibility, just as poor visibility, is a vital factor for planners of a military operation. Any such sudden change in 'favourable atmospheric conditions' can turn a well-laid plan into a nightmare. An attack, launched under the cover of fog, can turn into horror if the fog lifts and the bombers can spot their targets. But for the masses of apocalyptic believers, the bleaker prophecies of storm disasters still carry that thrillingly familiar ring: paralysis and panic. For centuries, intellectuals have laughed at the scared and the frightened. Now they themselves are beginning to head for the hills.

In the past, meteorological predictions were mainly by educated guess, and its prevailing conditions decided by God or Good Luck. Predicting the weather has always been a risky enterprise, and our credulity may still be taxed by the latest weather report. Today the world listens to the weatherman's outpouring on the global media. His weather forecast is an economic factor: farmers, truckers, seamen, airline pilots, even stockbrokers tune in to the man on the radio. '. . . *rain showers, accompanied by high winds, expected by noon* . . .'

The biblical flood may be the first recorded weather factor that has profoundly changed history. From those biblical days, if we dare believe historians and their contemporary accounts, the world has gone downhill. Mankind has always had to struggle against the elements more often than against each other. But when the two forces – weather fronts and human conflict, – collide it invariably leads to disaster.

An Act of God.

The lost legions of Varus

11 September, AD 9

'Varus, Varus, give me back my legions!'
Emperor Augustus, AD 9.[1]

It is the year AD 9, one autumn evening in the land of the Cherusci.[2] Above the majestic pines, the golden sky is full of swarming carrion birds, following a column of soldiers that winds like some giant snake on the trail through the primeval woods. For hours, three Roman legions have struggled along this narrow trail, more a goat-path than a cart track. The advance units have to force their way through masses of resistant undergrowth and clinging creepers; their bare arms and legs are cut and scratched, and now mosquitoes settle on the festering sores. Occasional stone heaps topped by bleached skulls, altars to a pagan god, point to a presence of native tribes of the region. But for the vanguard of Roman legionaries, only able to see a small section in front of them, all is peaceful and quiet; only an occasional squirrel or hare flits across the forest floor. And yet, everyone, from *tribun*

---

[1] Gaius Suetonius Tranquillus, second century AD.
[2] Braunschweig, or Brunswick.

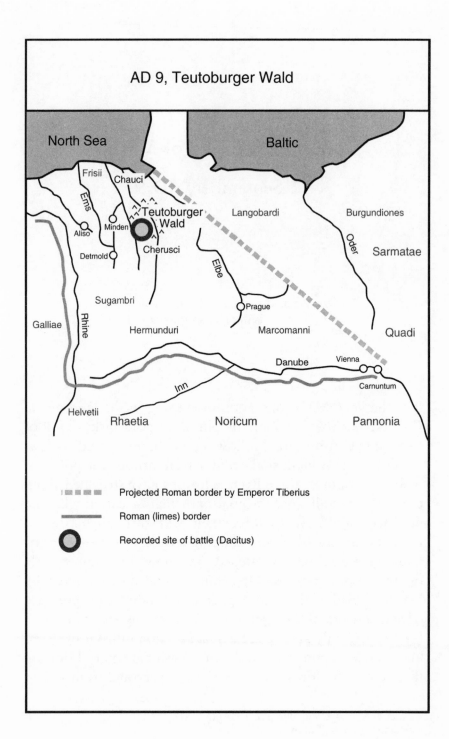

AD 9, Teutoburger Wald

North Sea

Baltic

Frisii

Chauci

Teutoburger
Wald

Langobardi

Burgundiones

Ems

Minden

Aliso

Cherusci

Detmold

Elbe

Oder

Sarmatae

Sugambri

Prague

Galliae

Rhine

Hermunduri

Marcomanni

Quadi

Danube

Vienna

Inn

Carnuntum

Helvetii

Rhaetia

Noricum

Pannonia

▪ ▪ ▪ ▪ Projected Roman border by Emperor Tiberius

─────── Roman (limes) border

◉ Recorded site of battle (Dacitus)

and *centurion* on to legionary, feels unease in these unfamiliar surroundings, hemmed in on either side by tall trees. The track is like a tunnel, overhung by an interwoven net of branches that form a vaulted dome with its natural penumbrae; a narrow passage between trees, too closed in for the archers to make use of their arrows in case of an ambush. The experienced *centurions* dare not tell their splendidly garbed *tribun*, a close relative of Emperor Augustus,[3] that it is most unwise to march into this hostile wilderness without sending out patrols to reconnoitre their front or protect their flanks. Another bend in the track, the last one hopefully and they must surely step out into the open plain. But behind that bend is yet another, and then another. The trail meanders along like a creek, from forest to swamp and from swamp into forest. The Romans feel out of control, as if borne along by a river's current. Swamps enclose them. A careless step to the side will spell certain death by being sucked down into the morass by the weight of their armour. And if they are not crossing a swamp, there is always that deep, dark, worrisome forest.

On the heels of the legions follows a haphazard procession of wagons, pack animals and push carts; women with babbling, suckling babies, cooks, money-lenders, prostitutes, and all the human flotsam raked together from military compounds that can be found anywhere in the realm of Emperor Augustus. With cries of anguish and curses, this mob pummels the ones in front to stay closed up with the legions. Their laden carts rattle with bone-crushing jolts over thigh-thick roots, only to sink into the deep ruts left by the supply wagons of the legions. Everyone prays for an end to the unholy wood.

The forest deadens all sense of time and space. The vanguard, made up of natives under the leadership of a Cherusci

---

[3] In 12 BC, on the death of Lepidus, Augustus became *Pontifex Maximus*.

nobleman, Arminius, advance around a bend; when the first of the Roman cohorts turn the same corner, the Cherusci are gone, swallowed up by the forest. Since Arminius and his local scouts are the only ones who know their way around these forests, the Romans halt in confusion when they come to a fork in the road. The day's march has exhausted them so they do not hear the sound of breaking branches, and, all of a sudden, several frightful, fur-covered creatures pop up in front of them. They carry spears and maces, their skulls are shaven and their eyes burn with fierce fire. The Romans are so surprised that not one moves until the weird creatures gallop off into the distance. A detachment of legionaries chases after the fugitives, but they've vanished. Their appearance is a clever ruse: it lures the Roman formations onto a trail, which leads them straight towards an ambush.

'They're here . . . quite near,' whisper the Roman legionaries. But where? They will soon find out.[4]

Half a century before, in 59 BC, Julius Caesar – fatalistically brave, totally cynical, and coldly cruel – began with the 'pacification' of *Gallia* (Gaul), and thereby pushed Rome's outer frontiers to the Rhine. His next ambitious project was to extend the Empire's border across the Rhine, to the big rivers of central Germany, and thus assure the protection of his *'acropolis italae'* (Upper Italy and Rome) and *Provincia Transalpina* (Provence) from the incursion by Alamannic tribes[5], who the chronicle of Dio Cassius described as 'a riff-raff of the basest kind'.

Having successfully stopped an invasion of 250,000 Helvetes by cutting the bridges across the Rhone at Geneva, he turned

---

[4] From records by contemporary Roman scribes, Tacitus, Velleius Paterculus, Dio Cassius.
[5] Quoted by Asinius Quadratus. (Alamanni, for *all men*, a loose league of tribes.)

north to smash King Ariovistus and his Suevian hordes in the Alsatian Plain. Next, Caesar led eight legions across the Rhine and pacified the region around *Colonia Agrippina* (Cologne) and *Bonna* (Bonn). At *Augusta Treverorum* (Trier), 200,000 Asipetis were no match for Caesar's highly disciplined 50,000 legionaries. Faced by Rome's military might, many of the tribal chieftains slipped away to escape captivity. Caesar promised clemency and presents, organised a great feast to which he invited all the leaders who had gone into hiding. Once they had sat down at his table, Caesar's legionaries cut off their heads. After which deed he set upon the leaderless tribes and massacred them.[6]

The Roman Republic died with Cicero and the Empire began with Julius Caesar, an empire based on the spirit of conquest and which owed its unity to the permanent presence of its soldiers in the confines of its enormous territory. Its military prestige was the cement of military power. Rome's legions were omnipresent, striking at their enemies without pity, flattering their allies, barring the route to barbarians. With great sovereignty, Rome distributed war and peace. *Pax Romana.*

At the time of Caesar, many Germanic tribes had moved from their forest redoubts into the open plains, and established villages on agricultural plains, primarily along the main rivers. This was to lead them into conflict with the Romans; when out in the open, barbarians proved no match for the well-disciplined Roman war machine. When, in the following year, Caesar crossed the Rhine near Confluentes (Koblenz), he defeated the Sugambri, a tribe that Caesar described thus: 'Their life is made up of hunting and military pursuits, eager for toil and hardship. They eat milk, cheese and flesh, and show no interest in agriculture. Their leaders may well fear that their people could substitute agriculture

---

[6] Dio Cassius, *Roman History* (transl. by E. Gary, 1916).

for the conquest of the warrior.'[7] From this description we may surmise that the majority of Germanic tribes were of nomadic origin. Caesar was quick to discover that pagan tribes hated each other, and the shrewd politician and opportunist ably used this information to *divide et impera*, divide and rule. Caesar's assassination put an end to his plans for the ultimate conquest of Germany. After his death, his *divide et impera* diplomacy was abandoned, and instead the power of suppression, backed up with Roman spears, raised its ugly head.

The Germanic tribes, according to Tacitus[8], who was to become their intimate chronicler, were 'large of body, fair-haired and blue-eyed. They carried no body-mail, but were armed with short, lethal spears (*framae*), and fought as one solid body, thereby they could easily be decimated by a hail of arrows from the Roman archery.'

What set the barbarians apart from their Roman invaders was an unshakeable belief in their own, fierce gods, a belief contrary to the deepest conviction of the human spirit: 'The gods are doomed and the end is death.'[9] *Valhalla*, home to their divinities, was a truly fearsome gathering of helmeted warriors, whose main activity lay in the pursuit of war. *Valhalla* was a place of extremes, of burning fires and utter darkness. Such a martial heaven held no place for a goddess of love or one of beauty; its womenfolk were *Valkyries*,[10] riding into battle to do the will of Odin. He decided who should die, and the *valkyries* led the fallen heroes to eternal glory through the gates of *Valhalla* and kept their *met* (beer) horns filled: Baldur, the God of Light, was murdered by his blind brother Hod; Fricka, goddess of marriage, looked after earthly morals; Odin (or Wotan),

---

7 Caesar, *Gallic Wars*.
8 Tacitus (AD 55–101), *Germania*.
9 In the Old Edda, like the Book of Revelation.
10 *Val* stood for the slain.

the god of warriors and kings was unforgiving;[11] he even banished his own, disobedient daughter Brünnhilde to a fiery rock. Tyr was the God of War, and Freya was a splendid, golden-haired goddess who claimed half of those slain in battle, something as natural to a warrior as dying for a woman's beauty. But fiercest of all the gods was Thor the Hammer, lord of thunder. With his mighty hammer Möllnar, the symbol of lightning, he hurled thunderbolts to smite his enemies.[12] Thus, lightning and thunder became the voice of a god and an auspicious omen for victorious combat.

During battle, tribal custom demanded that the barbarians equal their headman's prowess, and by their own gallant action add to his glory. The freely elected tribal chieftain was 'father to his people', his word was law, and he wielded power over life and death. Yet he was no dictator,[13] and any decision affecting the whole tribe, such as going to war against their neighbours, depended on a council of elders. Once such approval was given, the headman became supreme commander. In that sense, Alamannic rule was a curious mixture of democracy and feudalism.

Any successful chieftain's principal weapon was stealth and trickery. To bring down an enemy, especially a Roman, by any means was acceptable and honest. 'Against such tribesmen, mistrust was the surest defence – for those who were trusted effected the most mischief.' How true Strabo's prediction was to turn out to be.[14]

The *legat* who marched Rome's legions to the River Elbe was Consul Domitius Ahenabarbus (AD 1). For this

---

[11] Already mentioned by Tacitus in AD 98.

[12] Thor gave his name to Thordag, or Thursday. His symbol, the hammer, was found as jewellery in many warrior graves.

[13] Hitler liked to portray himself as the leader of a Germanic tribe, but he was not.

[14] Strabo, or Strabon, Greek geographer (58 BC – AD 25), author of *Memoires historique* and *Geographica*.

feat, Emperor Augustus decorated him with the *ornamenta triumphalia*. His successor was Marcus Vinicius (AD 4), who had fought under Tiberius in his drive to the River Visurgis (Weser). Then followed Publius Quintilius Varus. He had been elevated in rank to *consul* in 13 BC, and took over the command of the Army of the Rhine in AD 6. His legions had crossed the border river to 'keep the peace'; instead they moved like a plague across the countryside, feeding themselves off the land and leaving nothing for those who tilled the earth. They carted off winter provisions, thus condemning villagers and their families to death by starvation. If stealing food wasn't enough, Roman tax collectors harassed the locals, and robbed them of anything of value. Rings, ornaments and personal arms were impounded and distributed among centurions and legionaries. Should a tribe dare to object, or refuse to pay taxes, Varus' soldiers strung up the occupants of whole villages on trees. Survivors fled into the dense forests, formed bands and lived off the land (which did little to ease the life of the villagers). They attacked Roman patrols, and the Romans responded by sending out punitive expeditions that spent their fury on innocent, defenceless villagers. But like all soldiery on soft garrison duty faced by a negligible enemy, their morale collapsed. While the ordinary soldiers raped women, their officers stuffed themselves with food, and afterwards even forced the villagers to carry their loot for them. Yes, there was much injustice, but Rome was far away, and the emperor's attention focused on his conquests in the east, or on surviving intrigues at court.

In 17 BC, the Sugambri tribe revolted and caught *Tribun* Marcus Lollius in a marshy region, where they inflicted a costly defeat on his soldiers, though more by ridiculing the image of its *tribun* than by lasting damage to Rome's military capacity. Velleius Paterculus reports: 'In all his wars, Emperor Augustus never received any ignominious defeat except in

Germany, under his lieutenants Lollius and Varus.'

This defeat sent a clear message to Emperor Augustus who became preoccupied with his imperfect frontier, the *limes*, bordered by the Danube to the south and the Rhine to the west. This left a huge, wide-open salient, which put emphasis on the importance of establishing a suitable connection between Rome's Rhine and Danube armies.[15] The emperor's strategic plan called for the establishment of a new, fortified river borderline, to run approximately from today's Bremen across Bohemia to Vindobona (Vienna).[16] He assigned a large body of troops to push his empire's limits far east, to the Weser River, and thus forestall the threat of a barbarian attack on Gaul, or south, across the Alps.

Assigned to the task were his adopted sons, *Tribun* Drusus, and his brother, *Tribun* Tiberius.[17] Drusus, a man of unbridled ambition, was not merely content to punish the breakaway Sugambri, but he also annexed the entire territory of the salient that lay between Danube and Rhine. He established his headquarters in Mogontiacum (Mainz). In 11 BC, his army set forth into the unknown territory from two heavily fortified positions along the Rhine. His advance took him east into the Harz Forest, into Thuringia, land of the Marcomanni. Then he swung north and entered Cherusci territory. After he had 'pacified' that tribe, he crossed Brunswick and was headed for the Elbe River, when his ambition came to a sudden end. In 9 BC, Drusus was thrown from his horse and broke his neck. Tiberius took command over the legions. Like his illustrious forebear, Caesar, Tiberius exploited the barbarians' great weakness, their inter-tribal

[15] Not achieved until Emperor Domitian established a number of strong points in AD 90.
[16] Similar in strategy to Napoleon's *Rhine Federation* (1806) to protect France's eastern borders against Russia and Austria.
[17] Sons of Livia, later wife of Augustus, who intrigued to have both adopted by Emperor Augustus as his sons. Tiberius followed Augustus in AD 14 onto the throne.

jealousies. Playing the various tribes against each other with promises and gifts, their warriors, though huge, blond, and fearsome to look at, failed to unite in a common front against the usurper. This became the decisive factor, one that the Roman general aptly used to bring his German campaign to a successful conclusion. Divided, the barbarians went down in defeat, time and again, before the Roman eagles.

By 7 BC, most of Northern Germany had become Roman. The tribes had been subdued, yet peace had not been achieved: in 1 BC, the Cherusci tribe went into open revolt, serious enough for Emperor Augustus to order *Legatus* Tiberius back[18] into Germany and confirm the authority of Rome. Tiberius collected an army with which he set off in AD 4. He vanquished the Cherusci and then their neighbours, the Langobardi (Lombards), with customary brutality, before he sailed as far north as Jutland, where his force got stuck in the snows of Scandinavia. Assembling a new army in Carnuntum[19], Tiberius crossed the Danube to attack the Marcomanni of Bohemia, while another force, under *Tribun* Saturninus, marched from the Rhine. The Marcomanni were saved from extinction by a revolt in far-off Illyricum and Pannonia, which called for Tiberius to abandon the Bohemian campaign and rush south to crush the rebellion.

Tiberius knew that it would be unwise to leave his newly conquered territories without protection. He left five legions to hold the forts which he had established along the big central German rivers. Command over this occupation force was handed to the *Tribun* Publius Quintilius Varus, a court-appointee, as lazy as he was stupid, and more accustomed to the leisure of the camp than to actual service in war.[20] Varus was the grandson of Mark Anthony by his daughter Antonia,

[18] His rank had been upgraded.
[19] Hainburg, near Vienna.
[20] Velleius Paterculus.

and had astutely wed the grandniece of Emperor Augustus. As Rome's corrupt *legatus* (governor) of Syria, he had amassed a personal fortune, selling favours to tradesmen and collecting tribute from the population. The Syrians knuckled down to his demands; the Germans did not.

With Gaul pacified, and the victorious campaigns of Tiberius which had left the German tribes without a leader, Varus enjoyed a 'soft job': his garrison life was one long series of feasts, gluttony, and high-class prostitutes, all paid for by local taxes. With it, he set a bad example for his soldiers, who turned indolent and lax. Not one of the five legions under his command underwent regular military training, and soldiers were used to steal cattle and bring in taxes. Legionaries took wives or simply kidnapped tribal women to make them their concubines, and military camps grew into shantytowns.

During his entire tenure as governor of Alemannia, Varus failed to discover the difference between the malleable Syrians he had dominated before and the ferocious barbarians he was trying to govern now. Whether he was just weak, or outright oppressive, has never been fully established. Whatever the reason, he dug his grave the moment he began to exact tribute from the tribes to fill his personal coffers. Gold was rare, and the Germans were not about to give it up willingly. Nor did they take it lightly when their wives or daughters were dragged off to service legionaries and bear their bastard offspring.

In AD 9, while Emperor Augustus's attention was focused on court intrigues at the Capitol, and Tiberius was kept busy in Dalmatia, a message reached *Legatus* Varus. In early September, unrest had broken out in the region between the Weser and the Ems Rivers, in a densely forested-region settled by the Cherusci. Irate villagers had dumped his tax collectors into a river, a report that Varus did not take entirely seriously since he knew that the Cherusci leader, Sigimur, was someone who had always kept the peace. But he had reckoned without the leader's son, Arminius, a firebrand, who Tacitus was to call 'the incendiary of Germany'. His notoriety was well deserved.

Arminius was born in 17 BC. From early boyhood he had acquitted himself bravely and earned the respect of his tribe. Together with his brother Flavius he had served in the Roman army, but little is known about him, except that he was tall and powerfully built, an aristocrat of the highest rank who had accompanied Roman *tribuns* for a number of years. At twenty-six, he had more than once shown his valour and intelligence in the service of Tiberius during the Illyrian campaign. For his bravery and leadership qualities he was raised to Roman nobility of equestrian rank ('*Iuvenis nominae Arminius assiduus militiae nostrae prioris comes, iure etiam civitatis Romanae . . .*[21]) and made a *praefectus* in the Roman Army. Yet there was one thing the Romans didn't know: Arminius was a fiercely patriotic German. Since childhood days, having been witness to a massacre of one of his tribe's villages by legionaries, this seasoned leader carried in him a fanatical hatred of all that was Roman.

For years, while serving under different Roman *tribuns*, Arminius had looked on helplessly at the tragedy that had befallen his people. Their sad destiny in defeat became an obsession. It gnawed at Arminius. Time and again, he reminded his father of the fate that awaited a subdued Cherusci nation. While his father counselled patience, a rage burned in the young man's chest; from his own military experience he searched for a way to buttress his people against continued Roman slavery, though this was not an easy task.

The Roman Empire was based on the spirit of conquest

[21] Tacitus.

and owed its unity exclusively to the permanent presence of its soldiers within the confines of its enormous territory. Rome's army was made up of professional soldiers, every one a Roman citizen (although few were Italians), uniformly dressed in short metal armour worn over a shift, shin protectors and helmet, and boots (*caligae*). They were armed with the *pilum* (javelin), a short sword for close combat, and an oval shield made of cowhide and painted in each legion's colour. A legion (division), under a *tribun*, was divided into ten cohorts (battalions) of six centuries (companies) each, commanded by a *centurion*. The *legatus* was a court appointed governor, superior in rank to the military.

Arminius knew from experience that facing the Roman war machine in open battle must inevitably lead to disaster. He had stuided the fate of Vercingetorix and his gallantly fierce Gauls, who went down to defeat before the highly trained, disciplined legions of Caesar (52 BC). The Germanic tribes were anything but disciplined, totally undependable, involved in petty rivalries, and could not possibly match the supremacy of Roman infantry, archery and cavalry. And finally, a headman couldn't order up a tribe like a *tribun* could call up a legion; a tribal chief had to send out secret messengers (who could be intercepted by Romans, or by jealous tribal chiefs), then pray that enough warriors would follow his call to make a stand. It was also a choice of the terrain for a successful confrontation. Rome's garrisons were strongly walled forts, invulnerable to attack. But outside their stockade, the emperor's legions were exposed, especially if caught in a place where they couldn't deploy into their standard battle formations.

In AD 8 Arminius had joined the *Legatus* and *Tribun* Varus[22] as the leader of a contingent of Cherusci auxiliaries.

---

[22] Both his administrative and military titles.

At the same time, he began to work out a devious plan, which would bring Varus into the open. To lure the bear from its lair needed a valid reason, such as an uprising or, as it happened in this case, the rumour of one.

Arminius soon discovered that Varus was no Tiberius. He held the *tribun* in justified contempt and was prepared to use the Roman's carelessness 'as an opportunity for treachery, sagaciously seeing that no one could be more easily overpowered than the man who feared nothing, and that the most common beginning of disaster was a sense of security'.[23] Varus had always failed to take the most elementary precautions, marching from camp without the necessary reconnaissance, and there was no reason to assume he would change his style. It was early fall, time for the return of Varus's three legions from their summer camp on the Weser to winter quarters in Aliso (Haltern) on the Lippe. Being in the *tribun*'s confidence, he knew that Varus was planning on a detour, to teach the 'rebellious villagers' a lesson. Arminius's only concern was the superior Roman numbers, and for that, it needed a bold plan, for his aim was nothing less than the annihilation of Rome's occupation forces. He had to bring about an alliance of all tribes. With that in mind, he cast aside his caution, began agitating against Varus, and secretly contacted the tribes.

Arminius had an uncle, Segestes, brother of Sigimur, who thought that the leadership of the Cherusci should be rightfully his, and failing to get the tribe's vote, had turned into an informer of Varus, the Roman. To make matters worse, Arminius had fallen in love with Segestes' daughter, Thusnelda, a fair maiden with flaxen braids. The young couple eloped, and for that affront, Segestes hated the young warrior.

[23] Velleius Paterculus.

Arminius knew that there was no room for complacency in a land with a long history of tribal conflict. He had met secretly with tribal elders, not only Cherusci, but also Amsivari, Marsi, Bructi, Langobardi and Chatti. After much argument and bargaining, he convinced them to lay aside their fratricidal strife and join him in one supreme effort to rid their homelands of the invader. Despite the suspicion and hostility from some of the leaders, a plot took shape. Arminius outlined his plan, which was voted and accepted. What must be a unique course in the history of early medieval Germany, the tribes purged their leadership of all cantankerous, undependable elements by electing Arminius as their sole chieftain. But such conspiracy was vast, and couldn't be kept secret, certainly not from someone as well connected as his uncle Segestes. 'Don't trust Arminius,' Segestes tried to warn Varus, 'he is plotting and you must throw him in irons or he will destroy you.' Varus, well aware of the bitterness between Segestes and his nephew Arminius, who happened to be one of his most reliable lieutenants, thought of this accusation as the vengeance of an old man to settle his personal feud, and so ignored the warning. If anything, it convinced Varus that there was no danger whatsoever. As ultimate irony, the 'trustworthy' Arminius was handed command over the vanguard to guide the columns through the inhospitable forest region. Thus, Varus provided Arminius with the opportunity to lead three Roman legions into a trap.

The first week of September, AD 9, began without a hint of the coming disaster. Having spent their summer pleasantly enough on the banks of the Weser, the legions expected to reach their winter quarters within a week's march. They had been told that their *tribun* was planning on a minor detour to teach some rebellious villagers a lesson. Before the long columns set out, Arminius dispatched messengers to his allies, to congregate with their warriors in the Teutoburger Wald.[24]

One autumn morning, Varus rode out of summer camp at the head of a mighty force, the *XVIIth, XVIIIth* and *XIXth Legions*, plus three *ali* of cavalry and six *cohorts* of auxiliaries. *Cataphractarii* and *clibanarii* (heavy cavalry) in full mail[25] followed the foot soldiers and archers with their colour-coded shields (a colour for each unit and legion). Altogether, well over 20,000 heavily armed men trailed by a confused and chaotic wagon train of spouses and camp followers.

The trap was in place.

In those distant days, the forests between the Weser and Ems were made up of primeval growth with pines well over one hundred feet tall. Through this dark and sinister wilderness led only primitive trails, trampled out by wild beasts since the age of time. Such tracks were narrow and slippery, and crossed with thick roots, which had to be cut to allow the passage of the heavy carts. The weight of their armour and a stifling humidity made the legionaries sweat under their leather jerkins. And yet, despite the oppressive heat, they could feel a chill inching its way to their bones. They knew that the barbarians were around, unseen but observing. Centurions, standing out in their bright crimson tunics, called for more speed, trumpets blared, and legionaries tightened the straps on their helmets and steeled themselves for any ordeal that lay ahead.

From the moment that Arminius and his Cherusci scouts vanished, the Romans were lost. The legions stumbled deeper into a chaotic wilderness of fallen trees and foul-smelling swamps. Despite earlier reports of hostile tribes in the region

[24] Named after the tribe of Teutons, the original name for Deutschland (or land of the Germans), and located between the Rivers Weser and Ems, in a triangle formed today by Detmold, Minden, and Osnabrueck.

[25] Riding without stirrups as did all horsemen before the medieval knights.

and the mysterious disappearance of his pathfinders, Varus still refused to send out vanguard patrols. Counting on his vast military superiority, he blundered on blindly. Any commander committing such folly is guilty of gross negligence. While Arminius was aware of the *tribun*'s plans – his march route would lead him invariably through the Dörenschlucht (Dören Gorge) – Varus had no idea of the whereabouts of the Cherusci.

On 9 September AD 9, Arminius put his plan into action. His tactic was to harass isolated forward and rear units, decimate them and drive the main host deeper into the forest where they would be bereft of room for manoeuvre. A Roman front unit was the first to get buried under a rain of javelins and rocks. The attack came so unexpectedly that most of the legionaries died instantly, done to death by hordes of wild-eyed warriors, jumping on their hapless victims from cliffs and trees. Those who escaped the slaughter ran back to give warning. 'Cherusci! Cherusci!' Their shouts created panic among the thousands of camp followers that now jammed into the military units for protection. 'The legions were not proceeding in any regular order, but were mixed in helter-skelter with the wagons and the unarmed.'[26] Adding to the confusion, more sporadic attacks from the cover of the dense forest caused increased agitation and casualties among the legions. These hit-and-run attacks went on for most of the first day; the tribesmen struck, then faded into the cover of their woods. By late afternoon, the legions reached an open plain. Varus finally called a stop. Guards were put out and fires lit around the camp. The Cherusci did not attack that night.

Early next morning the Romans broke camp. Varus ordered to set fire to his cumbersome wagon park. Once again, the trail led into dense forest. No sooner had the columns entered the

[26] Dio Cassius, *Roman History* (transl. by E. Gary, 1916).

woods than the barbarians struck. The centurions ordered a
retreat. This was a bait, and Arminius recognised the ruse;
however, before he could stop his over-zealous warriors, a
number of Cherusci had already chased after the Romans into
the open plain. With it, the Cherusci gave up the advantage
of their chosen terrain. Out in the open, the disciplined
Roman formations and their accurate archery soon made
the difference.

Arminius, forced into a situation not of his choosing,
was pulled into the fray. The warriors' initial charge was
carried out with such frenzy that it nearly broke through the
Roman line. The energy and spirit these savages possessed
unnerved Varus, standing well protected behind the shields
of his legions. He was paralysed with fright and incapable
of reaching a decision, but his lieutenants soon had the
situation under control. The legions quickly formed into
phalanxes. Like deadly porcupines, bristling with lances and
swords, their inter-locked shields raised above their heads
shielded them from the shower of javelins, while the Roman
archers had their day. With devastating results, they dispatched flights of arrows into the densely packed attackers.
Once the barbarians' attack was blunted, trumpets blared,
and Roman *triari* and *principes* advanced in close order. The
better-disciplined legions waded into the tribes. With great
clash of arms, the Cherusci showed an obstinate valour and
fell where they stood.

While the Roman *tribun* remained safely in the back-
ground, Arminius was in the thick of battle, wielding his
broad sword. But his men had reached their limit; even his
best fighters had come to the end of their strength. That
they remained on the field was in tribute to their iron-
willed leader who had ordered them to crush the Romans.
On that open plain many brave warriors died before their
battle horns sounded retreat and the remainder fled back

into the woods. As for the Romans, equally exhausted, they failed to follow up on their victory and destroy the danger.

Arminius was in a quandary. He was berated over his call for retreat, the utmost dishonour for a warrior. Some dared to call him a coward. Others again resented that he hadn't given them the opportunity to sack the undefended treasure carts. On the open plain, he had lost a great number of his bravest fighters, many of them interrelated, and now he was held responsible for their losses. A number of headmen accused him of trying to undermine their own authority. In a way, Arminius had as much to fear from his own allies as from the spears of the enemy. He cajoled, preached patience and outlined his strategy. One more day, only one more day, he asked for, and their dead would enter *Valhalla* avenged. They would attack again the following day, but this time deep in the woods, on territory favourable to them.

For the Romans, the rest of the second day remained quiet. *Tribun* Varus was convinced that he had inflicted a resounding defeat, that the barbarians had had enough and were already far away. While his legionaries lit fires, tended to their wounds, and celebrated their victory, once again he failed to send out scout patrols.

A silver moon sailed through the sky and the night was chilly. Arminius could not tear himself from his dark thoughts. How many a good warrior had he sacrificed! Could the rest launch another assault? Whatever the situation, it had to be the final attack; he had no more reserves at his disposal. Was this the end? A brave man always had the chance to sell his life dearly. In this hour of finality, Arminius was alone. One more time he would have to lead his people into battle, and probably suffer death. He leaned back against the trunk of a gnarled pine. The disc of the moon grew paler before it vanished behind a fluffy cloud. The first rays of sun seeped through the canopy of the woven crowns. The morning of the third day was dawning.

Their superior number, and the stillness of their surrounding, lulled the Romans into a false security. Shortly after dawn they broke camp. To reach their fortress on the River Ems, the only trail open to them was through the '*saltus teutoburgiensis*', the Teutoburger Wald, and through the sinister Dörenschlucht.[27] Reassured by a feeling of having already achieved victory, the legions marched in good order of five abreast along the twisting path. What followed behind was less orderly, an unruly, noisy, highly frightened mob. Varus's main force, held back to allow the vanguard to reach the valley, became utterly disorganised when this raggedy mob piled into them.[28]

Arminius placed his warriors on both sides of the Dörenschlucht, a ravine bordered by steep, wooded slopes. From high up on a cliff, he watched the Romans file into the trap. He was about to signal the attack when an event took place that was to decide the outcome of the battle. In the moment that he needed it most, help came in the most unexpected manner. The first indication was a grey cloud. Soon the sun was hidden behind an ugly black mass.

For the Romans there was only silence, that heavy, damp

[27] Tacitus, *Annales*. Varus battle of 9–11 September AD 9, the exact place of the battle is today a discussed question, most likely located between the Dörenschlucht (Dören Gorge) and Hermannsberg (Mt Arminius).

[28] From Gaius Suetonius Tranquillus (*Book 56*): 'And so the plan unfolded. The leader [Arminius] escorted him [Varus] as he set out, and then made their excuses for absenting themselves ... the Romans had with them many wagons and pack animals as they would have in peacetime ... Meanwhile a violent downpour and storm developed so that the column was strung out even further. This also caused the ground around the tree roots and the felled trunks to become slippery, making movement very dangerous, and the tops of the trees to break off and crash down upon them, creating confusion. While the Romans were struggling against the elements, the barbarians suddenly surrounded them on all sides at once, stealing through the densest thickets as they were familiar with the paths ... the Romans were overwhelmed by their opponents, they suffered many casualties and were quite unable to counter-attack.'

silence before a storm. The sky was so near that it faded
into the earth. A metallic light filtered through the clouds
and outlined sharply the tangle of trees, transforming the
landscape into nature's chaos. The dark cloud mass raced at
the legions with its rain-charged electricity, for them, an evil
omen. The legionaries listened to their inbred anguish. For
reassurance, they gripped their swords. A human enemy, they
could understand; but only a god, in their case, Mercury,
controlled the weather.

Suddenly the horizon exploded with electricity. The heavens burst into flames. Flashes of lightning gave off ghostly,
split-second pictures of bluish trees, followed by ear-splitting
crashes. When the storm struck, it came with unaccustomed
violence, leaving no doubt about the power of nature. For
the Romans it was too late for explanations of natural
causes. The rolling thunder shocked them into inactivity.
They implored their gods and raised their shields to ward
off the evil demons. The ground shook. Terrified by this
irresistible attack of heavenly bolts, women shrieked and
old men fell to their knees, never having witnessed such a
fury. Lightning followed by showers of sparks smashed into
trees and split them asunder. Those who fled for protection
beneath the pines were cut down when lightning struck the
treetops. Howling gusts uprooted massive trunks, and buried
legionaries and camp followers alike. A hailstorm battered
the legions, stones the size of robins' eggs clanged off metal
helmets. To protect themselves from the incessant pounding
they raised their shields. Soon, the shields' leather covering
was so thoroughly soaked and so heavy that the soldiers could
no longer hold them up. Panic-stricken horses threw off their
riders and bowled over the packed cohorts along the narrow
path. Terrified soldiers flung themselves to the ground, dug
their fingers into the earth and prayed for the thunder and
lightning to stop. But nothing would stop their gods' fire that
poured down from the heavens on the superstitious Roman

legions. That day, Jupiter was not with them; it seemed that the sky itself was seized by a frenzy to destroy all that was Roman.[29]

The situation was quite different for the Cherusci. Their moment had come, heaven had sent a message. While the Romans interpreted the violent storm as a menace of the gods, for the Nordic warriors the *Thunder of Thor* was a sign of divine assistance. Arminius said out loud what all thought: 'In *Thor*'s name!' He raised his sword; a battle horn blared, followed by hundreds more. What, moments before, had been a dense forest, erupted into movement. Bushes moved, men jumped from behind trees and rocks. In an instant, the slopes converging on the trail were thick with barbarians. Lightning burst from the sky and turned the dark forest into a great bowl of brilliant flashes, a wood filled with hordes of fearsome, tall warriors, howling *'Thor!'* and coming down the slopes. *'Thor! Thor!'* went up the cry while their downhill charge built up to a furious momentum. *'Thor!'* With lowered spears and swinging clubs they crashed into the utterly confused and disorganised Romans, strung out along a narrow forest trail.

'Varus's legions were prevented from going forward and even from standing securely, and moreover deprived of the use of their weapons. For they could not handle their bows or their javelins with any success, nor their shields, which were thoroughly soaked,' wrote their chronicler Dio Cassius.[30]

The legionaries, shocked by the unexpected downburst, which their superstition translated into the wrath of Mercury, suddenly stared at a forest erupting. An entire nation had gathered to drown in blood all those Romans they had had to endure under the yoke of Roman governors. The intermittent blue flashes gave the Romans an impres-

[29] In the description by Tacitus in his *Annales*.
[30] Dio Cassius wrote his *Roman History* towards the end of the second century AD.

sion of a vastly superior number of barbarians rushing at them, yelling their blood-curdling war cry, wielding their spears and clubs, and assisted by bolts of heavenly fire. All along the narrow valley floor it was a similar picture. In great, wild leaps thousands of yelling Cherusci and their allies came thundering down the slope and crashed into the startled Romans, spearing the hapless legionaries like chickens on a spit. The force of this indescribably brutal onslaught was too much for even the most stouthearted of Romans; its initial impact was as devastating as it proved decisive.

Blood flowed in the rivers. The legions, already under shock from the unexplainable, violent fury of the elements, thought their gods had abandoned them. Rain swirled in solid sheets, slashing their faces and near blinding them. The incessant roll of thunder numbed their ears. But Rome's legions had been trained to blind obedience. Some units formed, then wheeled to face the enemy. For this the trail was too confined, it allowed no room for manoeuvre and their superior numbers counted for nothing. Roman archers nocked the arrows, but their bowstrings were wet and limp, and the distance too close to prove effective. Driving rain and spilled blood turned the battle ground into slithery mud. Robbed of their solid footing, the legionaries were prevented from taking up their ordinary defensive posture behind a wall of shields and planted spears. The violence of the hand-to-hand combat increased; the Romans fought on in a last act of desperation, but their open formations were no match for the fury of the barbarians' battle-axes. Nobody could withstand an onslaught conducted with such rage for long. The Romans didn't. Sections were separated from the columns, isolated, encircled, and savagely done to death.

The battle had got completely out of control, everything had happened too fast for Arminius to influence its outcome.

He watched the destruction of his former masters-in-arms with his mouth set in a grim line. No pity was expected and none was given. The savagery of the attack rammed wide gaps in the long columns; the fire and fury of the barbarians broke up the Roman columns into small units which could no longer support each other. Without co-ordination the legionaries struggled back; they landed blows with their swords and threw jabs with their javelins. To no avail. Up and down the narrow forest path, barbarians brought down clubs and battle-axes on the helmets of Romans, isolated into ever-tightening circles. Their screams for help were drowned by the howling tempest. The tribes' sharp, short spears and their stone mallets completed the massacre of the strung-out, disorganised Romans. The legions were lost, trumpets sounded retreat, but even that was no longer possible. The outcome was made final when the *Tribun* Vala Numonius, commanding the Roman cavalry, fled the field. This opened a gaping hole between the legions through which the tribesmen poured.[31]

The rest of the bloody encounter turned into carnage most horrendous. Varus's men were cut down by the thousands, heaps of the slain lay everywhere. Surrounded by a mounting pile of corpses, every Roman was fighting his own last stand on ground made slippery by blood and rain. Some legionaries tried to hack their way through, but were pressed back. Very few escaped with their lives. Most of those who tried, and raced off into the forest like mad horses, using every last ounce of strength in their desperate run, tripped over tree roots and were caught by their pursuers. For the wounded, suffering from only minor cuts or thrusts, there was no chance of help; soon they would be dead, with their throats cut, or from infection.

Almost as quickly as it had arrived, the thunderstorm

[31] Velleius Paterculus.

subsided, and the sun broke through the clouds. In a small clearing, protected by the shields of his last remaining officers, stood the *Tribun* Publius Quintilius Varus, clearly visible in his pristine white toga, red cape and golden helmet. All around him lay death – lifeless, staring eyes and open mouths – while the savage masks of men without pity grimaced avidly and-tightened the circle around him. '*Thor! Thor!*' They could have thrown their spears to do away with Varus, but no, they wanted him alive. He would become their trophy, sacrificed on a pagan altar to appease their horrid gods. For the Roman *tribun*, everything was lost – a Cherusci had outwitted him and shattered his authority; there would be no reinstatement to power by his emperor and no pardon from his enemies. He gave out an agonising cry, planted the hilt of his short sword in the ground, and fell on it. The officers followed his example and took their lives rather than be dragged off into barbaric captivity.[32] A wild cheer of triumph went up from the Cherusci and their allies.

Now that victory was theirs, the first signs of the sinister process of a breakdown in tribal discipline began to show in sudden outbursts of wild temper. The barbarians began to fight among each other, tribe against tribe, clan against clan, man against man; over trinkets, swords and armour, over women; over the booty and the treasure of Varus. Others went on a rampage, slaughtered the wounded Romans and stripped them bare – all without the slightest emotion. Holding up their children, the women begged for pity. None was granted. Legionaries, unfortunate to have fallen into captivity, were buried alive, crucified, or sacrificed on a pagan altar. And, finally, the barbarians hacked off the head of the dead *tribun*, impaled it on the tip of a lance and presented it to their leader.

[32] Dio Cassius, *Roman History*.

'The trail was stained with blood and crammed with corpses, and not one man escaped.'[33] Arminius stood by and did nothing to prevent his warriors from continuing their barbaric behaviour. Plunder and rape were part of warfare. His men had endured and, ultimately, triumphed. But he shared none of their jubilation. His eyes were raised to the sky, giving thanks. Because he knew that he had been granted victory by that cruel God of War, standing by his side with that sudden and violent thunderstorm.

'Hemmed in by forests and marshes, struck by a violent upheaval of nature, a Roman army was exterminated almost to a man by the very enemy whom it had always slaughtered like cattle.' Thus the Roman chronicler Velleius Paterculus recorded one of the decisive battles of antiquity.

When news of the *clades variana* disaster (Varus battle) reached Rome, Emperor Augustus 'rent his garments and mourned greatly because he feared that the enemy would now march into Italy.'[34] In utter desperation, so it is reported, Augustus banged his head against a wall and screamed out in anguish: '*Varus, Varus, give me back my legions.*'

As a direct consequence, many Roman fortresses were given up and Germany was freed from its Roman occupation force. Still Augustus panicked; he feared that Arminius and his Alamannis would cross the Rhine and incite a rebellion among the Gauls. He had nothing to fear, the Germans stayed on their side of the Rhine. Emperor Augustus died in August AD 14, and was followed by his stepson, Tiberius. In AD 15 the new emperor dispatched Germanicus, son of Drusus, on a punitive expedition to Germany; when the army reached the region of the '*saltus teutoburgiensis*' (Teutoburger Wald[35]), Germanicus was to discover a grisly scene: bleached

[33] Tacitus, *Annales.*
[34] Dio Cassius, *Roman History.*
[35] Tacitus, *Annales.*

bones, broken javelins, bodies sticking from the ground and skulls nailed to trees.[36]

While the Romans recognised the military genius of Arminius, the council of Germanic tribes, fearful of his growing dominance, replaced him with the impetuous Inguiomerus, who led them against Germanicus and his eight legions. In AD 16, at Iclistavisus (Minden), their encounter ended in a Roman victory. This time, the tribes foolishly attacked the tight Roman battle formations on the open plain. Following their defeat, Arminius was brought back 'from retirement'. He resisted Roman encroachment and Emperor Tiberius was made to realise that the value of a *Provincia Alamannia*, reaching to the Elbe, bore no comparison to the endeavours necessary to assure victory over the Cherusci. During the winter of AD 16, Tiberius called a halt to the German campaign, because he was afraid of a resurgence of Rome's nemesis, Arminius. Rome's overriding concern was to prevent at all costs both Illyria (Balkans) and Alamannia (Germany) rising at the same time. For Rome lacked the necessary means for a war on two fronts.

Arminius understood that the unity of Germany depended on a coalition of his northern tribes with the centrally located Marcomanni under King Maroboduus. While the Cherusci and their allies defended the Rhine border, the Marcomanni did the same along the Danube. As proof of his victory over the legions, Arminius sent the head of Varus to the Marcomanni ruler. King Maroboduus, a sinister, highly suspicious potentate, became so worried about the rapidly increasing predominance of Arminius that he sided with Rome. As proof of his loyalty to the emperor, he forwarded the head to Augustus. Arminius raised the northern tribes. In a bloody battle, Arminius defeated the Marcomanni in AD 17. Maroboduus fled to Italy where he died in AD 41.

[36] Germanicus' expedition, and his findings, were described in Tacitus *Germania*.

Much was written about Arminius by Roman scribes, who could hardly put down the valiant warrior without making painfully clear the incompetence of Rome's own generals. But it is obvious that he would never have obtained the title of 'supreme commander' had he not possessed adequate qualities.

He was an inspired leader but never a conqueror. Driven by a desire to banish bloodshed among the tribes, Arminius laid the first stone for a union of all Germanic clans. Following his victory over the Romans, he became the undisputed spokesman of the northern tribes. But his idea of a single Germanic patriotism, heart-thumping and stirring, was untimely and unrealistic. Once victory over arch-rival Rome had been achieved, the idea of German unity lost its galvanising appeal, and his grandiose plan, the unification of Germanic tribes into one great nation, came to nothing.

In AD 19, an ancient tribal feud was rekindled. To settle the dispute, Arminius called for a council of elders. The day of the meeting he did not wear his body-mail and the great warrior was forever silenced by the dagger of one of his own. With him died a visionary whose life-long ambition had been to unite Germany into one big nation. It took another eight hundred years, and Emperor Charlemagne, to finish the task Arminius had begun along a slippery forest path.

As fitting tribute, another German unifier, Otto von Bismarck, had a statue of Arminius the Cherusci erected near the site of the historic battle.[37]

The *clades variana*, better known as *Battle of the Teutoburgian Forest*, is one of the most important battles of history, as it marks the turning point of Roman penetration into Central Europe. Though other expeditions (under

[37] In 1875, by order of Kaiser Wilhelm I, on the Grotenberg (Autobahn near Bielefeld).

Germanicus) reconquered some of the fortified places, the time of Caesarian subjugation of pagan tribes was a thing of the past, and an early autumn settled on Roman conquest in the lands beyond the Rhine. The legions of Varus were never replaced. With the prospect of an easy conquest of Germany gone, the Romans retreated behind the principal rivers of Europe, the Rhine and the Danube.

Rome ruled for another five hundred years, but never again over Germany. Had their empire's frontier remained along the Elbe, the course of European history would have undergone a profound change. By extending Rome's borders to the Slavic countries, all of Europe would speak a Latin-based language. Germany would be *Alamannia*, just as France would have remained *Gallia*. Perhaps the two great nations of Germany and France would have lived alongside each other in peace, although this seems a highly unlikely proposition. As for *Britannia*, 'this island of ours would have never been called England',[38] and pilgrims from its shores might well have 'brought forth onto a new continent' a Latin-based culture.

Dis aliter visum – the gods thought otherwise.[39]

The fact is, that on an autumn day two thousand years ago, the Norse god of weather helped along the tenacity of a warrior prince, and together they made world history.

---

[38] Edward Creasy, in *Fifteen Decisive Battles of the World*.
[39] Virgil, *Aeneid*.

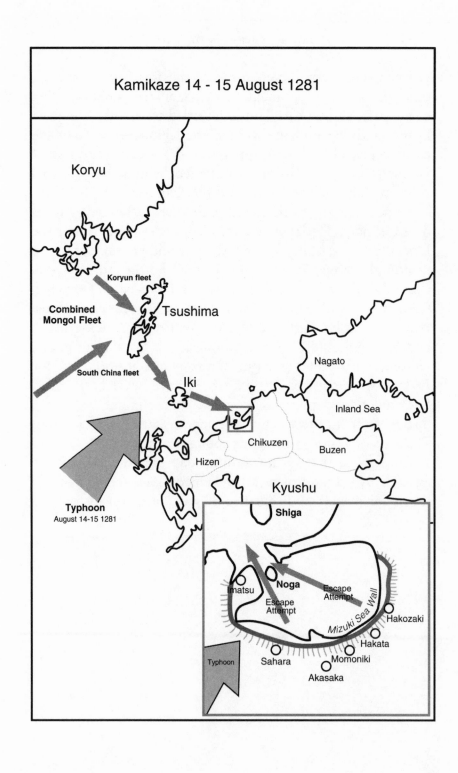

Kamikaze 14 - 15 August 1281

Koryu

Koryun fleet

Combined Mongol Fleet

Tsushima

South China fleet

Iki

Nagato

Inland Sea

Typhoon
August 14-15 1281

Chikuzen

Buzen

Hizen

Kyushu

Shiga

Imatsu

Noga

Escape Attempt

Escape Attempt

Mizuki Sea Wall

Hakozaki

Hakata

Typhoon

Sahara

Momoniki

Akasaka

The Divine Wind

15 August 1281

'This Nippon never did, nor ever shall,
Lie at the proud foot of a conqueror . . .'
William Shakespeare, *King John*.

Somewhere east of China, over the endless Pacific Ocean, the sun burns down on an oily sea. The air is superheated and sucks up dense vapours; the first wisp of a fluffy cloud appears in the leaden sky. The cloud increases until it builds into a dense grey mass, drawing up more moisture, engorging itself with millions of tons of water. The cloud mass reaches higher and higher, until it bursts open like the petals of a gigantic flower. The earth's rotation begins to propel this water-laden mass into a circular motion, accelerating ever more, until it is turned into a whirling thing with a momentum of its own. Faster and faster and faster, a madly spinning disc several hundred miles across. A monster is born, bent on death and destruction.

And lying directly in its path, that 14 August 1281, is the biggest armada ever to sail the seas; 3,500 ships, with hundreds of thousands of Mongol invaders aboard, all bound for the shores of Japan.

China, centre of the universe, had always been divided into a Southern and a Northern Empire. In 1234, the Northern Kingdom of the Kin dynasty was overrun by the Mongol hordes of Genghis Khan,[1] while the southern Empire of the Sung resisted the Tartar onslaught until 1279, before it fell to Kublai Khan. In the west, the Mongol Empire stretched to the Black Sea; the Russians were dragged into slavery, and their capital, Moscow, reduced to ashes. Two centuries of Mongol servitude left its permanent imprint on Russian character, especially in war. In 1241, the Mongols defeated the Teutonic Order at the battle of Liegnitz, and filled eight sacks with the ears of the slain knights.[2] In the east, he had crushed not only China, but also the Koryu king. As well, the kings of Tonkin, Cochin-China, Pegu, Bengal and Tibet had been forced into abject vassalage by the Lord of Mongols. From his new conquest of Korea, Kublai stared across the sea and set his eyes on the island chain of the Empire of the Rising Sun.

It was the time that the Earth passed through a shower of falling stars. A Mongol court astrologer interpreted the event as an auspicious omen, while the Japanese saw in the heavenly missiles a foreboding of great calamity. Kublai decided to act with a steel glove covered by velvet. With an easy victory in mind, he dispatched a delegation to the Kyoto court of Japanese Emperor Kameyama. It never got there. The Kamakura Bakufu *shogun*, military strongman and real decider of Japan's fortunes, intercepted the Khan's emissaries. The message from China was as threatening as it was insulting.

WE, by the grace and decree of Heaven, Emperor of Great Mongolia, present a letter to the *King* of Japan.[3]

WE have pondered that from ancient time even the

---

[1] Born at Temujin, beside Lake Baikal, Siberia, 1167–1227.
[2] Gibbon.
[3] Italics to emphasise the insulting phrases, e.g.: The Japanese '*King*' was an Emperor.

princes of small states have striven to cultivate friendly intercourse with those of adjoining territories.

. . . The prince of Koryu and his people, feeling grateful towards US, have visited OUR country, *and while the relation between US and them is that of Lord and vassal,* its nature is as felicitous as that of a parent and child. Of this, no doubt, you are well aware.

WE beg that thereafter you will establish friendly relations with US. Is it reasonable to refuse intercourse with each other? If not, *it will lead to war,* and who is there who likes such a state of things?

Think of this, *O King!*

The tone of Kublai Khan's message so galled the Bakufu cast of *samurai* that the *shogun* had to step in and restrain them from putting the Mongol envoys to the sword.

The imperial court of Japan had been reduced to the crumbling vestiges of a thousand-year-old empire. It held no shortage of corrupt court jesters and honorific advisers to an impotent emperor. They were fearful of the 'Yellow Peril', whose scowling ghost of brutality provided an enduring and haunting imagery, and counselled their *tenno* (emperor) to accept some form of nominal vassalage. Fortunately for Japan, the real power was no longer in the hands of the august descendant of the Sun-Goddess Ameterasu, but seated at Kamakura, with the Bakufu *Shogunate*[4] and its appointed military governors. The present *shogun* was the youthful Hojo Tokimune who rose to the Chinese challenge with his personal example. *Shogun* Tokimune's iron-fist dictates were to have profound implications for Japan's future.

As a first step, Tokimune called up 'all men worthy of bearing arms, and put to death all those who refuse'.[5] Mongols

---

[4] Established by Minamoto no Toritomo in 1185, who received the title *seji taishogun* or destroyer of barbarians.
[5] From the *Azuma Kagami*, the Bakufu Chronicle.

abducted two Japanese minor noblemen[6] from the island of Tsushima,[7] delivered them to Kublai's court in Peking where they were shown 'great courtesy and all the magnificence of the Mongol Emperor'; after which they were brought back to Japan to persuade their countrymen of the benevolence of Peking. Neither their account of a Chinese paradise nor the soothing, accompanying words from Kublai Khan changed the bellicose mood of the Japanese. The honourable knights of *bushido* remained steadfast in their will to defend their independence dearly. Like any island nation that is protected by the sea, there was always the expectation that they could achieve this. It was well known that the Mongols were not a seafaring people like the Chinese, with their long tradition of trading by sea. The Mongols had to rely entirely on Chinese and Korean shipbuilders and mariners, both vassals they couldn't trust. This dual structure, Mongol army commanders suspicious of their Chinese navigators, was a key to subsequent events.

In 1273, Kublai Khan issued orders to the King of Koryu to build him a thousand ships. The Koryu monarch could not possibly fulfil such an enormous demand, and said so. The Mongol emperor dispatched 5,000 of his wild horsemen 'to help convince the Koryu king'. Kublai, sure of easy victory, assembled 40,000 troops. A severe winter and a famine in Koryu delayed his invasion plans, and he had to wait for spring. More time was wasted on a final diplomatic effort. His ambassador demanded the stubborn islanders accept vassalage or face the terrible anger of the Mighty Khan. Unceremoniously, the Khan's personal envoy was kicked out, and the war was on.

The honour code of *bushido* made a Japanese *samurai*

---

[6] Their names are given as Tojiro and Yajiro, but nothing else is known about them.

[7] Tsushima became famous for the sea battle fought between Japan and Russia in 1904.

equal to the very best the Mongols had to offer. Japanese warriors fought under the rules of their honour code of *bushido*. 'It was a *bushi*'s [knight] habit to proclaim his name and title in the presence of the enemy, to dispirit the foe. His enemy, advancing to cross swords with him, would perform a similar ceremony of self-introduction. Yet a skilled swordsman did not necessarily seek out single combat; he was ready to ride into the thick of the foe without discrimination. But the general feature of a battle remained individual contest, and when the fighting ceased, each *bushi* proceeded to the tent of his lord to submit for inspection the heads of those he had slain.'[8]

The Japanese ground troops were to suffer heavily from the formidable Mongol crossbow, which the Tartar horsemen[9] handled with great mastery, even while in full gallop. Every rider went into battle with 60 arrows, of which 30 were made of light shafts for long distance, and 30 with heavy shafts for close armour penetration.[10] But when it came to sheer courage and fighting spirit, the Japanese had no equal. Within striking distance, they were certainly superior to their enemy.

While the *shogun* could call on a potential of 400,000 warriors streaming to his banners from the islands, the Khan dispatched a mere 25,000 of his élite Mongol 'horse marines'.[11] Added to this were 15,000 unreliable Koreans who held no great love for their Tartar overlords. Kublai Khan grossly misjudged his army's strength. Killing defenceless Chinese and Korean villagers was one thing, taking on Japanese *samurai*, willing to die for honour and home, was a different matter. He got his first taste in November 1274. The Mongol armada had landed at the Japanese offshore island of Tsushima, where its

---

[8] Quoted from Captain Brinkley, *Japan*.
[9] Oman, *The Art of War in the Middle Ages*. The Mongol crossbow preceded the English longbow of the Hundred Years War by a century.
[10] Yule, *Marco Polo*.
[11] Other than special troops, Mongols always kept their horses, even on an ocean crossing.

local commander and 200 islanders put up a valiant struggle and held off General Lin Fok Heng and his 25,000 invaders for several days. After the last defender had fallen, the invaders butchered the entire population of Tsushima, committing a grave psychological error, since this brutal act showed the people of Japan they could expect no clemency. This only strengthened their will to fight that much harder. A week later, the Mongols landed on the island of Iki, and from there crossed the channel to Kyushu,[12] one of the Japanese main home islands.

On 18 November 1274, the invasion fleet entered Hakosaki Bay, only a few miles from Dazaifu, Kyushu's capital. The local Japanese defenders were too thin on the ground to put up any lengthy resistance and the Mongols could have walked right across the island. Instead, they remained on the coastline, where they split up into raiding parties. Parts of the Mongol army sailed on, unloaded their horses on a sandy strip near the coastal town of Hakata, and put the town to the torch. From there they rode on to Akasaka, and further up the coast to Imatsu. On their way, they massacred the local fishing population. The promise of easy spoils got General Lin Fok Heng distracted from his main objective. This delay allowed *Shogun* Tokimune's local warlords to round up all available men on Kyushu, while the *shogun* rushed at the head of his army from Kamakura to bolster the island's defences. Before he could take any significant part in the hostilities, the local lords[13] had already attacked the Khan's hordes.

On 24 November, a major confrontation took place in front of the Mizuki Sea Wall[14] near Hakosaki. What really took place that day is buried in the mists of time. There are no accurate accounts, other than that the battle lasted

[12] The northern coast of Kyushu is made up of the provinces of Hizen and Chikuzen, and the off-shore islands of Goto, Iki and Tsushima.

[13] Matsura, Shimadzu, Kyushu, Kikuchi, Shoni and Otomo.

[14] Built six centuries earlier by Korean labour.

for eight hours and losses were great on both sides. At the outset, the Japanese attacked with fanatical obsession, while the marksmanship of Mongol archers took a heavy toll. Once the *samurai* got in close among their enemy, they wielded their double-handed blades with terrible efficiency. Soon the Mongols lost their taste for continuing the fight; they abandoned their vassal Koreans, who were slaughtered like cattle. Shortly before nightfall the Tartar general took a decision; he knew that in darkness their arrows were useless, while the *samurai* could apply their razor sharp swords with deadly result, while more Japanese reserves poured onto the battlefield. He decided to fight in daylight the next day; and ordered his men to embark for the night on the vessels standing offshore. To cover their retreat, they set fire to the Hakosaki shrine, an impressive wooden structure. Under cover of heavy smoke, the Mongols managed to withdraw without further losses. While the Japanese rushed in to save their sacred shrine, the weather changed. With devastating fury, a storm rammed into the ships as they were taking aboard the Mongol army. Decks were running with water, masts snapped, crushing sailors and soldiers, and the helmsmen fought to bear away from the dangerous shallows. Ships broke up or foundered, drowning a great number. Those struggling to get on board grabbed for rope ladders and were smashed against the sides of ships. Others, waiting ashore to be picked up had no chance as monster waves rolled over them. One ship tried to get into the open. It rose on a crest, then came straight down on a shelf and broke its back. Another was driven onto a sand spit. Local fishermen, whose villages had been put to the torch only days before, pulled its crew and some 300 soldiers from the sea before they put them to a cruel death. Most of the 13,200 Mongolian casualties were caused by drowning well after the battle on land.

With the emergency at an end, Japanese priests took credit for the victory. At the moment of great peril, everyone from the emperor down had been praying to God to help destroy the invaders, and God had listened. But once the danger was past, and the Mongol fleet foundered on the rocks, many forgot their God. Not so, said the priests. Pointing to the storm, the priests claimed that their prayer had been heard, and that it had not been the selfless heroism of *samurai*, but monks' prayers which saved Japan. They demanded that a large portion of the monies set aside for armaments should flow into their monastic coffers. Yes, agreed the emperor, the gods were still necessary; the monasteries were issued with liberal grants of land, and their temples gilded and restored. Such largesse condemned those who would have to endure any future attack to unreasonable hardship.

Across the sea, Kublai Khan refused to admit defeat. While his advisers blamed the setback on the fury of the elements, the Khan had learned his lesson. Next time would be different, because, as surely as he was the Ruler of the Universe, there would be a next time! And so he began to plan a second, much more powerful invasion. For this, it took an armada vast enough to carry an army of several hundred thousand.

Along the seacoast, from Southern China to Korea, Kublai Khan ordered every seaworthy vessel to be commandeered, some of them quite small for an ocean crossing. 'Each vessel will require 20 mariners, and will carry 15 horses with their men belonging to them,' wrote Marco Polo.[15] Since the Khan's last invasion attempt had stripped the Koryu kingdom of ships and manpower, and their forests had been cut down to build the fleet of 1274, there was no more timber to build another fleet. Kublai summoned the Koryu king to Peking and, under penalty of beheading anyone who dared obstruct his will, ordered the construction of 1,000 ships. Wood was brought overland from China and manpower was supplied from the penal colonies. Thousands of slaves died

---

[15] Yule, *Marco Polo*.

from famine and maltreatment, but the armada took shape. The end result was still insufficient for the Khan's grandiose plans; this lack of shipping space was made up by his conquest of the South China Empire (1279), which netted him 3,500 more vessels.[16] By late 1280, everything was in place and the armies of Mongols and their vassal nations assembled at various embarkation points. It was a most impressive force that gathered under thousands of colourful dragon banners.

Meanwhile, the Japanese had not been idle. The Tsushima Straits had stopped being the exclusive domain of the Chinese. Japanese privateers and raiders took to the sea in a 'mosquito fleet'. Their ships were small, but not their successes. With their swift vessels, they robbed the slower Chinese traders; and when the time came to be useful in the defence of their nation, they followed the call and intercepted troopships on the way to their assembly points. Captured ships were burned at sea, the crews thrown overboard and left to be eaten by sharks.

In the spring of 1280, spies informed *Shogun* Tokimune of the final preparations for a new Mongol invasion. The enfeebled Japanese Emperor Uda II, a sixteen-year-old demi-god, who listened to advice from his frightened favourites while philandering with his *shirabyoshi*, the court prostitutes, was willing to enter submission talks with the Khan. And again, the iron-willed Tokimune stopped his emperor. As he had so successfully done in 1274, the *shogun* put his nation on a war footing. Japan was steeling itself for the coming spring. The question was no longer: Would the Mongols come? But: When?

As the Khan in Peking geared up to impose his will on the island nation, so the *shogun* countered the move with

---

[16] The overall number of major ships was probably nearer to 300 or 400. The rest, to make a comparison, might have been like the evacuation of the British Expeditionary Force from Dunkirk in 1940, where everything from cruiser to tramp steamer to sail boat was used to cross the English Channel.

a solid defensive strategy. It was assumed that the Mongols would choose roughly the same invasion route and attempt a landing in the nearest estuary, on Kyushu. Tokimune ordered the existing Mizuki Sea Wall to be strengthened. The population came out voluntarily to dig deep ditches which were designed to prevent the rider hordes from crossing inland. Special wooden towers were put up for archers. Tokimune established defensive districts that could rush to each other's assistance. He created a local militia made up for the first time from all walks of life; blacksmiths forged swords, lance tips and arrowheads; fishermen trained in naval warfare; and peasants practised the use of arms, an art ordinarily reserved for the warrior cast. The *shogun*'s final order, but one that was to prove vital, was for all able-bodied men to take up the practice of archery. Competitions were held, and the winners honoured. The Japanese soon achieved mastery in the art of the bow that could favourably compare with that of their enemy.

June 1281. Last preparations were under way for the great Mongol invasion, the men boarded the vessels, and the fleet set out from Masampo. Under the command of the ruthless General Hwan Baku, Tsushima Island was conquered without much ado. On 10 June, Iki Island fell, and on 23 June the first sails of the vast armada appeared off the coast of Kyushu. They came in through the narrows, past the spit of Shiga, and made for Hakosaki Harbour. The Japanese had providently manned the newly strengthened Mizuki Wall with whatever manpower was readily available, but could hardly believe their eyes when they saw the masses of Mongols pouring ashore. They were prepared to put up a sacrificial stand, hold out as long as they could against a concentrated attack, and try to delay the hordes of Kublai Khan from their march inland. But they knew that it was hopeless.

There is little or no documentation available of what really took place in that seven-week period, from the initial landing in June, leading up to the dramatic events in the middle of August 1281. It is only recorded that the Mongols did not cross, or were prevented from crossing, the Mizuki Wall, and that they failed to turn the Japanese coastal defence.[17] It must be assumed that, once again, they dispersed their initial efforts along the sea shore, without engaging their crushing superiority in a single thrust. The Mongols split into individual raiding parties to attack soft targets, such as monasteries, which held a promise of great riches. Whatever the circumstances, the fight seesawed throughout the summer. It was a stand-off. The only surviving records show that Japanese losses, especially around the Shiga Peninsula, were excessively high. This alone indicates that battles must have been many and furious.

By the beginning of August, the Mongol commander decided to assemble his entire force to launch an all-out attack against at the Mizuki defences. He sent out his ships to collect his widely dispersed forces. Having failed to establish a bridgehead on shore, he ordered the army to remain on board their ships, anchored off Takashima Island (Hawk Island), until the day of the concentrated invasion. The Japanese were now so thin on the ground that they could not expect to survive one more assault, especially a concentrated strike by a vastly greater foe.

But when even the mightiest collide with the gigantic forces of nature's destruction, a stench of death is in the wind. That fateful 15 August 1281 changed history and added a new expression to the world's vocabulary: *kamikaze*. In the moment of their greatest need, the fickle luck of warfare sided with the Japanese: the Mongol attack had been set for the very afternoon a typhoon struck.

For days, the weather had been building up in the Pacific.

---

[17] This success led to a dangerous historical precedent for their defensive strategy of 1944.

Over the super-heated Pacific, huge volumes of vapours lifted from the ocean's surface, forming into towering clouds before the mass began to swirl around a 'dead eye'. The constantly shifting jet streams of the upper atmosphere herded the storm in a north-westerly direction towards the Straits of Korea. This whirling disc reached Japan by late afternoon of 14 August. At about the same time as the Tartar armada was headed for shore to unload their troops, the wind increased in intensity, as did the sea swell. Some of the bigger ships found it impossible to reach their disembarkation points by sail and had to be pulled in by rowboats; others found themselves dead to windward in a channel too torturous for manoeuvre, especially around the sandspit jutting out from Shiga Point. Hundreds of ships had already jammed into the lagoon, while more vessels, fighting a strong undercurrent, soon bottled up the narrow entrance into the bay. Ships nearest to shore had lowered the planks in order to transfer men and horses into smaller landing craft when the first squalls struck. The sea began to get choppy. Chinese captains stared at the sky and tried to warn their Mongol overlords of the looming danger. But the land warriors had no idea about the fury of the elements and refused to listen to the seafarers. Their priority was to get their men ashore for the planned attack.

The wind increased, and bigger waves broke through the narrow mouth of the inlet. Soon ships bobbed around, straining on their anchor ropes. The sky turned into a black of swirling clouds, torn asunder by violet and orange flashes in a divine bombardment. From the blackness of the horizon, a thin white line bore down on the ships at anchor, stretching as far as the eye could see; the first monster wave, with the sea behind it a cauldron of boiling water. In their anxiety to get away from the shallows and reefs, captains bellowed orders; seamen hacked through anchor ropes. With a roar the white water rolled over the shallows, the sandy spit, and into the bay. It picked up in its giant fists many of the smaller ships and smashed them onto the rocks. The wave thundered into the rock cliffs, from where it was thrown back, and its massive cross-sea threw the ships about like flotsam. Everything was caught in the maelstrom; even the biggest ships heaved like tiny toys on each mountainous wave. Tons of water spilled over the vessels and swept their decks clean. Horses broke loose and jumped overboard, men grabbed for ropes only to be crushed against the ships' sides. Lightning flickered constantly and illuminated an extraordinary scene, an armada foundering in the fury of a typhoon.[18]

The hundreds of vessels that had survived the initial onslaught were now caught inside an estuary with no room for manoeuvre, ships wallowed on gigantic waves, to plunge down into the trough or into each other. Sails entangled, masts snapped, beams cracked, ships and people were pulled into the vortex of the sea.

Equal panic and confusion reigned among those who had already been put on land. They were caught by the monster waves that washed over the shallow beaches, and sucked them back into the ocean.

The typhoon's fury continued unabated all night, and well into the following day. By first light, ships that had miraculously survived the night of terror tried to make for the exit from the estuary. They had one chance in a hundred, because there were simply too many ships and too many wrecks imprisoned in the grip of a strong undercurrent, which sucked them inexorably towards the narrows. In their frenzy to escape the boiling breakers, ships smashed into each other, broke up on submerged rocks, or were stranded on sandbanks, where each consecutive wave heaved them further inland. The Shiga Narrow was blocked by sunken vessels, and the shoreline was littered with broken timber and horribly mangled corpses of men and beasts. Those who

[18] After pictorial scrolls painted by period artists.

did make it into the open were carried off on the foam of the sea, never to be seen again.

The disaster was complete. Its victims have no known tomb.

'A storm rose from the west and all vessels made together for the entrance of the bay. The tide was running strong and the ships were carried along irresistibly in its grip. As they converged on the mouth of the estuary, a terrible catastrophe occurred. The vessels were jammed together, and the bodies of men and broken timbers were heaped together in a solid mass so that a person could walk across from one point of the land to another on the mass of wreckage. The wrecked vessels carried the 100,000 men from South China.' Such was the account of the disaster as written up in a contemporary Korean chronicle.[19]

Some survivors made it to the island of Takashima. They had lost most of their weapons, and most of their leaders had drowned. The Japanese warlord Shoni Kagasuke, leading the fierce *samurai* of the *daimiyo* of Choshin, attacked them and butchered all but three thousand. With the death of their last general, Chang Pak, the great Mongol invasion ended. The calamity was so great that the Khan lost his taste for more adventures of this kind. Kublai Khan died in 1294, and his successor, Timor Khan, abandoned all further attempts to conquer Japan.

Japan rejoiced, its faithful flocked to their temples to give thanks. The real heroes were the thousands of self-sacrificing, nameless *samurai* who had fought off the barbaric hordes for seven long weeks and the iron will of *Shogun* Tokimune[20], who had saved Japan's national independence. But the priests claimed, with a certain justification, that the Empire of the Rising Sun had been delivered by the god of weather.

[19] From *History of Japan: The Mongol Invasion.*
[20] Tokimune died in 1284, and was followed as *shogun* by his fourteen-year-old son, Sadatoki.

Japanese never forgot the myth of the miraculous storm. It reinforced their belief that the Shinto gods protected their land. In their honour, they named the tempest *kamikaze*: the Divine Wind.

Japan's miraculous preservation through the fury of the elements, on that day in 1281, had far-reaching consequences for Asia. Rulers of the only military power in the Far East, which would have been able to counter-balance China's continental expansionism, kept their nation firmly locked up behind its fortified sea walls. Thus, Japan became a nation in isolation. For seven more centuries, its surrounding seas kept the Empire of the Rising Sun inviolate. There was to be one more foreign invasion, and one more *kamikaze*, or the Divine Wind.

That event was to take place six hundred and sixty-three years later.

Situation map of Paris

PARIS

Maison Robespierre

Rue St. Honoré

Tullerie Gardens

E   Tullerie   A

River Seine

B

C

F D

A   The Louvre

B   Conciergerie

C   Notre Dame

D   Hôtel de Ville

E   Place de la Revolution with the Guillotine

F   Place de Grêve

The night it rained on Paris

9 Thermidor, an II (27 July 1794)

'Rain is counter-revolutionary!'
Prince Charles Maurice de Talleyrand (1754–1838)

All day long, the clouds have been hanging low over Paris, this hot and humid summer's day, the *9. Thermidor*,[1] *l'an II*. The rumour of momentous events spreads from the *Convention* (National Assembly). It races along the lanes of the inner city to the rancid hovels of the suburbs, those hubs of permanent unrest, teeming with naked tots and fighting hags whose misery has made them grow old too soon. *'Grand gibier* . . . big game today.' *Grand gibier* is not a delicious meal of boar or stag, but refers to a person of importance about to lose his head. Not since April, when 'the vile Danton' – before his fall he was known as 'the great Danton' – went to the guillotine, has there been any affair of similar importance. Certainly, in the last three months, thousands have gone that way, but all have been aristocrats and enemies of the Revolution. Crowds begin to gather around their *maisons-sections*, the assembly halls of

[1] Thermidor was, in the revolutionary calender, the month of July.

each one of the city's forty-eight sections. The hovels empty themselves of rough looking men and their equally horrid spouses. '*Tous à la ville!* All into town!' Like a brook, which is fed by small rivulets into a mighty river, so is it this day with the mob of Paris. The human flood swells, nobody wants to miss out on the excitement, everyone has to be part of it. Without a leader, they converge from both sides of the river, tramp across the Seine bridges. Not a breeze to stir the air; the temperature rises. More and more press into the *Place de Grève*, people faint in the crush of sweating humanity. Dark clouds gather on the outskirts.

In a few hours these clouds will reach the centre of town, and the violence of the downpour will change history. This is something that the many thousands, gathered in front of *la Maison-Commune*, the city hall of Paris on the *Place de Grève*,[2] are not yet aware of, this sweltering 27, July 1794.

The French Revolution had opened the avenues of promotion to the common man. Merit, instead of birth or influence, was the new order for advancement. A young lawyer from Arras, Maximilien Marie Isidore Robespierre, had chosen his way prudently. By skilfully avoiding the pitfalls, he had climbed to the apex of power. To achieve this took more than just ordinary qualities. History cannot dismiss him only as a monster, or a fanatic without qualities. If he shed much blood, this was in his maniacal struggle for virtue, and for the success of the young Republic. Even Napoleon stated that Robespierre had been made the scapegoat of the Revolution. When history judges him, it may well find that he was no worse than his co-revolutionaries, and most likely better than the lot.

On 27 July 1793, Robespierre replaced the ailing Con-

[2] Today, Place Hôtel de Ville.

ventionist Gasparin as permanent member of the *Comité de Salut Publique*, the Committee of Public Safety or Executive Council.[3] With it began his meteoric rise to power. He soon managed to silence his greatest rival, Georges Danton. The break, between the two former companions of the Revolution happened shortly after the assassination of Jean-Paul Marat, in the salon of *l'Incorruptible* at 398 Rue Saint-Honoré.[4] It was from this sinister place that, with the stroke of a pen, the lives of so many had been snuffed out. One night in 1794, Danton stormed in and yelled: 'Your friends want my death!'

'And yours want the death of the Republic!' retorted Robespierre icily.

'We created the Revolutionary Tribunal as a protection, and you've turned it into an instrument of indiscriminate slaughter. You've used your cannon balls in Lyon, and your butchers in Nantes tossed the people into the Loire. All those who stand up against you, die!'

A thin smile crossed Robespierre's face: 'But you are wrong. Proof is, you're still alive.'[5]

Not for long. Like all others, Danton fell victim to the *Incorruptible*. Robespierre achieved this by simply outlawing the right to defence by an accused! On the suggestion by Louis-Antoine de Saint-Just, his evil shadow, Robespierre pushed the 'Law of the 22 Prairial', through the *Convention*. Never in history has a viler piece of legislation been enacted. It ignored every rule of law, and handed the power to a partisan jury to condemn without proof or trial. *Accusation was equal to condemnation!* Nobody was exempt from it, and that included the members of the Convention. This law terrified, as it deterred the enemies of Robespierre and he turned it into

[3] *Comité de Salut Publique* was created three months before, on 6, April 1793. It was abandoned in December 1795.
[4] It stood on today's site of the Café Robespierre.
[5] Weisz, *Gespräche der Weltgeschichte*.

his base of power.[6] The Conventionist Ruamps tried to block the passing of this legislation: 'If we allow this bill to pass,' he dared to pronounce before the final vote, 'there'll be nothing left for us to do but blow out our brains.' The Jacobins shouted him down, and Ruamps went to the guillotine.

This law created the Terror, with its great effusion of blood. Fouquier-Tinville, the public prosecutor, became its tool, and the guillotine became its instrument. The 5, April 1794, the day that Georges Danton, together with his close friends and supporters, went to the guillotine, signalled the beginning of the Great Terror. Over the next three months, 2,085 people suffered a similar fate. The Revolutionary Court was no longer a place of justice but a charnel house. The public prosecutor and his assistant jurors lost all sense of justice, even the feeling for humanity. A breastfeeding mother had her baby ripped from her on the platform; another delivered her baby in the tumbrel on the way to execution. A housewife asked for a *rouet*, a spinning wheel, and was denounced as having asked for a *roi*. She died. When Fleury, a pensioner, denounced the injustice done to his daughter, wrongly accused of a black market deal, he was shouted down by Fouquier-Tinville: 'This gentleman is in a great hurry. His wish must be satisfied,' with which he brought down the gavel and the man was beheaded, together with the rest of his family. A special gutter had to be dug beneath the guillotine to allow the rivers of blood to flow into the sewer, so great was the daily slaughter. For this horrid carnage, Robespierre, who the populace of Paris had cheered and anointed as *l'Incorruptible*, was held responsible. 'Death, always death, and the scoundrels throw it all on me!'

After three months of daily executions, the vast majority of Parisians longed for an end to the Terror. With it, they signalled Robespierre's fall. It is a lesson of history that the

[6] Following his execution, this was the first law to be repudiated.

great mass will accept just about anything as long as they are given something in exchange that makes them lose their memory of liberty. But the guillotine stood there, tall and fearsome, as a daily reminder of dictatorial suppression.

In the sweltering heat of July 1794, it was clear that Robespierre's Jacobins would not outlive the Girondins whose downfall they had brought about in June 1793. Joseph Fouché was the power behind the great Thermidor Conspiracy. Saint-Just had once said of Fouché that he wanted 'to make Liberty a prostitute'. The man who was to become the Duke of Otranto, and Napoleon's feared chief of police, said of *l'Incorruptible* after having watched Robespierre climbing to the top of a pyramid during the *Fête de l'Etre Supreme*: 'He invented God that he might be His high priest!'

Jean-Lambert Tallien, a sordid man, whose corruption was outrageous, joined the conspiracy. When Tallien's beautiful mistress, Therezia Cabarrus, was arrested (together with her best friend, Josephine de Beauharnais, the future wife of Napoleon), he knew he could find no pity in the stony heart of *l'Incorruptible*. Only Robespierre's overthrow could save his mistress. Paul Barras was another of the conspirators, as was Collot d'Herbois, the 'butcher of Lyon', and Billaud-Varennes, who 'mowed down men as another would grass'.

'The *Convention*, gangrened with corruption, has no longer the power to save the Republic,' stated Robespierre in what amounted to a declaration of war against its elected deputies. Had Robespierre acted in time, and done away with them as he had done away with his rival Danton, his rule might have been saved. Instead, indecision and lethargy paralysed him. Saint-Just tried in vain to arouse in him the will to strike down his enemies. But Robespierre, overcome by a languor brought on by the disgust that he, the virtuous, was so foully treated by the corrupt delegates, failed to respond. Until the day he signed his own death warrant when he addressed the *Convention*: 'We assert that there exists a conspiracy against public liberty. That it owes its strength to a criminal coalition which intrigues in the very bosom of the Convention. That this coalition even has accomplices in the Committee of Public Safety, and that some of its members are engaged in this plot.' The hall rang out with shouts of the delegates' assurance of complete loyalty to Robespierre. But then he added a fatal phrase which silenced the conventionists into fear. 'I know well who these calumniators are.' This insinuation created dread in the hearts of his sworn enemies. He had a list! Who was on it? Fouché, the man behind the scene, stirred up suspicion among many deputies that their names were on the list. Bourdon de l'Oise, who was convinced that his name was on it, jumped up: 'Such accusations must be clarified!' When Robespierre tried to reply, the conspirator Cambon shouted him down: 'This *Convention* must be told the truth. There is one man who strangles the will of the National Convention.' And in the sudden silence that followed, he pointed his finger. 'This man is Robespierre!'

Billaud-Varennes yelled: 'Tear away the mask!' The room broke out into frenzy: 'The list! Give us the list!' Robespierre went white, gasped for air, and stumbled from the room; he headed for the Jacobin Club to address his loyal supporters. 'We shall rid the Convention of these corrupt scoundrels,' he declared to their frenzied cheers. He had lost the first round, but not the battle. Tomorrow would be another day, and tomorrow he would smite the opposition. As he turned into his quarters, his landlady, Mme Duplay, met him at the doorstep. He looked up at the sky: 'Tomorrow will be a fine day.' And he was not discussing the weather.

While Fouché and his band of conspirators prepared the battlefield for the coming day, Robespierre went to bed, having left it to Saint-Just to plan the attack of *9. Thermidor*. Not an easy task, as Saint-Just had to face up to an influential member of the Committee of Public Safety, Lazare Carnot, who openly accused him of contriving a devious plot. Saint-Just replied maliciously: 'With you I will deal in a masterly manner.' He might just have done it, but for Fouché, who had brilliantly outmanoeuvred the triumvirate of Saint-Just, Robespierre and Couthon, by nominating one of his co-conspirators, Collot d'Herbois, as the *Convention* president for the crucial session.

On 9. *Thermidor, l'an II.* (27 July 1794) the weather was not at all as Robespierre had predicted. Clouds hung over the city and the humidity was stifling. The *Convention* opened its session at precisely eleven o'clock. The Jacobins had loaded the galleries with a friendly mob, who cheered wildly as Robespierre, in his famous robin-egg blue coat and yellow trousers, arrived early, accompanied by Saint-Just and Couthon. Sure of his forthcoming victory, he waved to his supporters. Saint-Just went to the rostrum to launch the initial attack, but before he had even finished his first sentence, Tallien shoved him brutally aside and brandished a dagger (which, so he claimed, had been sent to him by his beloved Therezia): 'Tear away the curtain!' A demand immediately echoed by the rest of the conspirators, especially by Billaud-Varennes, who yelled: 'The Jacobins are trying to murder the *Convention!*' Among the confusion and tumult inside the hall, Tallien advanced on Robespierre. *L'Incorruptible* was taken aback, tried to speak, but his voice failed him. 'The blood of Danton chokes him,' yelled Tallien. When Robespierre opened his mouth, the conspirator Collot d'Herbois, wielding the president's bell, drowned out his words. Over the pandemonium came a hoarse wheeze: 'President of Assassins, will you not hear me!' before Robespierre's voice broke in anguish. He looked to the Mountain, but saw only turned heads, he addressed the Plain, and they scowled. A certain Louchet, a deputy who had never before shown initiative or courage, suddenly rose:

'I demand the arrest of the traitor Robespierre!' It struck. For a moment there was only the silence of shock, before the hall erupted into a tumultuous demonstration. '*A bas le tyrant!*' When Robespierre tried to speak, a number of deputies yelled in chorus: 'Let the blood of the noble Danton choke you!'

Robespierre fell back on his seat, ashen faced and sweating. Only Saint-Just kept his calm. The president read out the already prepared order for the arrest of Maximilien Robespierre and 'his gang of scoundrels'. *L'Incorruptible* was led from the hall between two gendarmes. He muttered: 'The Republic is lost, the brigands triumph.'

With the palace coup a success, and Robespierre, Saint-Just, and Couthon arrested, the *Convention* took the most insane decision in the history of a revolution: a two-hour dinner break!

The tension, which had gripped the *Convention*, quickly communicated itself to the popular sections of Paris. While the mob from the gallery rushed all over Paris to gather support for their arrested leaders, the Jacobin Club dispatched messengers to the city sections to assemble 'a posse of strong men and women' on the *Place de la Maison-Commune*. Assisted by the cannons of the National Guard, and their leader, Hanriot, they would soon take care of that rebellious *Convention*.

François Hanriot, general of the Paris National Guard, was a habitual drunk and braggart. He entered his 'military career' as valet of an officer who had fled the country, before he became Marat's hatchetman. On 2, June 1793, on Marat's behest, he had raised the mob to storm the *Convention*, oust the Girondins, and install the Jacobins. A few days later, Marat himself was dead and Hanriot had quickly switched allegiance to Robespierre. For his betrayal, he was handed the command over the National Guard; the night before 9. *Thermidor*, he had personally assured Robespierre he would line up his guns on the *Convention* 'and blast those traitors to hell'. Then he headed for the nearest *bistro* to get drunk. When friends located him and told him that his arrest had been ordered, he jumped on his horse and galloped, wielding his sabre and wildly yelling 'Kill all the deputies!' towards the Tuileries, where he was pulled unceremoniously from his horse, trussed up and dumped into a storage room. As soon as the Commune heard of his arrest, two hundred heavily armed men went to his rescue. They broke down the doors of the *Convention* and freed Hanriot, still incoherently drunk. Without specific orders, the armed rabble loaded the 'liberated Commune commander' into a cart and departed, but did no harm to the deputies, who were just filing back after a pleasant dinner. During this confusion, François Hanriot, retired once more to '*L'auberge du Cheval-Vert*'.

Lazare Carnot, who had taken control of the Committee of Public Safety from the ousted Robespierre, had already countered any possible move by Hanriot and the *communards* by ordering loyal gendarmes to guard the ammunition stores. The interruption by an armed mob had pointed out to the stunned deputies the seriousness of the situation – a close call – which had to be immediately remedied, especially since Robespierre was no longer under arrest. His guardians, having received no specific orders to hold him any longer and most likely terrified by the gathering mob, had let him go. The deputies speedily issued a decree that was to tilt the balance. By declaring Robespierre an *hors-la-loi* (outlaw), anyone who came to his help would face automatic arrest and be executed without trial. The Conventionist Paul Barras was put in charge to carry out the decision. He sent *Convention* members to the various Paris sections to read out the decree. It showed an immediate effect. Of the 48 city sections, only 13 followed the call by the Jacobins to defend city hall, while 27 observed cautiously from the sideline the outcome of the power struggle. When the section leaders noticed a swing in the tide, due to the clever ruse to make Robespierre an outlaw, they eventually declared in favour of the *Convention*. For the first time, several of the leading Paris section heads dared to show openly their dissension with Robespierre's Terror. However, Hanriot's gunners had displayed more initiative. Together with thousands of *sans-culottes*, they had marched on the *Place de Grève*, better known during revolutionary days as the *Place de la Maison-Commune*. By 10 pm, and without awaiting instructions from their commander, thirty-two pieces of artillery had been placed on the approaches to the *Hôtel de Ville* and along the quays. At this time, all the *Convention* could command was one lonely company of gendarmes, armed only with pistols. During these crucial hours, the *Commune* held a crushing superiority in cannons – a trump card that certainly would have decided the issue – if only they could find a chief to take charge! While the *Convention* debated how best to handle this explosive situation, and lived in constant terror of the street mob behind locked doors, thunderclouds gathered over the city.

During all that confusion, where was the man who had set off the excitement? Robespierre had still not shown his face at city hall, though it was widely known that he had been released. He had fled across the river and had locked himself into the *Mairie* of the *5me Arrondissement*. For once in his life, he was scared, plagued by doubt and unable to reach a decision. What chance did he and his supporters stand by trial under his own Prairial Law? The outcome was a certainty: death. Could he still count on a last-minute rescue by Hanriot and his National Guard? While Paris exploded and members of the *Commune* were looking all over the city for him, Hanriot was slumped over a table in *L'auberge du Cheval-Vert*[7] in the Rue Geoffrey l'Asnier, within shouting distance of city hall, snoring. This left Robespierre no choice

[7] Danton had lived there during his first visit to Paris.

but to put his future in the hands of the mob, Marat's
fearsome instrument of terror. All depended now on the
reaction by the section heads and the street rabble. With
this bearing heavily on him and fully aware that he had
been declared an outlaw, he made his way to *l'Hôtel de
Ville*. He arrived there around 10.30 pm and acted with great
precaution, as he did not want to confound his supporters
and put himself into the same camp as those 'rebels inside
the *Convention*' whom he was now accusing of high treason.
Nothing was lost; but instead of acting and striking hard, he
allowed valuable time to pass.

All the elements for a full-blown civil war were assembled.
The *Thermidorians* of the *Convention*, supported by the
bourgeoisie and half the city's sections, Deputy Barras and
his detachment of gendarmes, Robespierre and his Jacobins,
Hanriot's cannons, and the *communard* mob of Paris. The
Place de la Maison-Commune, in front of the open windows
of the city hall's *Salon de l'Egalité*, became a hive of rumour.
The mood of the huge crowd grew angrier by the minute. The
rabble raised its ugly head, windows were smashed and shops
looted. All the revolutionary powder had been gathered: it
would need only the slightest spark to set off a bloodbath.
Around midnight, a report that many of the section leaders
had begun to side with the *Convention* started to circulate
in the tightly packed crowd. When this momentous news
reached the crowd, many of those who had been waiting in
vain for hours for a message from *l'Incorruptible* began to
waver. Arguments and fights broke out, and the first groups
began to wander off. Had Robespierre immediately addressed
the multitude from the open window, he could have changed
their mood. He didn't. And then the unexpected happened.

Suddenly, Paris found itself in the grip of a violent summer
storm.[8] The downpour increased in fury. Within moments the

---

[8] E. Hamel, *Histoire de Robespierre*.

mob was breaking up, people trudged through the lashing rain to drift home, splashing through puddles that had covered the pavement. Gullies had become rivers, the lanes leading from the *Marais* down to the Seine had become torrents, which tore out cobblestones and flushed down garbage and drowned dogs. Then the gunners pulled out, dragging their cannons behind them. They heaved them through the network of lanes leading uphill into the *Marais*, fighting their way against a torrent of rushing waters. Shadowy figures danced through puddles, jumping from stone to stone and over the rubble that had been washed down. Even the rats were abandoning the overflowing sewers.

The sudden rainstorm drowned Robespierre's last hope. For a spine-tingling hour, clouds unzipped and dumped a million tons of water onto the city. When Robespierre stepped up to the window and looked down on the *Place de Grève*, ankle-deep under water and utterly deserted, he knew that his cause was lost. His shield, the masses from the Paris sections loyal to him, had abandoned him. By one o'clock, the square was entirely deserted. Hanriot, who finally had been roused from his drunken stupor, couldn't locate his *cannoniers*. A downpour had destroyed a revolutionary dream and would now bring a dictator down.[9]

Inside city hall pandemonium ruled. A panic-stricken Couthon had arrived at city hall just after midnight. With Robespierre, he formed a *Comité d'Execution*, and together with Saint-Just he worked out a proclamation that called for assistance from the *Commune*, specially addressed to the *Section des Piques*, Robespierre's own constituency.

'*Tous les patriotes sont proscrits* . . . Brothers and friends,

---

[9] Madelin: 'Suddenly, the rain which had menaced since noon, came down in trombs and torrents. It gave the crowd an excuse to disperse. Hanriot could no longer locate any of his gunners. Robespierre had finally decided to sign a call to arms – too late.'

la patrie is in mortal danger. The wicked have mastered the *Convention*, which holds the virtuous Robespierre in chains. *Aux armes citoyens!* To arms! Death to the traitors!'

At around two o'clock, while Robespierre and Couthon were drawing up the proclamation, the Conventionist Paul Barras acted. A column of three dozen gendarmes, under Leonard Bourdon, approached the *Place de la Maison-Commune* with great caution. They expected to face a huge crowd and found instead a deserted square. Bourdon's gendarmes stormed up the grand staircase of Paris City Hall. As they burst into the *Salon de l'Egalité* they found a dozen people gathered around Robespierre. The man himself was sitting in a chair, having just started to set the first two letters of his name to the proclamation. Bourdon yelled: 'Give up, traitor.' To which Robespierre screamed back: 'It is you who are the traitor. For this I will have you shot.' The ensuing anarchy and bedlam set off one of the great controversies of the French Revolution. Who shot Robespierre?[10]

As the gendarmes of the *Convention* burst into the room one of them, a certain Merda, or Méda, fired his pistol from point-blank range. The shot struck Robespierre; it went through his cheek and shattered the jawbone. His face fell forward, onto the decree he had just begun to sign. The paper, bearing the first two letters of his name: R O . . ., was splattered with the blood gushing from his mouth, while his head fell forward.[11] One of Robespierre's closest supporters, Philippe Le Bas, pulled a pistol from his belt. Saint-Just, standing next to him, tore open his shirt and

[10] This is one of the most highly discussed events of the French Revolution. Was it Robespierre by his own hand? Or was it the Gendarme Méda who fired the bullet? It's a question left unanswered, since the participants in the drama could never agree on what really happened in those first minutes. So is Robespierre to be portrayed as a man of courage or as one who died by his own hand in an act of cowardice?'

[11] The paper still exists, on the bottom are the first two letters: R o . . . (on display in the Carnavalet Museum). Another gendarme claimed to have fired the pistol shot, a certain Dulac, but his story has been discounted.

called out: 'Brother, shoot me!' Le Bas just sneered and said:
'*Pauvre con* (Simplistic fool), I have more important things
to do.' With this, he raised the gun and blew out his brains.
Robespierre's younger brother, Augustin, threw himself out
of a window and broke his leg. Hanriot was somewhat
luckier, he fell from a window and landed in a deep pile of
manure; he remained there for hours, snoring off his binge,
before a gendarme heard him next morning. Couthon, a
cripple, grabbed a knife and slashed his veins. A husky
gendarme picked him up and threw him down the monumental marble staircase. Couthon tumbled down, broke any
number of bones and finally lay there, senseless. Robespierre,
blood-splattered, with his clothes in disarray, was laid out on
a tabletop, dumped onto an open cart, and dragged to the
Convention, where Barras made a dramatic entrance: 'The
traitor Robespierre is outside.' To which pronouncement
the president of the *Convention* rose and announced: 'The
proper place for the traitor and his accomplices is on the
Place de la Révolution!' Thus he designated Robespierre for
the guillotine.

The decisive battle of the French Revolution on 9. *Thermidor*
was not fought with cannons and bayonets, but with words,
treachery, fear, and a fluke of the weather.

The end came late next afternoon, 28 July 1794. Fouché
had delayed the time of execution to give the Parisians a
chance 'to witness the end of an ogre'. At 6 pm, the gate
of the *Conciergerie* swung open and three horse-drawn
tumbrels of Monsieur Samson, *le Monsieur de Paris* and
public executioner, drove out into the streets, lined by
a multitude of jeering Parisians. The caravan took the
well-established route to the guillotine, dubbed the *Via
Dolorosa*.[12] Until now, the hatred of many Parisians had

---

[12] From the main gate of the *Conciergerie*, crossing the Seine on the Pont Neuf,
and along the Rue St Honoré to the Place de la Concorde.

only been in looks and whispers, now they screamed their maledictions out loud. '*A bas le tyrant!* Down with the tyrant', yelled the same hysterical masses, who only weeks before had been on their knees before this *Etre Suprême*, the Supreme Being. Hanriot, still drunk, caked in manure with one eye hanging from its socket, lay next to a broken Augustin in the lead cart. The main attraction, Maximilien Robespierre, was forced to stand in the second wooden cart, bound to it by ropes to keep him from falling down. The assistant executioner slapped the two Normandy greys hitched to the tumbrel, and the procession set off. Gendarmes pointed to the disshevelled Robespierre with their sabres. A fallen, degraded human wreck, spat on, doused with foul refuse, a common culprit on the way to the guillotine. The pain in his shattered jaw must have been excruciating as the wooden wheels of the cart bounced over the uneven cobblestones of the Rue St Honoré, towards the Place de la Révolution.[13] The cart was brought to a halt in front of Robespierre's lodgings. A man had fetched a bucket of blood from a slaughterhouse and was painting the outside of the house of the Duplay family. Those horrid *tricoteuses*, so named because they sat around the guillotine and with glee observed the daily blood-letting while knitting (*tricoter*), now danced around the tumbrel whose wheels they would have dragged gladly, only the day before, over a thousand of Robespierre's victims.[14] The people behaved not only intolerantly and fanatically, but cruelly in venting their hatred. A woman climbed on the side of the car, struck Robespierre in his bandaged face, which made him wince, and yelled: 'Go to hell, with the curses of all the mothers of France.' At an intersection, the procession halted to allow a funeral to pass. A certain Madame Aigné had taken her

[13] Today's Place de la Concorde. The guillotine stood in front of the entrance into the Tuileries Gardens.
[14] G. Aubry.

own life as Robespierre's men had come to arrest her. She may have been his last victim.[15]

A crowd of eight thousand had congregated on the *Place de la Révolution*. The *gendarmes* had to make use of their bayonets to force their passage through the crowd. High above the people loomed Robespierre's own instrument of terror, the guillotine. One by one, the twenty-two were herded up its steps, to face Monsieur Samson and his two assistants. Couthon screamed and begged, and fouled his trousers. Most others had to be pushed or were carried to the bloodstained board. Their heads began to pile up in the baskets and their bloody corpses were unceremoniously dumped from the platform onto straw lined death carts. Only Saint-Just kept his dignity to the very end; he never spoke out in his own defence and mounted the ladder with a resolute step. At twenty-seven, he faced death with that same ice-cold insensibility that had made him the most enigmatic man of the Revolution.

The twenty-first victim of the blade was *l'Incorruptible* himself, Maximilien Robespierre. The blood of the twenty who had preceded him had formed a crimson pool around the base of the platform. For the first time, a hush fell over the square: only the neighing of a horse here, and a muted sob there. Men took a tighter grip on their sticks, women crossed themselves, murmuring: 'Here goes the devil.' The stares were fixed on an elevated platform and a gleaming blade. Samson's assistants hauled Robespierre's broken body up the ladder. His blood-smeared hands dangled over the arms of the executioners, his feet banged hard on each step. From his bandaged face stared a pair of eyes unseeingly towards a leaden sky. They pushed him towards the board when his knees sagged. They left him lying there as a symbol of a fallen

---

[15] That day, another 7,500 prisoners were still in Parisian jails, waiting to be executed.

tyrant, before they lashed him to the board, red and slithery with the blood of those who had gone before him. The assistant hangman tore off the blood-soaked bandage from the shattered jaw. Robespierre screamed out in pain. Samson gave a brief nod, an assistant tilted the board forward so that it came to rest between the two oaken uprights. With a dull thud the wooden neck-clamp dropped into place. Samson pulled down the lever and the blade fell. Everyone heard its whisper. A sigh went across the *Place de la Révolution*.

A tyrant walked through the gate of martyrdom into history.[16]

Robespierre was put to death according to his own constitution (Article 17):

'*Que tout individu qui usurperoit la souveraineté, soit a l'instant mis a mort par les hommes libres.* – That any individual who usurps the sovereignty of the state be instantly put to death by free men.'

The reign of terror died with Robespierre[17], a revolutionary whose actions were solely guided by the virtue of some obscure Supreme Being. With a reign of terror Robespierre wanted to assure a reign of virtue, and attain eternal peace through violence. Where causing bloodshed would trouble the ordinary citizen, this extremist marched boldly ahead. Until the day when some of those he terrified could stand no more the horrible anguish, posing themselves the question each morning: will I be next on the list? On 9. *Thermidor*, fear instilled in cowards the courage of a last hope.

That, and a sudden rainstorm brought down an incorruptible man.

[16] By an irony of fate, Robespierre's body was dumped into the same mass grave as Louis XVI before him.
[17] A final batch of seventy-two, Jacobins and supporters of Robespierre, kept an appointment with the executioner on the following day, 29, July 1794. For the rest, the prison doors were thrown open.

Frozen Dutch Fleet 23 January 1795

North Sea

Texel

marsdiep

Den Helder

Ice

Issel Meer

French Cavalry

Amsterdam

Holland

Germany

marsdiep

Ice

Den Helder

Ice

The frozen armada
23 January 1795

*'Till France is ready, nothing will provoke her
to quarrel with us, and when she is ready,
nothing will prevent it.'*
Prince William V, *Stadhouder* of Holland, 1787

'I demand your immediate surrender!' yells the young man,
sitting stiffly on his horse, a blue-white-red *cocarde* of the
French Republic prominent on his tri-cornered hat. Under
his black coat, open at the waist, show a pair of pistols
stuck in his belt. Defiantly, he stares into the open mouths
of huge naval cannons. Up on deck stands an admiral, with a
deep crease across his forehead. With a grim smile the senior
naval officer stares down at the plucky young horseman. He
must admit, here is someone who behaves with an air that
portrays well the revolutionary spirit sweeping Europe.

'Why don't we discuss such serious matters over dinner
aboard my flagship,' replies the admiral. The young man
with the *cocarde* accepts the invitation.

It is 10 am, this 23 January 1795.

When asked by the English ambassador about his fears of a

French intervention into Dutch affairs, the *Stadhouder* (state caretaker, or head of state), replied curtly: 'Till France is ready, nothing will provoke her to quarrel with us, and when she is ready, nothing will prevent it.' That was in 1787, at a time when Prince William V, *Stadhouder* of Holland, was among the most disliked personalities in his own country. For a valid reason: his despotism had so frustrated the rich merchants and burghers that they kicked him out. In 1786, he returned to power on the back of the English fleet. His lack of popularity was no secret to the French. Always out to cash in on given opportunities, they connived to gain benefit from the tense political situation in the Austrian dominion of Holland. With this in mind, the court of Versailles dispatched an envoy to contact the opposition party, the *patriots*.

The Marquis de Rayneval was shocked by what he discovered. He tried to warn his monarch of a possible revolutionary contagion. 'The fervour of the Patriot party here has made terrifying progress and if it is not stopped it is to be feared that it may cause an explosion which will have incalculable consequences,' he wrote in his dispatch. This assessment was enough to shake the French king. Lack of assistance from Paris put an end to the Dutch Barbacan uprising of 1787. Without the French, the 9,000 Patriot troops were hopelessly outgunned and outnumbered. On 13, September 1787, 26,000 Prussians marched into Holland, and the revolt was quashed at the point of their bayonets.[1]

In the aftermath of the failed uprising, Holland found itself in a state of confusion and uncertainty. But Prussian boots had not managed to trample Holland's revolutionary spirit. Its torch was taken up by young firebrands and carried into France. Two years later, the day a Paris mob stormed the Bastille, the prediction of the Marquis de Rayneval was fulfilled. For the next years, the French were preoccupied

[1] Schama, S., *Patriots and Liberators*, New York, 1977.

by their internal affairs. In 1792, the Duke of Brunswick and an émigré army marched on Paris; the march ended at Valmy (September 1792), followed by more French victories at Wattignies (October 1793) and Fleurus (February 1794).[2] These revolutionary successes rekindled the political discussions in Holland. Patriotic committees for insurrection sprang up throughout the land, and a delegation was sent to Paris for secret talks with the French.

In France, the situation was in ferment. The revolution was devouring its children. By the summer of 1794, the heads of Danton and Robespierre had fallen under the guillotine. A *Directoire* had taken control of state affairs. High on their agenda was the dual war against England and the Habsburg Empire. This war had to include Holland. Since 1713, the country was an Austrian dominion, while English royalty had family ties with the Orange family, and the dominion's *Stadhouder*, Prince William V van Oranije.

The survivors of the Barbacan Rebellion had gone underground and formed into secret chapters. Under the able leadership of Herman Willem Daendels, who had been an officer in the French revolutionary army at the battle of Valmy, the Dutch anti-loyalists numbered perhaps 40,000, poorly armed and not able to attempt another popular uprising.

In France, a struggle for power and the political crisis this had provoked made the heirs of Robespierre react true to the motto: 'When facing trouble at home, export it to your neighbour.' The French army was only too happy to act as the liberator of Holland. The problem was within the French army itself; it was in a state of near anarchy; its logistics were in shambles, its discipline on the decline. Robespierre's terror had left its mark on the morale of the revolutionary forces. During the upheaval, generals had been put into prison, corporals had been made generals; officers were revelling

---

[2] In both battles, General Jourdan was victorious against the Austrians.

in luxury while soldiers suffered extreme hardship. Whole units deserted. Those heroic defenders of *la patrie*, who had followed the *levée en masse* (popular call-up) of 1793, were nowhere in sight by 1794. The state of distress in the Thermidorian Armies became legendary. Yet a spirit of *'l'an II'* had survived in one unit, the Army of the North under General Charles Pichegru. He had taken command, when its former general, Lazare Hoche, was thrown into prison during the Terror. Pichegru had begun his career as an artillery soldier during the American War of Independence. He proved an able sergeant and had moved quickly through the ranks; but he was a mediocre leader when compared to his subordinate, General Jean-Baptiste Jourdan. Pichegru was one of those heroic revolutionary generals who not only had to worry about their heads during the Terror, but had also to prevent the armies of the enemies of the Republic from invading France. Or, in the words of Jourdan: 'A time of the greatest danger'.[3] He didn't realise how close the danger was.

Pichegru was a political opportunist; when told of Robespierre's fall, he wrote: 'We fight for France's liberty, but never will we become the tools of a tyrant.' His letter, taken as a sign of loyalty was warmly received in Paris. It showed a certain naivety on his part; a general was expected to look after his task, which was to fight a war, and not get involved in politics. In the autumn of 1794, while three French armies under Jourdan, Moreaux, and Michaud advanced on the Rhine, Pichegru received instructions from the new *Directoire* to take the initiative and invade Holland. A victory in the north was welcome, it would lead to territorial rectification, annexation, and the control over the vital Channel ports. 'And grab their navy, if you get a chance,' he was told as an afterthought.

It came as complete shock to the *Stadhouder* of Holland, as also to the commander of the English contingent, the Duke

---

[3] Jourdan, J.B., *Memories militaires de la campagne de 1794.*

of York, when Pichegru and his Army of the North suddenly swung towards Holland. While the English had counted on holding off just a few divisions, they found themselves with the prospect of facing an entire army, flushed by the victory at Fleurus. Yet even more worrisome was a rising unrest within the country. Once Jourdan's French had beaten back the Austrians at Fleurus, small parties of armed *patriots* attacked garrisons and blocked vital river crossings. This, the Dutch government couldn't allow; it ordered countrywide arrests. The leader of the *patriot* insurgents, Herman Willem Daendels, went to Paris to see the members of the *Directoire*. He pointed out that the French had to act fast or be responsible for a massacre of all their friends, disposed to carry out the Batavian Revolution.

On the military scene, things moved with great speed. General Pichegru took Brussels (10 July 1794) and Antwerp (22 July). The fortress of Ijpetren surrendered and all of Flanders fell into French hands. The setback at Fleurus left for the *Generality's* (Dutch) Army only the stronghold of Brabant, which could be defended to the very end by opening the sluice gates on the dykes along the coast. Pichegru pushed north, expecting to throw the British back across the Maas before the autumn rains set in. Following a skirmish near Boxtel, the Duke of York and his 28,000 troops locked themselves inside the walls of Hertogenbosch, while 22,000 Austro-Dutch defenders took up positions around Breda. The French could count on a formidable weapon within the country: the re-emerging *patriots* were gaining rapidly in power. By the middle of September 1794, their subversive literature swamped the streets. It included a new patriotic anthem:

> *As God shall will it, so shall there be,*
> *Liberty! Equality!*

Finally, on 18 October the *patriots* came out into the

open and declared: 'Before long, standing with our French friends and allies, we will rise as one man against the tyranny.'[4] But their allies were nowhere near to stand by their side. Pichegru had crossed the Waal and, instead of heading straight for Amsterdam, diverted to Nijmegen. The Batavian revolt collapsed, and on 18 October, six of its leaders were arrested. The police slipped up on one, the most dangerous of the lot. Herman Willem Daendels got away and ended up in the French camp. He pressed Pichegru to move speedily north, but the Frenchman ignored his request. This provoked Daendels to issue a general call to arms for his Dutch citizens, something which greatly annoyed the French general.

At the same time, the situation had become extremely precarious for Prince William who had already dispatched a mission to London, asking for urgent military assistance. Prime Minister Pitt was not interested, and said so. The foreseeable collapse of Holland was a good way to get rid of Dutch maritime competition in the West Indies, and this would greatly further British trade. Pitt's gambit was so obvious that the clerk of the Secretary to the States-General, jotted into the official ledger: 'A person until now known as a stout partisan of England, told me that only a traitor to the Fatherland could find anything to say in favour of England.'

Holland's destiny was decided in the *Convention* in Paris. Jean Lambert Tallien, one of the men who had brought about Robespierre's downfall, loudly claimed that 'we need Spanish and Dutch ships with whose help we would hasten to the banks of the Thames and destroy the new Carthage'. The army of Pichegru was ordered to march north.

The Netherlands was protected, as it had always been, by three major water obstacles: the Maas, the Waal, and the Lek. The retreating British had burned most of the

---

[4] Jorissen, *De Patrioten.*

bridges, and the French had no means to cross the rivers. To build floating bridges would require big boats, at least ten metres in length. Dragging such boats along the roads from France was both impractical and time-consuming. Heavy autumn rains had flooded the rivers and made a crossing on makeshift bridges a hazardous affair. The weather, and not the Austro-British armies, brought the French to a halt. Pichegru did nothing. He just sat in camp and waited. His relations with Jourdan, his junior, commanding the Army of the Rhine, were strained. When Jourdan asked assistance to take Mainz, held by 100,000 Austrians under General Wurmser, Pichegru delayed unreasonably. He argued that the point of greatest danger was on the Upper Rhine, posed by the British and Austrians based in Holland, ready to strike for Alsace. Only months later the reason for his delaying manoeuvre became clear.

While Jourdan, Marceau, and Bernadotte held back the Austrians on the Rhine, it began to snow in Holland. Pichegru's men had to sleep in the open without adequate covers. What made Pichegru decide against marching on became the subject for much discussion. First it was blamed on the weather, then on a doubt whether overall control could be achieved before the onset of winter. Also the constant worry that, as final resort, the Dutch or English would open the dykes to drown his army like rats in the raging flood. Perhaps he was not aware that the English had already been ordered to withdraw. With winter around the corner, the Dutch Campaign was limping to a close. Pichegru was ready to pull back when he received help in an unexpected manner. Frost set in; never before in the century had the temperature fallen so low. The natural defences of Holland, its dykes and rivers froze solid, much to the delight of children, who used the waterways for skating.

'*La Hollande est maintenant solide*,' wrote Daendels to Pichegru, to encourage a rapid advance into the heart of the country. 'Holland is now consolidated earth. The rivers that surround it, the floods that can protect it in time of crisis, are as hard as the frozen ground. Amsterdam is connected to Paris by a stretch of paved road.'[5]

On 2 December 1794, the Duke of York abandoned his troops and embarked for England. Still, Pichegru would not be hurried and continued to advance with extreme caution. By 27 December, his army had crossed the Lower Maas, on 8 January it was on the Waal, and, on 15 January, set over the Lek. All along his drive, he pushed before him an utterly dejected and discouraged British force, bereft of leader and provisions. Having suffered great loss, the English contingent finally withdrew from Hanover. Giving up the Lowlands, their historic springboard into Europe, proved a debacle for London. For the French, frustrated along the Rhine, the Dutch Campaign was an astounding and unexpected victory and a great morale booster. In one month, they had captured most of Holland, and Pichegru was lionised in the French press as a brilliant general and revolutionary hero. Yet Holland had not been conquered – it had simply given up.

Once the French crossed the Waal, the situation for the loyal Dutch forces became hopeless. The troops of the First Coalition were in complete disarray. A government call-up to arms *en masse* yielded a mere fifty men. On 16 January, it became clear that no further resistance could be offered against the advancing French, and that Holland would have to sue for peace. The Dutch blamed it on the English, who 'have ruined our manufacturers, devastated our trade and dragged us into a ruinous war contrary to our interests. The *Stadhouder* bears towards the English such hatred that he is willing to put on the tricolour *cocarde* and unite with them to exterminate this race [the English] for whom nothing

---

[5] Ernest Lavisse, *Histoire de France contemporaine*, Paris 1920: 'Les fleuves qui l'entourent, les inondations qui la couvrent des invasions sont dur comme la terre. Amsterdam est de plain-pied avec Paris.'

is sacred.' This devastating statement came from Volkier
Benedinck who had served as an officer in the British Army
during the American War of Independence.

The French entered Utrecht on 17 January, and just after
midnight of 18 January 1795, Prince William V fled by ship
from Haarlem to Harwich. The same night, the Republic of
Batavia was proclaimed. Count Clerfait, the Austrian general
commanding the Habsburg troops in Holland, summed it up:
'Never has a revolution been so rapid.'

The fact was, Prince William V had been given no option.
While Pichegru's army marched relentlessly north, each new
day heightened his anxiety. To protect his exit, he counted on
his war fleet to make for England. For this, he had ordered
his Admiral of the Fleet, Jan Hendrik van Kinsbergen, to
anchor the ships of the Dutch Navy in the Marsdiep, a
three-kilometre-wide strait, located between the mainland
of the Helder, and the island of Texel. Leading up to the
water was a broad zone of mud flats (*slikken*) and salt
marshes, cut up by tidal creeks, over which the sea tides
washed twice daily, and so prohibited the advance of an
army with carts and cannons. It was a good plan, but the
Dutch *Stadhouder* hadn't counted on the weather.

At the beginning of December weather played a key part in
events. A week of clear nights produced an unusual drop in
temperature. Within days the Wadden Zee from the Helder
to Harlingen became a solid sheet of ice. This eliminated any
hope of entering the Ijselmeer, Holland's internal sea. This
initial frost was followed by a furious north-western gale.
Fog and sleet hampered the fleet's movements. Still, with
great seamanship, the admiral managed to bring his vessels
into safe anchorage in the lee of Texel Island. For days, it
howled and snowed. When the weather finally cleared and
the sailors stared in wonder at a pristine landscape, they
found to their dismay that the exit from the strait into
the ocean had been blocked by an ice jam. Ice in front and

ice behind – fifteen ships-of-the-line, two cargo vessels, and several smaller cannon boats were caught in the strait. Admiral Van Kinsbergen realised that it would be at least a month before the channel was clear enough to make their escape into the open sea. Having tried, and failed, to blast their way through the ice jam with black powder[6] the admiral came to the sad conclusion that his ships were trapped, and that he would have to scuttle the fleet should the French try to take it. There was an additional problem: the Marsdiep anchorage was so shallow that it would permit the French to recover his valuable cannons. It forced him into a painful decision: instead of firing his gunpowder at the enemy, he would use it to blow up his beloved ships. Meanwhile, the temperature kept on dropping and, within days, the ships were solidly locked in a thick layer of ice.

In the middle of January, a piece of amazing intelligence fell into the hands of General Pichegru. It had to do with the Dutch fleet. He called a war council. 'Who are we closest to . . .' he stabbed his finger at the map, '. . . here?' Texel Island!

'General de Wynter and *la 4me division de Souham, mon general.*'

'I want them to march immediately for the Helder,' he ordered. He had just heard that the entire Dutch war fleet was trapped in the ice.

Commandant Louis Joseph Lahure, a Belgian student who had fled to France after the failed Barbacan rebellion of 1787, was in charge of a battalion in *la 4me division de Souham*. His unit was made up of 780 *fantassins* (foot soldiers), 128 hussars, and 39 gunners, with four small bronze cannons. They were nearest to the Dutch fleet. At midnight on 20 January a dispatch rider dashed into his camp with orders

---

[6] Ice cannot be blasted as an explosion has no lateral effect on ice, it can only be sawed.

to move immediately in the direction of Alkmaar and the Helder. The battalion reached the Marsdiep on the evening of 22 January. Across the frozen narrows, they could see a row of lights, but it was too dark to venture onto the ice; Lahure decided to make camp and wait for the morning. Though the night was bitter cold, Lahure forbade campfires. While the French were in bivouac, a solitary rider passed by them and made his way across the frozen strait. When he reached the flagship of the Dutch admiral, he was immediately shown into his presence.

'A most secret dispatch from the States-General of Holland, Admiral.'

Van Kinsbergen took the envelope, broke the seal and read the note. A shadow crossed his face and he shook his head. Then he handed the dispatch to his second in command, Captain Reyntjes.

'But . . . but that is . . . treason,' stuttered the captain.

The admiral nodded sadly. 'So it is, but we must abide by it.' A piece of parchment relieved him of all further responsibility as to what to do with his fleet in case of a French attack.

This was due to a dramatic turn of events that had taken place a few days before, on 17 January. The *patriots* had taken control of the *Staten Generaal* (States-General or state assembly), and had voted to cease all further hostilities immediately. To this purpose, dispatch riders were sent out to the various units, carrying the state council's order. 'And so it is decided by the States-General of Holland to instruct every military commander to put up no further resistance against the French troops.'

French commanders, like Lahure, had not been immediately informed of this.

For Commandant Lahure and his men, half frozen and huddled together under makeshift tents, the morning of 23 January dawned with a curtain of fog that had descended over the frozen narrows of the Marseiep. Lahure mused about his situation – a Dutch-Belgian, commanding French cavalry, attacking a Dutch war fleet at sea! What madness! How could he, with his thirty-nine gunners, dragging four six-pounders across the ice, take on fifteen ships-of-the-line with hundreds of pieces of naval artillery. His puny six-pound cannon balls would not put a dent into the solid oak of a battleship. This forced him into a bold decision; it had to be bold, though many would call it a foolhardy gamble. It was a case of best solution in a series of bad options. He realised that his greatest ally was the fog; it would cover his approach across the ice. He would leave the *fantassins* and guns behind, ride out with his one hundred and twenty *8me Hussars*, and hope for the best. He knew nothing about the conditions of the frozen channel, nor whether the ice would carry the weight of his men and horses. And that even before he had to face more guns than he had men! A frontal charge would be blasted backward by the big naval guns and his men would be blown off the frozen sea. With this unattractive prospect foremost on his mind, he issued strict orders for his hussars to follow him and not to break into any foolish, sabre-swinging charge. The flagbearer unfurled the revolutionary colours, Lahure took a brief salute, and one hundred and twenty-eight hussars rode out onto the ice. Soon the fog swallowed them up. Suddenly they found themselves directly in front of the fleet.

Lahure's luck continued to hold, the ice had not cracked and the Dutch naval batteries didn't open fire. The French cavalry rode up to the ships ... and an ageing admiral, who had expected the attack by a huge army, found his vessels surrounded by one hundred and twenty-eight hussars under the leadership of a former Dutch student. It is hard to imagine who would have been the more surprised: the admiral, looking down from the afterdeck of his battleship on a handful of riders, or the cavalry commander when an admiral-of-the-fleet proposed: 'Let's discuss such serious matters over dinner ...'

And thus it happened that on 23 January 1795, in a feat that has remained unique in the annals of warfare, cavalry captured a battle fleet on the high seas. The rest was negotiated over a candlelit supper aboard the admiral's flagship.

General Pichegru dispatched a note to Paris: '*La marine hollandaise est à nous.*' The Dutch navy was theirs! That news was electrifying, and Paris took to the streets, celebrating a great patriotic triumph. Pichegru became the man of the hour.

As happens so often in history, the real hero's name was never mentioned. Commandant Lahure and his resolute horsemen had shown great audacity and imagination. They rode out with no previous knowledge of the Dutch decision to cease hostilities; they only knew that out on the ice were the gaping mouths of guns directed at them, and that the Dutch navy had a great tradition of loyalty towards its prince. Years later, Napoleon bestowed on Commandant Louis Joseph Lahure the title of *Baron de l'Empire*. Lahure ended his career as a general, having served an emperor and, after Waterloo, two French kings.

A different fate was in store for '*l'hero de Hollande*', General Charles Pichegru. During a skirmish in 1804, French soldiers captured the coach of an Austrian general with two boxes of secret dispatches. From these it was learned that Pichegru had been all along in contact with the Prince de Condé and the Comte de Montgaillard, leaders of the *émigrés* and mortal enemies of the Revolution. Pichegru's refusal to come to the assistance of Jourdan, and his reluctance to advance faster and deeper into Holland, was not ill-will, but high treason.[7] While marching into Holland, he was secretly negotiating to open up an invasion route for the Austrian armies to march on Paris. The reason for his treasonable

---

[7] *Letters between Pichegru and Conde*, 1795, published in Vienna 1898.

act was never elucidated; perhaps it was prompted by a grab for power, or by jealousy over the military successes of Jourdan, his junior in line of command. Whatever his reason, the general could ill afford to contribute to the defeat of an army he hoped to have as his ally. Following this stunning revelation, Pichegru was arrested and thrown into Temple prison, where he was found strangled with his own tie.[8] The full extent of the *Pichegru Conspiracy* was never discovered.

In October 1806, Napoleon abolished the Republic of Batavia, created the Kingdom of Holland, and put his brother Louis on the throne.

The incredible story of the capture of the Dutch navy was embellished, and great feats of heroism were added.[9] There never was a sea battle fought by cavalry, and not a single shot was fired in anger. An admiral had been ordered to obey a ceasefire, which he did, and a cavalry commander reaped the spoils of a beaten foe that had stopped defending itself. The military history of France is sufficiently rich in glorious exploits that it does not need an imaginary battle to enhance its grandeur.

One fact is certain: without the sudden drop in temperature, and the ice in the Marsdiep, the Dutch fleet would have sailed for England to strengthen the British Navy – fifteen more ships for Nelson, and Trafalgar. As it turned out, Nelson didn't need them.

[8] 6 April 1804.
[9] *Archives de la guerre*, du 1er au 10 pluviôse, an III., per le general Salm, commandant 4eme division.

A brave called Tecumseh

5 October 1813

'Shall we let our people become annihilated without
 a fight?
Shall we abandon the lands given by the Great Manitou to
 his children?
Shall we leave behind the tombs of our ancestors?
 Never! Never!'
> Tecumseh, Chief of the Shawnee Nation, 1811.[1]

A sleek nuclear submarine cuts through the waters of Chesapeake Bay. Soon it will slip beneath the waters of the Atlantic to lie in wait somewhere in the depths of the world's oceans. Seen from the shore, this latest addition to the US Navy's nuclear arsenal bears no markings. Only its crew knows the name. It is the USS *Tecumseh*, named after an Indian brave who was once the scourge of the armies of America.

The Shawnee chief Tecumseh, hero of the War of 1812.

The saga of this brave began at the end of the eighteenth century. American pioneers were pushing deeper into Indian

[1] From a paper in the Tippecanoe Historic Council Library.

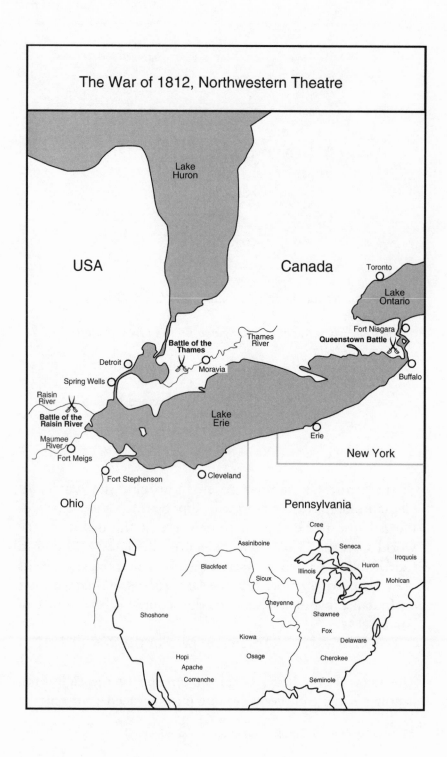

The War of 1812, Northwestern Theatre

territory. With their wagons and their families, they crossed through woods and swamps until they reached a wide river, the Wabash. Here were the traditional hunting grounds of a fierce tribe of American Indians, the Shawnee, whose territory extended from Indiana and Kentucky, into Michigan, and all the way north to the Great Lakes, which separated the United States of America from the British Dominion of Canada.

The story of Tecumseh, the great Indian warrior, begins in 1791, at a trading post called 'Keth-tip-pe-can-nunk', or, in its Americanised version, 'Tippecanoe'.[2] White prospectors traded sugar, salt, tobacco and beads, for furs with the Pottawattomie and Kickapoo tribes. To push back the Indian frontier and open new lands in Indiana and Michigan to white settlers, the trading post was razed to scatter the Indians. The eternal discord between Indian and white man was the question of who held title to the land. Force and violence nearly always settled this, and the white man had guns.[3] Faced with the profanation of their sacred hunting grounds, two Shawnee brothers revolted. Tenskatawa, who was to gain notoriety as 'The Prophet', and his brother Tecumseh had one ambition: to unite the tribes and oust the white man. While the Prophet installed his Indian followers at Tippecanoe in order to demonstrate to the white man his native birthright, Tecumseh, more farseeing, aimed to create a single Nation of Indians before tackling the settlers. With this in mind, he went as far south as Florida to incite the Seminoles to join ranks with his cause. 'There are those among us who will sell our lands! Why not sell the air, the great sea, as well as the earth? Didn't the Great Spirit create them for the use of his children? The only way to stop this evil is for the red man to unite in claiming a common and equal right in the land, as it was first, and should be now, for it was never divided.'

[2] Six miles north of Lafayette, Indiana.
[3] One of the noted exceptions is William Penn's treaty with the Indians.

And when the Seminole chief hesitated, Tecumseh spoke to him in anger: 'Your blood is white, and you do not believe I was sent by the Great Manitou. This will be my proof.' He handed the assembled Seminole braves a number of red sticks, one for each day, and said: 'Count well, because the day I return home, I shall stamp my foot on the earth and your ground will shake.' And it happened, the ground shook, and many Seminole warriors took this as a sign, picked up their cudgels and joined the Big Warrior to fight the white man.[4]

Once launched on his great unification scheme, Tecumseh travelled north for a pow-wow with the chiefs of the Illinois and Pottawattomie. 'The destruction of our race is near,' exclaimed Tecumseh to his braves, 'unless we put our quarrels aside and unite in a common cause against a common enemy.' His next travels took him as far afield as the land of the Delaware, the Ottawa, Miami, Chippewa, even the Iroquois of Quebec.

From Tippecanoe, 'The Prophet's Town', Tenskatawa called down fire and brimstone on white settlers for stealing the tribes' sacred hunting grounds and making braves drunk with their liquor. The militant activities of Tecumseh and his Prophet brother not only attracted over a thousand braves from the tribes, it greatly worried the settlers along the Indian frontier.

In early 1811, this growing native Indian threat was countered by the newly appointed Governor of the Indiana territory, General William Henry Harrison. He recruited a militia of a thousand men and armed them with muskets. While Tecumseh was still on his southern recruiting drive, Harrison and his men descended on Tippecanoe on 6 November 1811. They arrived just before dark and camped in the woods outside the Prophet's Town.

Tecumseh knew that the best means to harass the Yankees

---

[4] T. L. McKenney, in *History of the Indian Tribes of North America*.

lay in guerrilla tactics. His Shawnee knew the country, the Americans did not. In these 'wild and dark backwoods', American movement was hampered by cumbersome wagon trains and big guns, while the Shawnee travelled light. But the white man was also armed with muskets, while the Indian had only arrows and his tomahawk. With this in mind, Tecumseh had dispatched an urgent message to warn his brother never to venture into an open attack against a superior-armed force. But the Prophet refused to listen.

It was a cold and rainy night, with fires ringing the outer perimeter of the Yankee camp near Tippecanoe. While the American militia was asleep, albeit fully clothed, the Prophet exhorted his braves with a fiery speech. He assured them that a musket ball could never harm a brave. The tribes attacked at daybreak. Before the Americans could organise the Indians were upon them. In the next two hours, 62 Americans died. But the Shawnee and Winnebagos also suffered casualties – mainly from musket balls. This put them into such rage that they threatened to kill their Prophet. They abandoned Tippecanoe, which was put to the torch by Harrison's men later that day.

Although the precipitate action by his brother greatly frustrated Tecumseh, it helped to change his attitude. The men who had invaded their sacred hunting grounds were not only white men, they were white men from the United States! From that day on, he considered anyone American as his mortal enemy. It was to lead to wide repercussions: at the outbreak of the War of 1812, Tecumseh and his braves joined the British forces of Major General Isaac Brock, Governor General of Upper Canada.

War broke out on 18, June 1812. The territories of both belligerents, British Canada and the United States of America, were largely undeveloped. The American campaign relied as much on chance – the impact of the weather – as on strategy.

President Madison's plan called for the speedy taking of Montreal, but the New England governors refused to release their state militia for the effort. The inclination for war was much stronger in the 'Far West' – at that time the Indiana–Michigan territory – and the initial campaign drifted to the Niagara–Detroit region.

In the conflict, the British General Brock was opposed by the American General William Hull, Governor of the Michigan territory, who had already expressed self-doubts of his military ability before his appointment as commander of the United States' North-Western Army. A pessimist by nature, in matters of military strategy and tough decision he was no match for his counterpart. The campaign got under way; in order to reach its destination, Hull's army had to cross an area known as the Black Swamp, and also known for its hostile Indians, not to mention black flies. Adding to his problem was the unstable weather, when it rained, his wagon train got stuck in the mud, and once the rain stopped, hard-baked ruts made the tracks impassable. Rather foolishly he loaded his secret military papers aboard the schooner *Cuyahoga*, hoping thereby that they would reach Detroit by the faster sea route. Two days later, the *Cuyahoga* was intercepted by a British gunboat, the papers seized, and Brock had Hull's plans. It told him the size of his enemy's forces and about the morale of the troops.

Hull and his army stumbled on towards Detroit, harassed by black flies and Indians. Under cover of darkness, the 'savages' swooped down on his column, striking murderously before vanishing into the safety of the woods. While still on the march, Hull issued a declaration to the people of Canada in which he gave notice that any white man found by the side of an Indian would be immediately shot. This threat had its effect. Several hundred Canadians joined the Americans, and the situation now turned in favour of Hull. His next target was the Canadian Fort Malden, across the river from Detroit.

Hull's task looked to be greatly simplified when, under Colonel Lewis Cass, the vanguard found the British sentries asleep and captured the vital bridge over the Aux Canards River.[5] But instead of acting and marching on into Canada, General Hull was overcome with panic over supplies, and issued no further orders to the frustrated Colonel Cass, who withdrew his unit and gave up the river crossing. A few days later, Hull suggested a retreat to the River Raisin, and found himself faced with a mutiny by his Ohio volunteers. The situation got so bad that the contingent sent a petition to Governor Meigs of Ohio, demanding 'the arrest and displacement of their general'. Hull next retreated to Detroit with his thousands, while Brock rushed from the Niagara Peninsula to the relief of Fort Malden. For this he had only a tiny force of 260 militia and 40 regular redcoats of the *41st Regiment*. Given his numerical superiority in men and guns, Hull could have crossed the river and fought it out, and the war in the north-west would have been over. Instead, his retreat was hampered by torrential rains, which caused a great number of casualties from deadly swamp fever. One evening, the Indians dragged away some stragglers, and throughout the night the troops could hear them screaming, evidence enough of Indian torture, which sapped the morale of the commander and his troops.

A momentous encounter took place on 13 August 1812. Brock met Tecumseh. 'Among the Indians whom I found at Amherstburg,' he reported in a dispatch to Lord Liverpool in London, 'were some extraordinary characters. He who attracted most my attention most was the Shawanese chief, Tecumseh.'

When Brock explained that he was unfamiliar with the terrain around Detroit, Tecumseh drew a precise map on a

[5] This feat can be compared with the capture of the bridge over the Rhine at Remagen in January 1945.

piece of birch bark with his hunting knife. With a new ally and a thousand braves, Brock crossed the river to the American side at Spring Wells. From there, he dispatched an order to General Hull to surrender Detroit. He was counting on the American's fear of Indian atrocities. When Hull refused, Brock resorted to a ruse. He dressed his militia in the red uniform of regulars and made them parade where Hull could see them. Then Hull received a message that a relief expedition had got itself hopelessly lost in the woods and in one of the most disgraceful episodes in American military history, he surrendered his garrison on 16 August 1812. Major General Sir Isaac Brock marched his 260 soldiers unopposed into Detroit, while 2,500 Americans went into captivity. To show his appreciation and to honour his Indian ally, the British general slipped off his red military sash and wrapped it about Tecumseh's waist. The Shawnee responded by removing his beaded sash and presenting it to Brock. Then both embraced to the cheers of the soldiers and the war cries of the braves.

Before his surrender, a panicky Hull had sent orders to Fort Dearborn (Chicago) to evacuate the fort. A friendly Indian brave tried to warn its commander, Captain William Wells, that a great number of hostile braves had gathered in the region. Regrettably, Captain Wells obeyed General Hull's order, and on 15 August, a long column of soldiers, including wives and children, set out from Fort Dearborn. They were hardly outside their stockade when hundreds of Pottawattomie Indians set upon them, slaughtering a great number. The fate of Captain Wells was particularly horrid – his heart was cut out and eaten. This incident panicked the entire frontier population into heedless flight, and the Niagara border region was now ripe for the taking by the British and Canadians.

A further incident stopped this from happening. On 12 October, the American Colonel Solomon Van Rensselaer, in command of the New York militia, crossed the Niagara

River and attacked at the Queenstown Heights in Canada's Niagara Peninsula. General Brock, leading the counter-charge to regain a lost cannon, was struck mortally by a musket ball. Though the British went on to win this encounter, their troops were left without a leader.

A new threat was quickly emerging along the Wabash for the British unit holding down Detroit. A force of 2,000 Kentuckians was on the march. Tecumseh's Indians stopped them by using favourable winds to set the prairie on fire.

The weather intervened, and winter brought the fighting along the Canadian border to a halt. Tecumseh used this period to gather additional tribal support. His principal aim was not to aid the British fight – 'a white man's war' – but to protect the sacred hunting grounds for his red brothers. Washington leaders began to worry about the growing influence of Chief Tecumseh. It wasn't his thousand warriors that worried them, but the fact that these braves came from all of the north-western tribes. What, if on top of a war with Great Britain, America would have to face up to a co-ordinated Indian uprising? For that, the United States did not possess the military means. It is a fact of history that the British never realised the strong hand they had to play. London was far off and engaged in its struggle for survival against Napoleon. Brock, who had seen the virtue of gaining Tecumseh as an ally, was dead, and the new British commander, General Henry Proctor, was anything but a diplomat.

Fighting broke out anew on 22 January 1813. Proctor surprised some American units on the Raisin River and gave them a thrashing. Three hundred Americans were killed. Following the disaster at the Raisin River, the new US North-West Army commander, General William Henry Harrison, Governor of the Indiana territory and future President of the United States,[6] was forced to withdraw on Fort Stephenson. With the

[6] Elected in 1840 with a majority of less than 150,000.

road open for a British advance into Ohio, General Proctor marched on Fort Meigs, located at the mouth of the Maumee River, into Lake Erie. His force consisted of 500 regulars and 500 militia. But he could count on Tecumseh and 1,200 braves. For four days, Proctor pounded the fort with his heavy guns but Fort Meigs held out. When General Harrison was informed that a group of 1,200 Kentuckians under General Green Clay were on the way to relieve the besieged garrison, he rushed with his troops to their assistance. Before he could join Clay, the Kentuckians walked into a trap, cleverly set by Tecumseh. Six hundred militiamen were killed or captured by the Indians. When the Shawnee chief discovered that his warriors had begun to butcher their prisoners, he quickly intervened and his action saved many American lives on that 5 May 1813. What upset Tecumseh was Proctor's indifference to the massacre, and he spat at him: 'You are not fit to command, go and put on petticoats.' This phrase was to lead to a profound mistrust between a British general and an Indian leader. Where Brock had been the astute diplomat and brilliant strategist, Proctor was neither. He considered Tecumseh as nothing but an uncouth, bloody savage, infinitely below his officer cast and rank. He made this quite plain when Tecumseh pleaded to take the fort by a ruse. In front of his officers, Proctor yelled at the noble chieftain that he would never allow his soldiers to be used 'in that treacherous Indian manner'. After which insult, Proctor raised the siege. It must have come as a shock to him when most of the Indian braves drifted off and Tecumseh did nothing to stop them. For the Shawnee, this affair had shown them the extent of his inbred racism. This was a white-man's war!

Unfortunately, his grandiose plan for an Indian Confederacy was about to come to naught. The overture to the drama was fought on Lake Erie. After a decisive naval encounter on the lake, the British Great Lake Fleet surrendered. Proctor realised that without naval protection of his vital supply route, his position on the southern shore of Lake Erie had become untenable. One last time, Tecumseh rushed to his aid with a thousand braves. But Proctor, never a leader capable of bold decisions, decided to abandon the river line, and with it Fort Detroit. For his retreat to the Niagara Peninsula, he chose the Thames River Valley in the Province of Ontario.

In the meantime, Harrison had rallied some 4,500 men; Governor Shelby of Kentucky raised another 3,000. The last to join Harrison's corps was the one destined to play a key role in the upcoming drama. Congressman Colonel Richard Johnson, together with his brother James, had gathered around his banner 1,000 mounted Indian fighters, mostly adventurous and eager 'to do in the bloody redskins'. On 27 September 1813, the assembled force crossed from Middle Sister Island onto Canadian territory. Proctor ran, and Harrison ran after him.

To abandon the Detroit Frontier was to abandon their Indian allies who had fought all along beside the British. Tecumseh argued with the British General that not to take a stand was virtually to concede the loss of the entire territory of Upper Canada. He was well aware that his 1,000 braves were no match for the Americans in an open battle, and that he could not delay their advance, but he pleaded with Proctor to make a stand, first at Matthew Dolson's farm and then again at McGregor's Creek, but the British General cut him off and affronted him even further when he turned his back on the Shawnee chief.[7] Proctor was a man on the run and prone to panic, a narrow-minded leader who never considered his Indian allies to be the kind of fighters that could be relied on during an encounter with disciplined infantry, and furthermore they had nothing to fight for. He was wrong on

---

[7] Proctor was eventually court-martialled and cashiered.

both counts. Indians were first-class warriors, and by giving up their territory to an enemy, they had as much to lose as the white farmers.

There comes a point when even the best of soldiers get battle-drunk and exhausted from the permanent strain. For the British companies, this point had been reached. In addition came famine, storms, rain, and frost. 'Proctor's Army' had shrunk to 400 regulars, plus Tecumseh's 1,000 braves. The lack of men and supplies (Proctor had foolishly abandoned his guns, except one, and all his powder in Detroit) was wearing down the general's resolve, a feeling that quickly infected his already disheartened soldiers. With it he not only lost control of the conduct of the campaign, but also the control over his men, and the running of military affairs was now in the hands of Lieutenant-Colonel Augustus Warburton.

Harrison, in hot pursuit, learned about the British contingent's breakdown in morale. They ran so fast that 'the hounds couldn't catch them . . .',[8] so fast that they even failed to destroy the bridges after they had crossed them. Not so Tecumseh. At McGregor's Creek, he laid a clever ambush. His braves snaked along on their stomachs and camouflaged themselves in the treacherous darkness of the thicket. The first unit of American cavalry came along the road and waded cautiously into the creek. Some were swearing about their general's red panic to chase after the enemy. They were halfway across when the opposite bank erupted in a single volley that had men and horses fall wounded or dead into the water. The Indians reloaded and managed a second volley before the surviving horsemen raced back to the far bank leaving dozens of wounded riders and thrashing horses behind to drown. For Harrison, it was only a temporary hold-up, for his main party attacked with such verve and fury that they pushed the braves from their riverbank position. With the

[8] Title of a song.

Americans chest-high in the water, the Indians fired a final volley before they vanished into the trees.

That night, Tecumseh felt depressed. He had a premonition. 'What will become of my poor children?' he said to his friend Oshawna, chief of Sioux and Chippewa. Sitting with them around the fire was a certain William Caldwell, once a captain in *Butler's Rangers* but who now commanded his own unit of irregulars called *Caldwell's Rangers*. Caldwell held the leadership qualities of Tecumseh in great respect. He knew that Proctor no longer discussed his battle plans with the Indians, while the Indians considered Proctor a coward and his British soldiers as men whose fighting spirit had departed them. Even the official British historian though so. 'Numerical inferiority was not the only defect,' wrote Sir John Fortescue, 'for the men were so thoroughly demoralised. During their retreat they formed the conviction, which unhappily appears to have been justified, that their commander was more anxious for the safety of his family and his private property than of his troops.'

The Canadian winter was around the corner. It was cold that night around the campfires of the tired British soldiers. 'How long can Proctor go on running away? Mark my word, Harrison will force us to make a stand before we get to the Moravian Mission.' And so it was to be, early on the morning of 5 October 1813.

Harrison had finally caught up with Proctor's ragtag force. The Americans held a considerable numerical superiority, but that could be quickly offset by applying Tecumseh's ambush tactic. The place to make a stand was well chosen; a road leading through a field, with a small bog in the middle, and hemmed in on one side by the wide river and by a large, heavily overgrown swamp on the other. There, Canada's national emblem, the beavers, had been at work. They had cut down half a forest and used the logs to build a dam, which had flooded a substantial part of the ground. This again had considerably narrowed the field between wood and river.

The narrow approach stopped Harrison from bringing into play his numerical superiority. But there was another good reason for him not to engage his entire force. Although scouts had informed him of the British blocking position, they had failed to discover the whereabouts of Tecumseh's 1,000 braves. That greatly worried Harrison. He would be a fool to engage all his units before he knew where 'these savages' were hiding. Therefore, he handed the task of the initial assault to Colonel Richard Johnson and his 1,000 mounted riflemen. Their orders were to make a dash along both sides of the road and take out the 400 British regulars, who had formed up in a double line astride the road. Proctor had installed his unique piece of artillery in plain view, a small bronze cannon but without powder or shot!

Colonel Richard Johnson rode on ahead to study the situation. He discovered that the field between the river and the small bog in the centre of the field was too narrow for a frontal charge of his full complement of 1,000. Therefore, he split his force in half and gave one battalion to his brother, Lieutenant-Colonel James Johnson, with the order to hit the British line from the rear by leading his contingent forward, using the cover of heavy growth along the edge of a seemingly undefended large swamp.

During his long retreat, Proctor had hardly addressed a word to Tecumseh, but now he needed him. The Indian braves were the only hope that lay between the enemy and disaster. Under cover of darkness, and allied with *Caldwell's Rangers*, Tecumseh deployed his 1,000 muskets in a perfect ambush position, hidden in the heavy undergrowth and behind dead trees on the edge of the beaver swamp, well within musket range of the force that had to pass in order to attack the blocking position of Proctor's redcoats. The Indian volley would smash into the side of the attacking battalions with a result that would make the Great Manitou blanch, and thereby more than even the numerical odds. The set-up was perfect, the Americans would be slaughtered.

To the 1,000 braves, lying beautifully camouflaged on the edge of the swamp, an hour passed and nothing happened. They had seen some single riders (Johnson on his scout), but no large units. Just silence, the uncomfortable silence that only happens in forest and lakes. The braves lay quiet as corpses, but the men of Caldwell's force were beginning to get restive and wiggled around on the wet ground. The minutes dragged by and it seemed as if each minute lasted an hour.

Destiny, or the Great Spirit of the Winds, took a hand. While the two Johnson brothers divided their force, a natural phenomenon came to pass – not unusual for the fall season – one that was to decide the outcome of the battle. It had been a typical Canadian autumn night, when temperatures dropped to freezing and the sudden frost painted the trees across the land in the most beautiful patchwork of colours. The air had cooled rapidly, but not the water of the swamp, which kept its constant temperature. The day dawned in a nice, crisp morning. The sun rose and began to heat the surface of the swamp faster than the air. Water rose in the form of vapours which, mixed with the cold air, produced excess moisture that condensed on microscopic dust particles in the atmosphere just above the ground. This again increased the moisture content of the air beyond the saturation point and turned instantly into thick fog. Though the rest of the battlefield remained relatively clear, the braves on the edge of the swamp were caught in the fog and would have no targets to fire on because they couldn't see further than three feet.

It was precisely this blanket of dense fog that was to create so much havoc, and death. The braves peered with narrowed eyes into the murk. Vision was limited to a few yards. They could only pray that the Great Spirit would send them some wind to disperse the fog. On that October morning, the Great Manitou did not listen to his children.

That's when Johnson's cavalcade came downfield to charge the redcoat line.

From the outset, the Americans held the advantage. While Johnson's riders had gathered for the attack, the British took up their firing position. The first rank knelt down, the second rank prepared to fire over their shoulders. Because of the fog, Colonel Johnson's initial five hundred managed to dash unharmed past Tecumseh's ambush. In a fury, unmatched before in this war, they overrode the British line and turned its left flank. The situation, as confused as it had been, now became chaotic. Panic broke out in the tightly knit infantry ranks. The British fired twice – and surrendered! It had taken less than ten minutes to chase the redcoats from the field. Of the four hundred British soldiers, only fifty men of the *41st Regiment* got away with their lives. But all this was nothing compared to the pandemonium that was about to hit the foggy patch at the edge of the swamp.

Tecumseh, who had observed Johnson's cavalry charge from his vantage position in a tree, was thoroughly disgusted by the cowardly behaviour of the British soldiers. Suddenly his attention was drawn to a movement along the right flank. A second, large body of riders drifted slowly towards the edge of the swamp, still obscured behind a blanket of thick fog. It was the unit under Johnson's brother, Lieutenant-Colonel James Johnson. Tecumseh suddenly saw movement in the fog. 'Too soon,' he wanted to yell, 'wait!' Because of the battle noise around the redcoat line, which they could hear but not see, the braves failed to wait for his signal. Most likely, they didn't want to be branded as cowards. Whatever the reason, they now stormed forward, filling the air with their piercing war cries, and in the dense fog crashed headlong into Johnson's five hundred horsemen. Caught in the swirling mist, the riders jumped from their mounts; they had received no warning and now had to defend their lives as best as they could in the cold and the fog. Soldiers and braves were no longer people, but shapes, staggering around in a murky void. They engaged in a frightful hand-to-hand combat of shadows – and often killed their own neighbours. They used musket butts, hatchets and cudgels, hunting knives, bayonets, boots and bare fists. They hit and they slashed, bit, stabbed, and butchered each other with grim enjoyment. No pardon was asked and none was granted. Over the din of battle, Tecumseh's voice could be heard, encouraging his warriors. What took place in this dense fog was slaughter most frightful. The swamp was running red with blood. Tomahawks came down on heads and bayonets rammed into living flesh. Ever more men stumbled blindly into the fog to join in the flight, yelling, shooting, stabbing, dying. Others had only flight on their mind and were killed running away. A Kentuckian crawled off on all fours. An Indian threw his tomahawk after him, which struck him between the shoulder blades. Some fell wounded to the ground and died cruelly mutilated, scalped alive. The ranger captain, Caldwell, had his hands covered with blood as he had thrown away his musket and instead used his battle-axe to deal with one enemy after the other. Nearby, one of his men got shot in the face. It threw him back and he kicked out with his legs before he lay still. A Shawnee had his face crushed with a musket-butt, a horseman had his throat cut. Another brave was riding on the back of his enemy, growling like a wild animal and choking him with his bare hands. Suddenly a figure stumbled from the fog. It was Tecumseh, his arms wrapped around his body. When he saw his friend Caldwell, he opened his arms and displayed a gaping hole in his chest. Blood spurted like a fountain and foam was on his lips, most likely from a lung wound. Slowly, the great warrior sank to the ground. Caldwell ordered two Indians to take care of their chief. They applied a fistful of mud over the wound to still the flow of blood, then picked him up and disappeared with him into the fog. The Great Warrior was never seen again. With Tecumseh's death, the braves lost not only their leader, but also their will to continue the battle. They vanished into the swamp and the battle of the River Thames ended in an American victory.[9]

The question of who killed Tecumseh is a riddle for history.[10] There are many stories that his body was recovered, even mutilated by white men after the battle. It is almost certain that no white man ever saw the body of the Shawnee chief again.

Tecumseh was 'the noble Indian'. He never strayed from his creed, which was to protect the land of his ancestors and build one great, united family of all the tribes. With his death, the tribes' resistance faded and his dream of a United Indian Nation was forever laid to rest. Most tribes migrated west of the Mississippi. It is almost absurd that such momentous historic consequences should come from such an insignificant battle. But such is so often the course of history. While such mass slaughters as occurred during the Napoleonic wars decided little or nothing, an encounter of a few hundred – and an unexpected patch of fog – decided the destiny of the warriors of the forests and prairies of North America.

It can be argued that had Tecumseh proven victorious at the Thames River it is unlikely that this would have altered the course of history. Given his persistence, the American settler would have returned, his economic interest would have carried the day, and the sacred hunting grounds would have become integrated into the white United States of America.

*   *   *

[9] The war dragged on for another year. After Napoleon's defeat, the British reinforced Canada. Their most famous raid was the one into Chesapeake Bay which resulted in the sack of Washington, DC.
[10] For a while, Colonel Richard Johnson stood accused of having issued strict orders to kill him on sight.

Tecumseh, the 'Shooting Star' (in Shawnee) lives on in the heart of his people. To Americans he is still the most enigmatic individual to choose this course, and today he remains a central symbolic figure in a fable concocted around these faraway events.

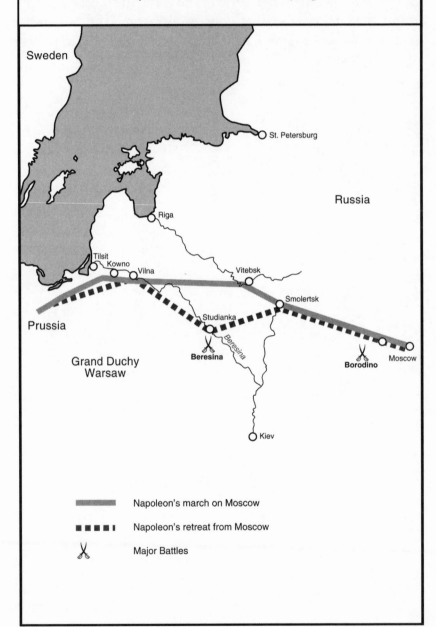

1812 Napoleon's Russian Campaign

Sweden

St. Petersburg

Russia

Riga

Tilsit
Kowno
Vilna
Vitebsk
Smolertsk

Prussia

Studianka
Beresina
Beresina

Borodino

Moscow

Grand Duchy
Warsaw

Kiev

Napoleon's march on Moscow

Napoleon's retreat from Moscow

Major Battles

Two bridges to cross

25 November 1812

'A plan which succeeds is bold, one which fails is reckless.'
Karl von Clausewitz (1780–1831),
The Campaign of 1812 in Russia

St Petersburg, 1812. 'Convey to your Emperor this honest notice that once the war has begun — one of us, either Napoleon or I, Alexander, must lose his crown.' Such was the message from Czar Alexander I of Russia to Emperor Napoleon's special envoy, Count Caulaincourt. His advice was unheeded.[1]

On the morning of 25 June 1812, the mightiest host the world had ever witnessed – 423,000 men with 1,150 cannons – crossed the River Niemen and invaded Russia. Napoleon thus launched himself on a landmark of destructive warfare;

---

[1] By signing the Treaty of Tilsit of 1807, Russia had agreed to join in Napoleon's Continental Blockade of England. But Russia couldn't follow through on its promise. Russian industry depended in great part on exporting shipbuilding wood, (which served to build England's navy), while it imported manufactured goods, such as cloth and woollens, otherwise unavailable. By 1810, the Czar ordered a stop to the import of French luxury items and at the same time opened his harbours to British trade vessels. A war became unavoidable.

he would have done better with an army half this size but of better quality. The *Immense Armée* of 1812 was no longer the *Grande Armée* of 1805; its fighting force was made up of French regulars, *les grognards*, but also of a great number of regiments of foreign levies of uncertain valour. His generals – with the notable exception of Murat, Ney and Davout – no longer carried the *esprit* of Austerlitz, this *charge à l'outrance*, nor the rage to fight and conquer. They were jealous of each other's preferential position at the Napoleonic court, and the size of fortunes they had plundered during a decade of conquest all over Europe. Only Napoleon's own grandeur was untainted, having never suffered defeat. Count Caulaincourt, with his intimate knowledge of Russia, as the French envoy to St Petersburg, tried to warn his Emperor:

'Sire, beware of the vastness of the Russian countryside and the ordeal of its winter.'

Napoleon replied sternly: 'Caulaincourt, you imagine yourself already frozen. I have no intention to remain that long.'

Napoleon's plan was simple: head straight for Moscow and force Czar Alexander to knuckle down to his demands. For this he divided his huge host into three columns, advancing on a parallel course on Russia's capital. Facing the French were three Russian columns of vastly inferior strength under Barclay de Tolly and Bagration. Because of Czarist court intrigues their two best generals, Benningsen and Kutusov; had been sidelined from a command; fortunately for the Czar and Mother Russia, Marshal Kutusov, Napoleon's most dangerous opponent, was retained as strategic military adviser.

Kutusov had faced Napoleon before, in 1805. The day after the Austro-Russian debacle at Austerlitz, one of his officers had spoken contemptuously of the French Emperor. Kutusov stared him down: 'Young man,' he growled, 'who gives you the right to jeer at one of the greatest men of history?' He now advised his Czar to employ a strategy of constant harassment without giving Napoleon a chance to lure the weaker Russian armies into battle. Lightning, pinprick raids by cavalry units into the French flanks, combined with a scorched earth policy to deny the advancing adversary food[2] and shelter. This strategy soon showed its results. Fatigue and hunger began to reduce the effectiveness of the French, its forced levies deserted in droves, and sporadic attacks so slowed Napoleon that he lost his race to catch up with Barclay's main force at Vilna.

The first in a series of blunders happened at Vilna. Instead of vigorously pursuing his main foe, the king-maker Napoleon spent some weeks in Vilna trying to solve the question of restoring a friendly Kingdom of Poland. It has been said that this was not the only reason for his delay. One of the Polish envoys was a woman of exquisite beauty, Maria Walevska, and the French emperor fell victim to her charms.[3] For the love of a woman he delayed the advance of his army.

From Vilna, the *Grande Armée* advanced unopposed. For the first time in his career, Napoleon felt unease, reminded of the fate of the Swedish warrior king, Charles XII, who allowed himself to be sucked into the immensity of Russia before suffering a disastrous defeat at Poltawa. While Napoleon failed to catch Barclay, his brother Jerome was unsuccessful in trying to force the second Russian column under Bagration into battle. Napoleon wrote a furious note: 'How can I make war in this way when you compromise the success of the entire campaign.' He relieved Jerome of his command and gave it to Marshal Davout.

Meanwhile, the pillaging *Grande Armée* had managed to

[2] Napoleonic armies lived mainly off the land.
[3] She bore him a son, Alexander Joseph, who became a minister under Napoleon III.

offset any support their Emperor could have achieved from the newly liberated Russian serfs, for any village that had been left untouched by the retreating Russians was now plundered of all food, thereby putting the local population in danger of starvation. But also the condition of Napoleon's army had become precarious. White Russia, among the poorest agricultural regions of Europe, could not provide the means of feeding half a million soldiers. Soon Napoleon's army lived on boiled rye porridge. Horses fared even worse; Napoleon had violated the age-old rule never to enter into a campaign before the grain had ripened. Over five hundred ammunition wagons and their guns had already been left behind and soon part of his cavalry were without horses. To add to his worries, dysentery and fever claimed the lives of thousands, horses died by the squadron and conscripts threw away their arms to return home.

By 27 July, near Vitebsk, Napoleon thought to have cornered the two wings of Barclay de Tolly and Bagration, but in a masterly move the Russian generals managed to slip away during the night and, by next morning, Napoleon stormed into an abandoned enemy camp, stripped of everything. He conferred with his chief strategists, Berthier and Murat, who strongly advised their Emperor to halt the campaign, go into early winter quarters in Smolensk, and continue his campaign the following spring. For a time, Napoleon agreed, but two days later he changed his mind with a significant remark:

'I've made my generals too rich, they think only of pleasures. They've grown sick of war.' He wanted to destroy the Russians, and found it inconceivable that Czar Alexander would give up Smolensk or even Moscow without a fight.

At Smolensk, he finally did catch up with the Russians. He dispatched Marshal Junot across the Dnieper River to cut their retreat along the Moscow road. But Junot hesitated and, following a vicious two-day bombardment, Napoleon marched into the shell of a city while Barclay had managed, once more, to give him the slip. With the fall of Smolensk, Napoleon had reached the point of no return. He sent Ney and Murat to chase the Russians to Valutino, where Barclay lured them into a trap and inflicted some 6,000 casualties on his pursuers. Once again, Napoleon's marshals pressed their Emperor to put the army into winter quarters, and again he refused, especially after he had met with an emissary of the Czar.

'Why are there so many churches?' he asked Count Balachov.

'Because our people are most religious, sire.'

'Bah, not in these days. So tell me, which is the best road to Moscow?'

'All roads lead to Rome, sire. As for yourself, you may take any road; they all lead to Moscow. The Swede Charles XII took the one via Poltawa.'

The threat was clear. Poltawa had been the end of the Swedish adventure, their king was lured into the depths of Russia and annihilated by Czar Peter the Great. Napoleon fully realized that his army could also disappear in Russia's vastness, like the waters of a mighty river being sucked into sand. Soon the weather would change, and what then? The weather made him decide. Moscow, with its promise of plush quarters and plenty of food, was only two hundred miles away.

'The imminent danger forces us to push on to Moscow. I have exhausted all other counsel by my advisers.'

25 August. The leader of a troop of levies, the German, Roeder, noted in his diary: 'A decision has been taken. We march on. Even should the Emperor reach Moscow, unless he can first strike a decisive blow and put the Czar's army out of action, he will not be able to hold the city during the coming winter.' That same day, the Czar finally appointed the sixty-seven-year-old Prince Kutusov as his commander-in-chief and ordered him, contrary to the general's counsel, to make his stand.[4]

7 September 1812, Borodino. Napoleon's army had reached the banks of the Moskva River, only one day's ride from the Russian capital. They found their route to the city barred. Kutusov had used his time well, his troops were heavily entrenched. Behind a formidable earthwork, dubbed the *Grande Redoute* (Grand Bastion), he had installed twenty-seven pieces of heavy artillery. More cannons supported this redoubt on two nearby hills, which could enfilade any attacking unit with deadly crossfire. Behind the hills, Kutusov posted his 120,000 men and his formidable battalions of Cossack cavalry. The chill of the night had given way to a grey, hazy morning. While Marshal Kutusov and his men sank to their knees and prayed to an effigy of the Virgin of Kazan, carried past their lined-up battalions, Napoleon, plagued by a feverish cold, sat in his tent with his head in his hands. He had just received news that Marshal Marmont's army had gone down in defeat to Wellington at Salamanca in Spain.

'What is war?' he asked himself; 'the task of barbarians where all depends on being the strongest at a given point.' The moment the sun made its appearance, Napoleon stepped briefly outside the tent. His mood cheered. 'The sun of Austerlitz,' he stated. But it was not so, the sun was in the east, and in the east were the Russians. Through his spyglass he studied the hills before him, then turned to his aide, General Rapp.

'Do you believe in our victory?'

'Certainly, sire, but a bloody one . . .'

'So, let us then open the gates of Moscow!' With this he gave the order for attack. Fearing that Kutusov, like Barclay, would try to slip away, the emperor rejected Marshal

---

[4] Clausewitz wrote: 'Kutusov would not have fought at Borodino, where he obviously did not expect to win. But the Czar forced him into it.'

Davout's suggestion to go at the Russians with a flanking attack. Instead, he ordered an assault straight up the centre, onto the village of Borodino, covered by the Russian batteries on the *Grande Redoute*. The guns thundered, the earth trembled. Elite French battalions advanced with their usual *élan* and took Borodino, then stormed uphill into the blazing mouths of cannons on the *Grande Redoute*. The Russians, taken by surprise, as they had never expected a frontal assault, were thrown from the hill. In the course of the action, Marshal Davout was wounded. Marshal Ney took the strategic *Three Arrow Heights* and silenced its battery. But the assault on the vital hills had been costly in men and depleted the French battalions. When his marshals asked for reserves and Napoleon hesitated, the impetuous Ney exploded: 'Why doesn't he go back to the Tuileries and leave his generals to do the fighting.'

Kutusov recognised the opportunity and launched a furious counter-attack, which threw the French from the *Grande Redoute*. For a moment, the outcome of battle hung in the balance. Napoleon ordered his batteries to lay a deadly curtain of fire on the *Grande Redoute*, and Murat, ably assisted by Ney, led his *cuirassiers* in a mad cavalry charge uphill to retake the hill. By 3 pm the battle was decided. But at what horrifying cost! Almost 75,000 men had died, three times as many as would at Waterloo![5]

Now was the moment to chase the Russians and annihilate them once and for all. Napoleon still had the *Garde Imperiale* at his disposal, but he refused to release them. 'I shall not have my Guard destroyed. At eight hundred leagues from France I do not risk my final reserve. With what should I fight tomorrow.'

In 1805, at the summit of his glory, he would never have hesitated to take a positive decision – at Borodino he failed.

[5] The losses at Borodino: 28,000 French and 45,000 Russians.

And so, Kutusov and his Russians, badly mauled but still intact as a fighting force, managed to slip away. Murat stated best what all had on their mind that day: 'I no longer recognise the Emperor's genius.'

At Borodino, Napoleon won a pyrrhic victory and lost the Russian campaign.

The morning after Borodino, a Russian prisoner warned Napoleon: 'Sire, in a month our cold will make your finger-nails fall out.' To his regret, the Emperor failed to heed the prophetic words. He dispatched Murat with his cavalry to ride into Moscow. They faced no further opposition. Kutusov had come to a decision. 'As long as a Russian army exists we preserve the hope of stopping him. But if the army is destroyed, not only Moscow, but all of Russia will perish.'

If Napoleon had thought that with Moscow he had captured the beating heart of Russia he was badly deceived. The victor rode into the city expecting a deputation of *boyars* suing for peace. Instead he discovered the towers of the Kremlin amid a sea of flames. Rostopchine, the governor of Moscow, had ordered its population evacuated and the city put to the torch.[6] Napoleon had conquered smoking ruins, with neither food reserves nor winter quarters for his depleted forces, badly in need of a rest. When the flames reached the Kremlin and threatened its powder magazine, Napoleon was forced to flee the Czar's residence and bivouac with his forces outside the city.

Before and during Borodino, he had lost half of his army. Now he was faced with the prospect of a rapidly approaching winter without adequate housing for his troops, without hay for his horses, without bread for his men. It was October, and the situation became more desperate each day. He knew

---

[6] It is not certain how or when the great fire started. Some historians claim it was on the day *after* the first French units moved into Moscow. It may have been an accident by the French themselves that started it.

that wintering in a barren Moscow would invite disaster. Therefore he dispatched a letter to the Czar, offering peace. His offer remained without reply.

The Czar's problem was how to hold on to power. Showing weakness would mean the loss his crown. 'Russia is lost, unless a miracle happens,' he lamented to his crown adviser. But for a miracle it was almost too late. The fact was that the French were in Moscow. The Czar failed to see what his able field marshal counted on most: a change in the weather.

Kutusov had been weakened when he lost a great part of his army, but, as a Russian, he could always count on one ally to stand by his side in the moment of need: 'General Winter.' This eternal ally of Holy Mother Russia would arrive soon, as sure as day follows night, and November follows October. In the meantime, the old fox Kutusov devised a genial plan. By positioning his troops astride the shorter route of a predictable French withdrawal, he could force Napoleon to retreat along his original northern invasion route, passing through the same scorched, barren countryside, with no hope of finding food for the men or grain for the horses.

On 19 October 1812, Napoleon marched out of Moscow.

Then an incident, and the weather, took a hand.

20 October. Into Kutusov's camp dashed a dispatch rider from St Petersburg. The Czar's order was short and to the point. 'Attack Napoleon!' But this time the old marshal refused to obey his monarch. He knew what the Russian winter could do to an enemy in full retreat: that Napoleon's men had no chance of reaching safety before the cold set in; that the undefeated *Grande Armée* was doomed! 'Let the cold come!' he said to no one in particular. Within two weeks, 'General Winter' was on its way.

Four days after Kutusov received the Czar's orders for an immediate attack, the Russian scouts of General Docturov, operating south-west of Moscow, sighted a French column, and erroneously identified it as a minor foraging party. Napoleon, in fact, had set out in a south-westerly direction, taking the shortest possible route back to Poland, and this was his advance guard under Eugène de Beauharnais. Docturov soon discovered that he was in no position to stand up to Napoleon's main force. He set up his 84 cannons and dug in his 12,000 men on the outskirts of Maloyaroslavets, some 50 km from Moscow, to block the *Grande Armée*'s retreat. On 24 October, it came to a pitched battle in which the Russians lost 6,000 men to the French's 5,000, while the town was taken and abandoned in five consecutive assaults. A French bayonet charge decided the outcome. Kutusov arrived too late with his main force; he chose not to engage Napoleon in a drawn-out battle, but left a blocking force behind.

Maloyaroslavets was a French victory, but one of the worst kind. Napoleon was in a rush. With winter closing in, he could ill afford the time fighting his way through Kutusov's battalions, which he (rightly) assumed were positioned all along his southern route. This made him decide to take his army on the safer but longer northern route, through Mozhaisk and Smolensk. Which was just what Kutusov had intended him to do.

For the French the situation had become precarious. Napoleon rode out of town with 108,000 men and 569 guns, but with neither supplies nor food. They set off expecting to forage along the way. But there was nothing to forage, there was precious little left after the pillaging of their summer campaign. Hunger plagued the French soldiers, and extensive food raids were made impossible by Cossack patrols that killed anyone who strayed from the main column.

The last days of October were clear and the nights cold. The temperature dropped below freezing, and for this the French were not prepared. Napoleon had not counted on spending a winter there, and had led his armies into Russia dressed in their summer uniforms. When the sun hid behind dense clouds and snow covered the countryside that was when their real suffering began. The wind blew thick snow-clouds across the flatlands, horses and men sank ever deeper into the snow, and the poles which had been planted to mark out the road were not visible in the driving snowstorm. A long column of exhausted, famished, feverish men snaked along the Russian winterscape, driven on by the fear of falling into the hands of Cossacks, following relentlessly behind. The wind howled and the temperature continued to drop. The men suffered from frostbite, and they wrapped burlap bags around their feet and their faces.

'It is so cold that the crows tumble frozen from the sky,' wrote a *grenadier* in his diary; 'our nostrils are choked, our mouths filled with lumps of ice, and the ice needles, which the wind drives into our faces, make us blind. Pray for us, 'cause tomorrow it might be too late and no one knows what awaits us.'

The soldiers of *la Grande Armée* stumbled across a devastated landscape, many using their muskets as crutches. Where they passed, the endless track became signposted with corpses. The army had lost its pride. Cossacks ruthlessly pursued its remnants on sturdy little Siberian ponies used to the biting cold. Any straggler caught by these terrible horsemen was stripped and pushed along at lance point until he fell dead to the ground. Others were doused with water, tied to trees and left to freeze. The French were still a long way from Smolensk where they hoped to find food and shelter.

On 10 November, this 'Army of Ghosts' stumbled into Smolensk. But a blunder by the quartermaster corps denied the exhausted troops food, clothes and gunpowder. Reserve units had eaten up all the food, winter clothes had never been ordered, and the gunpowder had been left in the open and made unusable. One thing became desperately clear – to spend the winter in this burnt-out shell of a town, bereft of stores, with no communication with France, was out of the question. Reports arrived of Russian troop concentrations, both regulars and irregulars (partisans), across their escape route. Five days later, Napoleon ordered a further retreat towards the west. They had to reach France's vassal states in Germany before the real Russian frost was upon them.

Mauled during several successive encounters, or lost in the snows of Smolensk, Napoleon's army had shrunk from a half-million to some 50,000 men. The Emperor took personal charge of his poorly clothed and fed horde. He had the carriages burned, and harnessed the remaining horses to the few artillery pieces he had left.

On 14 November, Kutusov waited for Napoleon at Krasnoi. Napoleon threw in his pampered Guard battalions who went through the Russian Cossacks 'like a hundred gunships through a fishing fleet'.[7]

By 25 November, Napoleon's remnants reached the banks of a wide river, the Berezina. Its water was covered with ice floes. It was here, near the village of Studianka, north of Borizov, that Kutusov was waiting for them. The only bridge across the raging, ice strewn flood had been burned by Cossacks, and the river was too deep to ford. A perfect site to annihilate Napoleon. With a river in front, and no way to cross it, Kutusov's Russians were poised to end once and for all the myth of the invincibility of the Corsican upstart.

'The end of Napoleon is irrevocably marked, it is here, in the icy waters of the Berezina, that his meteor will be extinguished,' the Russian general assured his troops.

Napoleon was caught in a trap. His situation was outright precarious. An unfordable river, with Russian guns behind him and on the opposite shore, and with a starving, freezing army in full retreat. For the first timer in his brilliant career,

---

[7] Quoted by Davidov, a Russian general, in his account of the 1812 campaign.

all the elements of a disaster were assembled. He had to cope with the terrain (the river) and a ruthless enemy. But worst of all with the weather factor.

Near the village of Studianka, Napoleon ordered General Eblé, his chief of sappers, to throw up two bridges across the icy waters. The challenge to his engineers was near impossible. And yet, in a show of sublime devotion to their emperor, three hundred French engineers obeyed his order. With unsurpassed heroism bordering on plain suicide, they braved the icy waters, and anchored wooden pillars, which they tied together with ropes. The covering of the bridges was made up of wagon platforms and wall boards torn from log cabins. The three hundred sappers sacrificed their lives (most froze to death), having to stand up to their necks in the chilly flood, braving ice floes and occasional cannon shot. By the light of torches they worked throughout the night; rickety wooden structures took shape and by noon of 26 November, two bridges spanned the river, an incredible feat given the means and techniques of the time.[8]

The same day brought a howling snowstorm, which filled the valley of the Berezina. All landmarks disappeared and the ground was covered by snow so deep that the heavy artillery pieces sank down over their axles. But the storm brought for the French some desperately needed respite; in such a storm, not even Russian cavalry could launch an attack. A great number of French, together with their artillery, managed to cross on the congested bridges. The fording operation proceeded at a trickle pace, about 500 men per hour, with the bridges frequently collapsing and in need of constant repair. Passage of supply wagons and cannons further slowed the operation. On 27 November, more French managed to cross, but now the structures had been so weakened that passage became

---

[8] A hundred and thirty years later advance German panzer units reached the site and found the remnants of Napoleon's bridges.

perilous. Under the incessant pounding of ice floes slamming into the wooden pillars and the thousands of marching boots, the bridges gave way twice. Men and horses tumbled into the floods, but each time more sappers went into the icy waters to repair the bridges. These heroes died either of exposure or were crushed by ice floes, and their corpses swept off. Their names are not recorded, but their deed is.

By the afternoon of 28 November, the biting wind that had whirled up clouds of snow, and thus obstructed the view for the Russian gunners, dropped and the air was suddenly clear. At this time, the reserve corps of General Oudinot had completed its crossing. Only the rearguard corps of Victor was left behind on the opposite bank, trying to protect the huge mass of stragglers. That's when Kutusov's advance units under General Wittgenstein appeared on the high riverbank. Cannon balls began to smash into water, wooden bridges and human flesh. The French stragglers, caught on the approach to the bridges, panicked as more shells crashed into this jostling, pushing mass with devastating result. Cossack battalions dashed for the jammed up bridges and drove a great number of French into the icy floods, where they were caught by the strong current and swept along, or crushed between colliding slabs of drift-ice. Very few made it across, and those who did, and climbed up the riverbank, dripping with water, froze within minutes into pillars of ice.

While this slaughter was going on, a new danger appeared in the form of a Russian corps under Admiral Chitchganov, who had inadvertently stumbled into Napoleon on the other side of the river. Napoleon's batteries made short shrift of the Russians, which left the field leading down to the river strewn with thousands of corpses. While this action was in progress, pressure was increasing on Victor's corps on the opposite shore, and the bridges were rendered impassable by a steady hail of cannon ball from Wittgenstein's accurate artillery. Suddenly, the firing stopped and Wittgenstein's cavalry made for the bridges. Those of the French still left behind made for the bridges in a clumsy run, their shoes sliding on the crystalline ice in their desparation to escape the lances of the Cossack battalions. That's when something terrible happened – in front of them, the bridges went up in flames.

Napoleon was faced with an appalling choice. In order to save what could be saved, he ordered his sapper commander, General Eblé, to set fire to the bridges. At the same time he dispatched a message to Marshal Victor to save his brave cavalry and lead them across the raging flood. The *cuirassiers* forced their steeds into the river and hung on to their saddles. Some made it but many didn't, dragged under by their heavy steel breastplates. This final escape still left thousands to their fate on the opposite shore, where the ferocious Cossacks rounded them up and hacked them down. (After the spring thaw, Russian peasants found 36,000 bodies of slain French.)

That the French managed to salvage anything from this disaster points to the great sacrifice of some engineers and the effective leadership of Napoleon. Where other leaders would have failed, Napoleon had won perhaps his greatest personal battle. He had saved part of his force. But what a force! On 29 November, the emperor sent a dispatch to Paris: 'Our Army is not a good sight today.' The Marquis de Chambray put it more dramatically. 'On the shores of the Berezina ended the career of *la Grande Armée*, a force which for two-decades had made Europe tremble; it ceased to exist in a military sense, its only safety now lay in headlong flight.'

Worse was yet to come. Russia had frequently been called the *Weather Kitchen*, providing a demonstration of nature's power and man's vulnerability. An army in retreat moved into the implacable world of the intolerable Russian winter. At the beginning of December, a screaming wind whipped across the wide-open plains of Russia and the temperature dropped to a numbing minus 32°C. These jets of icy wind battering down on the men carried the roar of the brutal weather. Cold and wind multiplied. At first the men felt panicky, then desultory as time went on. The storm snapped at them unabated, whipping at sleeves and trousers. Their condition deteriorated savagely, their vision disintegrated into flickering lights, the gruesome ravages of frostbites were to be found everywhere. The phenomenon of the 'winter mirage' added many casualties. Wooden poles marked the track leading through high snowdrifts. Many began to suffer from a cold-induced hallucination. There was an even more devastating element, one testing the troop's morale. All me down to a question of lead buttons. In the Napoleonic army braces, attached to lead buttons, were used to hold up uniform trousers. In the extreme cold, these buttons became brittle and disintegrated, and soon soldiers were walking with trousers around their ankles. Added to this was the torture of button-less fly-flaps, where the wind whistled in, causing stomach cramps, diarrhoea, and death. Not a morale-booster.

Stumbling ghosts faltered, wondering why they should continue forward, facing that shrieking, banging gale of frightening malevolence. But when they looked to the road sides, they saw a grim warning for all those who wanted to give up. Their unfortunate comrades had seen poles where there were none, and had walked off into the whiteness to their peril. The line of their retreat was strewn with corpses, hard as wooden planks. If they stumbled, they hauled themselves to their feet and staggered on. The living knew they had to move on or enter their own frozen eternity. The snow was granulated ice and didn't bind. Every step was like walking on loose sand. Like some giant sand blaster, the storm whipped their faces with its needle-sharp pellets; they couldn't turn their heads, they had to keep their half-shut eyes on the man in front, their only contact in the darkness, *grognards* of the Old Guard and young recruits alike. While the young were stronger, the older made up for it by determination.

Their beards were clumps of ice, the howling storm snapped at the rags wrapped around their heads. Their arms hung limply, with no strength to raise a musket, their mouths were agape, fighting for breath. They felt the cold creeping up from their feet. Another day, another night, and the ravages of frostbite would fell them. When they stumbled into the shelter of a half-burned hut or a cave, and laid down for the night, huddling up to each other to share bodily warmth, they found on waking they'd been lying with corpses.

The storm continued unabated and bone-chilling, and death would come quickly unless they kept on moving into the freezing darkness. They pointed their shoulders into the gale and blundered onwards in brain-numbing fear of an enemy they didn't understand, 'General Winter'. And so they staggered on, a hundred, a thousand, ten thousand . . . An army of ghosts, never before defeated in battle, was headed for its demise.

On 4 December, the remnants of a once proud army struggled into Smorgoni, near Vilma. The Emperor called his commanders to a meeting.

'I must save what can be saved, and this I can only do from Paris.'

With that, he handed overall command to Prince Murat and bid farewell to his generals. Accompanied by his ambassador, Count Caulaincourt, he set off for Paris.

'The Russians should be viewed by everyone as a scourge,' he said to the count. 'Any war against Russia is wholly in the interest of the older Europe . . .' and, after a pause, he added: '. . . and civilisation.' During darkness on 18 December, a defeated Napoleon entered Paris through his monumental *Arc de Triomphe*.[9] The remnants of his army slogged on, through the infinite silence of forests, beneath glittering

[9] Erected on his orders to celebrate the glory of Austerlitz.

ice-crystals hanging from trees. Many just sat down in the deep snow and waited for the end, others huddled under a blanket, knowing that by the following morning their tombstone would be a mound of snow. None of them would be buried; they would lie frozen in fields and forests until the spring thaw turned them into food for the thousands of crows. What had been the glory of an Empire, an undefeated army of a half million men that had crossed the Niemen just six months earlier, had been reduced to isolated bands of haggard scarecrows, starving and wrapped in rags, who finally recrossed the same starting point.

On 13 December, a great mass of ragged soldiers and cavalry without their horses stumbled into the border city of Kowno. To the local quartermaster it became clear that to feed this half-crazed mass in any organised manner was out of the question. When he tried to set up a distribution centre, his guards were pushed aside. The hungry hordes, stormed the storehouse, plundered it, and stuffed themselves to bursting and then to vomiting point. Worse was the fate of those that had torn open bags of flour, and, in their hunger, ate it by the handful. They suffocated when the thick mass clogged their mouths and entrails. For no good reason, a few soldiers threw their torches into barrels of oil and set the warehouse on fire, thus roasting half of their comrades and depriving latecomers of their share of food. But that was only the beginning. By late afternoon, marauders located a cellar with hundreds of barrels of French brandy. They smashed holes in the barrels, poured the amber liquid into buckets, then indulged in a wild drinking spree. Others simply laid themselves under the spout of a barrel and opened their mouths. They ended up drunk, then stumbled blindly out into the snowdrifts to lie down and snore. Any sleeping drunk, wearing usable clothes, was stripped naked and left to freeze to death. And so, having escaped the dreaded Cossacks, they had reached safety only to lie condemned to death from cold by their own comrades.

Around midnight, a *troika* bearing a French war chest arrived with its escort. The casks and bags of gold were unloaded in the middle of the Town Square and surrounded by an armed guard. But the night was so cold that the guards began to walk around to keep their feet from freezing, or to go for a bit of foraging themselves. This left only a few men to guard the hoard. It didn't take long for the heavily guarded pile of bags to be noticed by the rabble. For a while, the guards managed to keep a semblance of order with muskets and bayonets. Scarecrow soldiers gathered around the bags filled with pieces of gold, when shots were heard from the outskirts of town, and a scream of 'Cossacks!' went up. Men rushed around in panic, every one headed for the bridge across the Niemen to seek safety on the opposite shore. In the confusion, some soldiers, rather than stand and fight off the pursuing Cossacks, jumped the treasure guards, stabbed them, and then stuffed as much gold into their pockets as their threadbare coats would carry. Greed took hold of them, fights broke out, and more throats were cut. The shooting was getting nearer, and the first sabre-wielding Cossacks appeared. Since the bridge across the Niemen was jammed solid, many of the robbers tried to make their escape across the floating-ice-covered river. Most were drowned, dragged down by the gold in their pockets.

Stripped of their clothes and left to die by their own comrades, with their throats cut for gold, or drowned by their own greed, thus perished without grace the remnants of the *Grande Armée*.[10]

'It is no longer possible to serve under a maniac,' wrote a disillusioned Murat in his secret diary after he had reached the safety of Gumbinnen in East Prussia.

Napoleon's chief of staff, Marshal Berthier, had to report:

[10] *Unter Napoleons Fahnen, Erinnerungen aus den Feldzuegen*, 1809–14.

'The whole army is completely disbanded, even the 400 men who are all that is left of the *Garde Imperiale*. Twenty-five degrees of cold and heavy snow on the ground are the cause of the disastrous state of the army, which no longer exists.'

Napoleon wrote during his exile in St Helena: 'The most terrible of all my *batailles* was the one of Moscow.'

The day after the debacle of the Berezina, Marshal Ney dispatched a hurried note to his wife: 'What's left of the Army marches in broken ranks. It's but a mob without purpose, famished and feverish. I cover their retreat. 'General Famine' and 'General Winter', rather than Russian bullets, have conquered *la Grande Armée*.' Three weeks later (December 14), the same Marshal Ney led the rearguard over the Niemen; he had barely one thousand men fit for action.

Napoleon had failed to listen to the advice of his wise men.

'General Winter' did the rest.

An ironic smile crossed the face of Prince Talleyrand, eternal king-maker who evaded the guillotine, served four monarchs, and betrayed them all, when he said after having read Napoleon's dispatch from the icy wastes of Russia: '*C'est le commencement de la fin* – it's the beginning of the end.'

The lucky survivors eventually sneaked back into Paris, in small groups and during the hours of darkness. Perhaps they were ashamed to be still alive. 'What returned was the ghost of *la Grande Armée*,' wrote Count Philippe de Segur. 'And yet, they felt they had been beaten only by nature.'

Despite not losing a single battle during the entire campaign, Napoleon's invasion of Russia turned into his greatest defeat. His retreat from Russia set the stage for revolts against his oppressive regime across an entire continent. Several months thereafter, when engaged in his greatest battle at

Leipzig, one which was to go down in history as 'The Battle of Nations', he no longer fought Austrians or Russians, but all of Europe.[11]

The rest is history.

A history which was to repeat itself in precisely the same manner, along the same roads and in the same villages, forests and fields, by another man who thought he could fight the enemy and the elements, and who had skipped history classes.

A 'Napoleon with a telephone and a panzer'.

That event took place 129 years to the day that the great Napoleon had crossed the Niemen and began his ill-fated march into Russia.

'If the destruction of Napoleon's army was more complete than it need have been, his fault was not in his having penetrated too far, but in the late period in which the campaign opened, the sacrifice of life occasioned by his tactics, the lack of due care for supplies, and lastly, in his delayed march from Moscow.' (Karl von Clausewitz).

[11] England had sent a rocket unit.

The Great Potato Famine

September 1845 – July 1849

The stink of famine
Hangs in the bushes still
In the sad Celtic hedges
Desmond Egan

In November of 1844, a message was received by the British government of Prime Minister Sir Robert Peel that a disease of unknown origin had attacked and destroyed in large part the potato crop in the United States. This report was filed away as 'The American Potato Blight' and nothing was done about it.

In mid-summer of 1845, the potato harvest of Ireland promised to be a bumper crop. The weather had been ideal, hot and dry. In mid-July, the *Freeman's Journal* was jubilant: 'The poor man's property, the potato crop, was never before so large and at the same time, so abundant.'

But the vagaries of the Irish weather were well known. One day, at this particular time, it was bright sunshine, people strolling about in shirtsleeves, and the next, Dublin woke up to the densest fog in memory. The temperature dropped, it was cold, and vision was limited to a few yards. People going to work peered with narrowed eyes into the murk, desperately searching for the way to their places of work, trying to expel the uneasy feeling that had begun to beset them. What had happened? This was July, not February!

People were no longer people, but shapes, staggering around in a murky void. They kept close to the side of the streets, groping along the walls of houses and, where these ended, trailing across the street, hoping to find another wall on the other side. Dubliners had received no warning and had to handle as best as they could the cold and the fog. They piled coal into their fireplaces to warm their homesteads. Then came the rains, day after interminable day.

It was no better in the countryside. It rained, on Galway, on Kerry, on Limerick and Donegal. It rained biblical, three long weeks of continuous cold weather, dense fog and downpours. Yes, 1845 was an unusual summer for the Irish farmer. His fields were gorged with water, his beasts drowned and his cabin flooded. An unreal situation in a world that had gone mad.

More than the hardship it put on the population, the weather hit the potato plant. And the potato was not immunised against rot, a prevention that would be discovered only seventy years later. The scientific world of the time was caught helpless. Dr John Lindley, the leading authority and professor of botany at the University of London, declared: 'A fearful malady has broken out among the Irish potato crop. As for cure of this distemper, there is none. We are visited by a great calamity which we must bear.'

On 13 September 1845, Dr Lindley's article appeared in the bible of agriculture, the *Gardener's Chronicle and Horticultural Gazette*. An excerpt said: 'We stop the press with very great regret to announce that the *Potato Murrain* has unequivocally declared itself in Ireland. Where will Ireland be in the event of a universal potato rot?'

What the paper did not print is what it did not know.

That this was only the beginning of the trouble. Yes, there had been over twenty potato failures before, from frost or curl, but none so severe as that which struck Ireland in the autumn of 1845.

The villain was a tiny spore that strangled the potato plant. One thing became sadly clear, that with the change of climate there would be no bumper potato crop this year. Ireland depended on the potato. One year of poor harvest and people would be starving before spring, so much was certain. Most were left with a few miserable offerings, enough for a month perhaps, but not enough to survive the winter. The villagers had no doubt that there would be hard times ahead. For all except the landlords that is, because whenever things got rough they took the ship to England.

With the successful conclusion of the Napoleonic Wars, the English Empire had become the mightiest power on earth, imposing their brand of *Pax Britannica* across their vast dominions. Especially hard hit were their neighbours on the Emerald Isles. The English owned the land and the Irish worked it. English landlords imposed their law and Irish peasants endured it.

The situation between landlord and tenant peasant was a vicious circle. Not only did the tenant lack capital to improve his farming, furthermore sure of seeing his rent raised if he ventured on the least improvement, he was careful to make none, nor to try to improve the quality of his 'spuds'. If there was a succession of bumper harvests, the landlord immediately raised the rent and then refused to return to the old rate because he found it most inconvenient to curtail revenue to which he had accustomed himself.

The tenant, working a plot not sufficiently large to feed his family, had to look for outside work to pay his rent. A continuous struggle for survival made these wretched people apathetic and turned them from sluggard into drunkard, while their wives became slovenly and their children pallid and dirty. Like a dagger festering in the wound, they blamed all their misery on the English usurper. If a tenant got himself evicted as a bad payer, the reputation followed him and he could never find another tenant plot. This left him the option of emigration, but for that he lacked the means to buy passage for himself and his family.

Given this oppressed and poverty-stricken rural population without incentive, given landlords who thought only of profits but not of improving their crops, given the fickleness of Irish atmospheric conditions, a disaster was predictable. To start planting varied crops would have been the sensible prevention, but common sense was forgotten when it came to profit sheets. Thereby Ireland depended entirely on a single produce, and, should that rot, its people were condemned. The first signs were not long in coming. In October 1845, the *Freeman's Journal* published a letter from a local priest: 'It grieves me to inform you that the rot is making frightful ravages even in the potatoes, which about eight days ago were intact.'

The noted botanist, Dr Lindley, stated, following his sponsored inspection tour of Ireland, that owing to the continuous rain, the potatoes were gorged with so much water they could no longer absorb it and were rotting.

Today it is certain that the fatal potato disease crossed the Atlantic in a shipment of cereals from America; at the time, its origins were unknown since the original warning had never been passed on. The *Phytophthora infestans*, or potato blight, was discovered only in the twentieth century. It is a minute growth, a spore fungus of great destructive power. It multiplies at a frightening rate and the spores from a single infected potato plant can destroy thousands of other plants in a very short time. Though rain is not the direct cause of the blight, it is the cause of its spread, because without humidity the fungus starves and does not multiply. Thus, the climatic conditions in Ireland of 1845 provided the ideal conditions for the rapid spread of the blight.

Daniel O'Connor, the elected Irish member, tried to warn the Peel government to take preventive measures, when he pronounced in the House of Commons: 'The people are not to blame. It has pleased Providence to inflict this calamity on them.'

The Lord-Lieutenant of Ireland, Lord Heytesbury, explained it away in a much colder tone: 'The season has been so ungenial and the absence of sunshine so remarkable that the potatoes have ripened imperfectly.'

It shows that the man worried more about the potato profits than about the wellbeing of his subjects, whatever their social position may have been. What plan did he, the representative of the British government, undertake to help the Irish? If one can believe an article that appeared in the *Freeman's Journal* of 29 October 1845, which reported on the Lord-Lieutenant's frosty reception of a deputation from the Irish respectability: 'They may starve! Such in spirit, if not in words, was the reply given yesterday by the English Viceroy to the deputation which prayed that the food of this kingdom be preserved, lest the people thereof perish.'

Prime Minister Robert Peel had already made available £100,000 for the purchase of American Indian maize to be shipped to Ireland, and his decisive move helped overcome the initial stage of the famine in early 1846. But then a bitter fight broke out among his ministers, and the Cabinet blocked any further aid. This impasse left him only one way to combat the famine: repeal the *Corn Law*, a legislature passed to protect the price of British-grown cereals. This unpopular move split the government and brought down

Robert Peel.'[1] Or, as the ageing Duke of Wellington put it: 'Rotten potatoes have done it all, they put Peel in his damned fright.'

Winter came and with it came the hunger. A great calamity had struck the village. There was no more food. None. All the potato stocks had been exhausted. There were so many sick, and so few resources. As the days passed, the despair mounted. The courtyard in front of the manor house, with its windows and doors tightly shut, was packed with weeping women and dying children. A scarecrow in tattered rags shuffled back and forth. She looked the very spirit of death, filthy and louse-infested. A priest dispensed last rites. The village was dying, just like all across the country villages were dying.

The blight continued unabated into the following year. The year 1846 was much worse than 1845. After a clement spring, cold gripped Ireland anew, from Donegal to County Cork, and record rainfalls drenched the Emerald Isle from County Kildare to Galway. Dirt roads turned into impassable mud. Transportation came to a standstill, emergency food could no longer reach its destination. In the cities, this was felt when food prices were jacked up with an explanation that shortages had become critical. Meanwhile, the constant rain doused the fields and the sun, in the few days it tried to peek through the clouds, had not enough strength to dry up the ground. Violent thunderstorms and torrential rains drenched the country and spread the blight. It soon became apparent that the people were not equipped to survive unless immediate steps were taken. Yes, 1846 was worse, because unscrupulous dealers were buying up anything edible and putting it on the market at highly inflated prices, much too steep for the poor Irish. In their desperation, a crowd stormed the local workhouse at

[1] No other government could be formed to face the crisis, and Queen Victoria refused to accept Peel's resignation.

Listowel in County Kerry, screaming: 'Bread or Blood!'

Charles Edward Trevelyan was, in title only, the Assistant Head of Treasury. In fact, he was the boss. Despite the fact that he held the Irish in great disregard, he was handed the authority to oversee the Irish food relief programme (placed under the Treasury's control). He refused to open food relief depots: 'The only way to prevent the people from becoming habitually dependent on Government handouts is to bring the operation to a close,' he said and ordered government stores to be closed on 15 August. With this step he became one of the leading characters in the unfolding Irish drama.

By August 1846, as blackened potato fields increasingly made their appearance, there was still hope: minor portions of the countryside were flush with golden wheat, which could have been redirected to famine relief. However, grain in Ireland was not considered food, but money to pay the rent! Heaven help the Irish peasant who failed to pay his tenancy fee; he faced immediate eviction, which was conducted with utter brutality by the landlord under protection of the law.

Trevelyan and his compatriots earned undying Irish hatred when he refused to stop these food exports from Ireland. He declared that he would not interfere with the law of supply and demand: 'We cannot encourage the idea of prohibiting exports, perfect Free Trade is the right course.'

And thus, by September 1846, food produce was exported from a starving Ireland to England and other European ports. According to official papers, at the height of the Famine of 1846, Ireland shipped to England: 250,000 quarters of grain, 700,000 hundredweights of barley, and 1 million quarters of oats and oatmeal.'[2] Another report'[3] confirms this and gives the exported quantities as 18,169 tons of wheat, 8,990 tons of barley and 102,938 tons of oats. And so, while the Irish

[2] T. Hayden, *Irish Hunger*.
[3] Edwards and Williams, *The Great Famine*.

died of hunger, English corn traders amassed a fortune.

A famous French chef, Alexis Soyer, put up a soup kitchen in front of the Royal Barracks in Dublin. But thin, handout soup was hardly a replacement for the Irish worker, used to meals of 14 lbs of potatoes. While the Soup Kitchen Act provided food for three million Irish, Trevelyan's secretary came forth with a statement:

'There is much reason to believe that the object of the Relief Act is greatly perverted and it is frequently applied solely as a means of adding to the comforts of the lower classes, and of assisting the farmers and employers, instead of being, as intended, a provision for the utterly destitute.'

Trevelyan went even a step further. He declared that 'this extravagance has to stop' and that the English tax-payer carried the entire burden of the famine, therefore all relief under the Soup Kitchen Act would cease by September.

'It is my opinion that too much has been done for the people. Under such treatment the people have grown worse instead of better.' All that could be done had been done, and the rest should now be left up to *the operation of natural causes*. Charles Edward Trevelyan was knighted for his labours.

'Heaven only knows when these things are to end,' wrote a local clergyman in desperation to his bishop, 'for we scarcely have seen even the beginning of the misery that awaits our unhappy people.'

So it was. To still their hunger, they baked pancakes from sawdust, scraped the glue from wallpaper and boiled it up as thick soup. The sick did not need medicines, they needed food to recover. People died everywhere – in their hovels, along the road and in the fields. Most corpses weren't buried and the spectre of epidemics grew from day to day.

The year 1847, or as the Irish were to call it, Black '47, was about to commence. The famine had brought on unemployment on a scale never before known. The summer began superbly and it was believed that the dread of hunger was finally over. But another ghost loomed over Ireland. The people, weakened by hunger, were an easy prey to epidemic diseases. A nation was not only dying of starvation but becoming the carrier of that infectious, mortal disease, typhus.

The typhus plague swept across the island. The Lord was unswayed by the cries of His children to intercede for forgiveness of their sins, which, so they strongly believed, had brought about this new calamity. The death toll from typhus, an epidemic spread by lice, rose. The illness began with vomiting and agonising boils appeared before gangrene set in. Besides typhus, relapsing fever was another deadly illness, also transmitted by lice. It started with high fever and profuse sweating, and ended mostly in death. Even that was not the end of it, there were other equally fatal diseases such as bacillary dysentery (bloody flux)[4] and infectious diarrhoea, which first struck through children devouring old cabbage leaves or foul turnips to still their hunger. And of course there was always the hunger oedema, which led to a swelling of the limbs, and death.

The few sick wards available gave off the awful stench of rotting flesh, which drove back the medical personnel. The real heroes were the doctors and their voluntary helpers, as well as the priests; their courage was without description, fully aware of the risks they took coming into daily contact with highly infectious patients and parishioners.

To stay put was to court certain death. Therefore, the entire country was on the move. The people left their homes and they left their fields – anything to escape the horror and find a better life. It led to the largest mass exodus in

---

[4] The *bloody flux* which decimated medieval armies.

European history. The Irish emigration to North America must be considered today as the most important effect of the Great Famine. The real rush to leave Ireland began early in 1847. At the beginning of the year, over a quarter of a million emigrated from Ireland, and not only the destitute and poorest, but also the better off, planting the seeds of Irish hate towards the British government and setting in motion the 'Irish feeling'. The survivors of that terrible famine carried within them a survival instinct and a will to seek their fortune, but only a lucky few achieved what they came for – a good life and happiness on a new continent. Most ended up as poor as they had been back in Ireland, working for slave wages in the rapidly expanding industries, such as laying tracks for the railroads or filling the ranks of the depleted regiments during the bloody American Civil War.

Travelling to the Americas was expensive. A family of six had to pay a £6 fare to Quebec or £21 to New York. The way the US Consul in Belfast excused this difference in price was: 'To America go the people of good character and means, to British North America the evil and ill disposed.' The great difference in fare decided most Irish to go first to Canada and then simply to walk across the unguarded American border.

Huge masses jammed the quaysides. They camped there for weeks, trying to get passage. Dishonest passage brokers cheated the poor of their savings before they were allowed to go aboard. The Atlantic crossing from the many ports along the Irish and English coasts turned into a nightmare. Overcrowded below-deck quarters, a haven for lice which spread disease, where those suffering seasickness vomited over each other because they were too weak to reach the deck, where the smell of urine was all-pervading and the water supply was often undrinkable because the water casks had been used to transport vinegar.

A well-off young gentleman from Limerick, Stephen de Vere, took passage to Canada and observed the lower-deck passengers on the crossing: '. . . They are huddled together, without light, without air, wallowing in filth and breathing a foetid atmosphere, sick in body, dispirited in heart, the fevered patients lying between the sound in sleeping places so narrow as to deny them a change in position, by their agonised ravings disturbing those around them . . .'[5]

They called them coffin-ships. The *Elizabeth and Sarah* out of Killala had no toilets and its thirty-two bunks were shared between 276 emigrants. Many did not survive the hardship of the voyage; on the *Larch*, out of Sligo, of its 404 passengers, 108 died at sea. The voyage of the *Loosthawk* took seven weeks; 117 of the original 348, perished. Not all of them from fever, sometimes alcohol was offered for sale and this always ended in bloody fights with people being thrown overboard. The *Virginius*, out of Liverpool, sailed for nine weeks to cross the Atlantic. Of the 476 emigrants, 158 died on the high sea. And the *Agnes* arrived with 427, of which only 150 survived after quarantine, the rest fell victim to typhus.

The *Montreal Gazette* called for strict government measures to curb 'the inundation by the poor and destitute Irish'. A persistent fear of importing the fever into North America forced the Canadian government to build a quarantine station on Grosse Isle on the St Lawrence River. An eyewitness reported that the poorest of immigrants were slung into boats, then rowed to the beach where they 'crawled ashore and died like fish out of water'. Some 109,000 arrived on Canada's Grosse Isle in the spring of 1847, of which 2,500 were ill with fever and locked up under appalling quarantine conditions. By the end of the year, 20,000 had died of fever within sight of the promised land.

The tenants had no more fields to till, and the people of Ireland could no longer pay for their tenancy. Relentless

[5] C. Woodharn-Smith, *The Great Hunger*.

severity in collecting the rent came on top of the hunger. Eviction followed upon eviction; 500,000 were kicked out of their homes during 1847. A certain Christian St George from Connemara had his tenants evicted 'without even a rag to cover them,' Captain Hellard, the Poor Law Inspector of Galway who was sent to enforce the law, reported furiously. Roofs were ripped off, cabins demolished and people weak from hunger were stunned by the brutality. In retaliation, some tenants rebelled and killed sixteen landlords. London panicked; was not the new English labour movement of the Chartists led by an Irishman, Feargus O'Connor? With millions unemployed at home, what if the spark from Ireland touched English shores? The government quickly dispatched an additional 15,000 troops to make sure this didn't happen. Owing to the bungling by London, the political situation in Ireland was heating up.

Not only were the peasant tenants in despair, but some local resident landlords were close to ruin by high rates, without receiving rents. Their tenants were either dead or had emigrated. The break-up of society was a serious threat. Lord Clarendon, the newly appointed Lord-Lieutenant of Ireland, took one look at the situation before he dispatched an urgent message to the Home Secretary, Sir George Grey, in which he expressed his fears that the country was faced by a wholesale calamity which would bring eternal shame on the British government. His warning remained unheeded.

The year 1848 became one of revolutions throughout Europe. This was no different in Ireland. One might have thought it was a strong fatalism in their peasant blood that made the Irish resigned to a given situation. But that was not so. In the present hardship, the Irish had found a purpose. They might live on the fringe right now, but it didn't always have to be that way. Some were prepared to throw off the yoke of their English landlords. They would not wait much longer for this to happen. Four men led the way, William Smith O'Brien, Thomas Francis Meagher, Charles Gavan Duffy, and John Mitchel. They were joined by a number of peasants and workers, loitering day after day without hope of either employment or betterment.

But fury against injustice was futile. What mattered was picking the right moment. The year 1848 was not yet the right time for an all-out Irish rebellion. Arrest began under the new Treason Felony Act. John Mitchel was sentenced to fourteen years of hard labour, Meagher and Duffy arrested and thrown into Newgate Jail. Dublin, Cork, Drogheda and Waterford were put under the Crime and Outrage Act. On 29 July 1848 the Irish Rising came to its unbloody conclusion in Widow McCormack's cabbage patch in Ballingarry. William Smith O'Brien's parting words were spoken with bitterness:

'Let the fact be recorded in Irish annals that the people preferred to die of starvation at home, or flee as voluntary exiles to other lands, rather than to fight for their rights and liberties.'

Death came once again with the rain, silent and lethal.

The Irish were a God-fearing people. Their religion was Catholic and it began in the womb of the mother. Anything else was against God's law. God always had His will, the old died and the young were born. But this time it was different, this time the babies were stillborn and the young as well as the old died. Because in the year of Our Lord, 1848, the potato blight was back with a vengeance.

The trail of misery stretched across the land. An endless column of scarecrows stumbled under the protective covering of blue mist, towards the harbour, the ships, and vague hope. They carried on their backs their meagre possessions; some pushed wheelbarrows with their old folk. Their hands were coarsened with toil, their bodies worn out. Most didn't even think beyond their immediate situation how they would possibly live through the next few days, even hours. How wonderful it must be not to feel hungry any more. To say only once: I've had enough to eat.

They were numb, there was neither open lamentation nor silent sorrow at their parting. With their cloth bags, suspended from knobbly canes perched on their shoulders, they marched across the land without meeting a soul. The more they walked, the worse was their spirit. From time to time they passed some peasant hovels, but these were empty, their doors standing wide open. Had these hovels of the poorest been humanised by the sight and sounds of even a few children playing, it wouldn't have seemed so grim. But there was no sign of life, only a silent landscape with acre upon acre of black-leafed potato plants. The Irish peasant had abandoned his home and his fields, and deserted the plains. Only the thought of making it onto a ship, to escape to another world which would offer them shelter, kept them from sitting down and dying like the others. Even their priests were silent, they had no more comfort to offer to the soul.

There was lamentation all across Ireland. Oh Lord, kill me and put me out of my misery! There were lots of rumours about witchcraft, and the responsibility of evil women for the horror that had befallen Ireland. But this was a Christian and, more so, deeply Catholic nation. Satan, the devil, burning fire and eternal hell. Christ was suddenly very close to all religious people, and also to those not too close to church, because Christ was not only forgiveness but, even more so, He was hope. For most, the only hope there was. *He* knew what the Irish had to suffer, and *He* was always there. Just seeing a man wearing the collar helped change the attitude of many. And yet, the congregations were getting thinner. Some had died, some had simply gone away. Those who still had the faith to come to Mass squeezed ancient relics in their hands, hand-carved crosses – Holy Patrick save us! They raised their eyes heavenwards: 'Oh God, let eternal sleep overcome me.'

Outside his landlord's house, a man lay down, his head pillowed on his arm. Everything within him was peace and tranquillity and there was even a gentle smile on his face. That's the way he died. Another peasant they found hanging on a tree in front of his destroyed cabin next to his two daughters, dead from starvation. They were carried to the churchyard on ladders or in baskets and thrown beside the nearest ditch, left there to the mercy of dogs, which had nothing else to feed on.

'Six famished and ghastly skeletons, to all appearance dead, were huddled in a corner on some filthy straw, their sole covering what seemed a ragged horse cloth and their wretched legs hanging about, naked above the knees. I approached and found by a low moaning they were still alive, they were in fever – four children, a woman, and what had once been a man.' So lamented an Irish justice of the peace to the Duke of Wellington, begging for the duke's representation of the true situation to Queen Victoria.

In the fields, the rotten leaves from the unharvested potatoes had dropped to the ground and carpeted Ireland with a black layer of grief. This was now already the third year and the country was stripped bare. The bark of trees was boiled up as a soup or chewed raw; then the heat killed the bark-less trees, leaving them as the only eloquent witnesses to the horror. The fields had been dug up with bare hands for the last turnip, the last carrot. Cats, rats, squirrels, everything served as food. A few terrified dogs, which had escaped the farmer's axe, roamed around this pitiless solitude. Heat and rain, bugs and lice tortured the columns of slinking scarecrows. Could anything be worse than famine? The pain of hunger was unbearable, that awful gnawing pain tearing at the insides.

While many contemporary scribes exposed these tales of horror, others tried to separate myth from reality. Most came to the same conclusion: the overriding reason for the disaster lay in the inability by some members within the British government to handle the situation. That the English aristocracy in Ireland wasn't behaving with great tact comes from a note in the Dublin society pages. At the height of the famine, the Lady Mayoress of Dublin gave a splendid ball at Mansion House: 'Dancing continued until a late hour of the night and refreshments of a most *recherché* description were supplied with inexhaustible profusion.'

After three years of continuous crisis, the Irish were so exhausted that even the slightest mishap was bound to set off yet another major catastrophe. It happened in the first days of December 1848. Some were to claim afterwards that it had been brought about by a sailor who had stumbled off his coffin-ship, others, again, said it was a destitute man arriving from Scotland. In any case, the man attempted to force his way into an overcrowded workhouse in Belfast. There was no space for another beggar and a scuffle broke out. This brought him into contact with others, and he infected them with the most deadly of all epidemic diseases, Asiatic cholera. From this workhouse in Belfast, the illness raced across the country, and for all practical purposes, Ireland was now put under total quarantine from the outside.

The Central Relief Committee declared that 'we are truly sorry that it is now out of our power to offer ourselves as the distributors of bounty to our suffering countrymen . . .' (Lord John Russel, the new British Prime Minister). Thereby, the British government decided that enough was enough, and abandoned the Irish to the Trevelyan principle of 'the operation of natural causes'.

A sweet, almost rancid odour of rotting potatoes and death pervaded the country. The poorest were the ones who starved first. And because they were the weakest, any disease hit them quick and hard. (The cholera epidemic lasted until the middle of 1849.) They died in their hundreds of thousands, there was no one around to take care of the many dead and certainly no one to show grief. The island was littered with corpses, and few received a Christian burial. Volunteers helped with the disposal of the many bodies in trenches dug outside the villages. Still the Irish hung on, a nation that refused to become extinct. But a look around the countryside showed up the emptiness, a world gone mad.

By the fall of 1849 the potato blight finally receded. What killed the unknown disease remained a mystery. But even the fact that the famine had abated across the island was not reassuring. Too much damage and too much horror had been inflicted. This was not a zone of war with its destruction by gunpowder, this was nature's giant forces that had created such desolation; more destructive than a thousand cannons, a wasteland where millions of hard-working people had once tilled the soil. When some official parties from Dublin made the effort to visit the area, perhaps their visit was intended to show some human presence.

There was great need to restore authority. It was generally feared that Ireland would never again recover from the terrible fate that had struck it down, and that it would end up as nothing but an agricultural appendix to England. Even that wasn't assured, and for a long time the agricultural production of Ireland suffered from the aftermath of these terrible years, because the countryside was deserted and the fields abandoned. After the Great Famine, the repopulating of the countryside took more the aspect of salvage than resettlement. There were a few incidents and a few trials, but most of them were overblown as the population was simply too weak to stand up and fight. Certainly too weak to do an 'honest day's work'. These people had suffered too much, they were destitute and lacked everything. Those who hadn't already gone wanted to leave for America, the Golden. For the Irish, there was no way of turning back. They never had much choice in the matter.

Death across the countryside had been the immediate result

of the years of the Great Hunger, but almost as disastrous was the fact that over two million able-bodied men and women had emigrated and thereby emptied the island of its prime labour force. One and a half million Irish went by ship to the United States. Since North America had finally put up stringent health barriers and would not take in the sick, the emigration to North America went back down to a trickle. Perhaps that was what finally saved Ireland.

The tragedy had run its full course. A hitherto unknown fungus, in combination with the vagaries of the weather, almost destroyed a country. A million had perished horribly,[6] many of them needlessly. The neglect by British officials to come to the assistance of their people in dire need – some of it due to the bungling by minor administrators,[7] and the lack of comprehension or compassion by the controllers of the relief fund – was considered by the Irish as genocide. Men like Trevelyan compromised British long-term interests in order to impose their own version of short-term economy. Any hope for a brotherly relationship with their neighbours was buried on the potato fields of an emerald island.

And yet, it was an act of God. If the Lord was compassionate, He was also cruel and had punished his Irish children. The Irish never gave a thought that prevailing weather patterns – rain, fog, and cold – in combination with the untreated potatoes, were as much to blame for their years of hunger, as was the lack of compassion from the outside.

The rebuilding of Ireland has taken well over a century. But the memory of *The Great Famine* remains in Irish folklore, as does their hatred for those whose irresponsibility – so they feel – led to one of the great dramas of European history.

[6] In a census conducted in 1841, Ireland's population stood at 8,175,124. But another census, only ten years later, gave the population as 6,552,385. Deducting the emigration figure and the estimated yearly increase due to births, the death count of the famine came to over one million.
[7] Their bungling was not specially reserved for the Irish, it also led to the demise of the British forces before Sebastopol (Crimean War) during the winter of 1855.

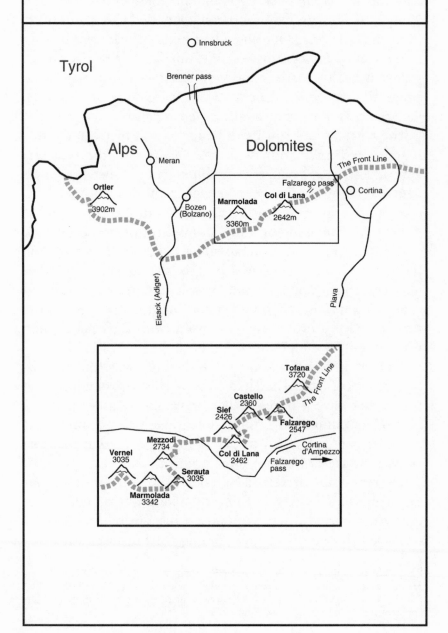

The War in the Alps 1915-1918

The white death

13 December 1916

'*Walsche foch'n müassn mir giahn
Es ischt ja s'schianste Wetter.*'

('Italians we must go and fight
For that, it's the nicest weather.')
Song of the *Tyrolean Standschützen*, 1915

Snow, snow, and more snow. It had been snowing and storming for a whole week. It had its positive side: the enemy gunners had to stay under shelter. It was Friday, 13 December and the day of Santa Lucia. Surely a lucky day, not quite as cold as it had been for the last two weeks, with the occasional ray of sun bouncing off the pristine glaciers and the snow-covered valley lying below the 1st Battalion of the *Tyrolean Kaiserschützen Regiment 3*. Their artillery spotter nest was at 3,300 metres, though the rest of the battalion was further down where the glacier met the cliff. Now they had to dig out their snow-filled trench. Well over two metres of fresh snow had fallen, and in some places the storm had piled it up to six metres. The powder snow was so fine it didn't stay on the shovel. What the heck, it was a nice day and all was calm. The rest of the men passed through the ice tunnel from the rock cave, which also served as their bomb shelter, storage room and sleeping quarters, and began to dig. After having been cooped up for a whole week, a little work was not bad for the morale. They smoked and shovelled and joked. They failed to pay attention to the *foehn* (warm mountain wind) that was beginning to melt layers of snow. This sudden change in temperature transformed the summit slopes into an unstable mass that hung above the glacier without a base to support its enormous weight. In other words, a blueprint for disaster.

At 11.07 am, the man on observation duty in the bunker of wooden beams and piled-up rocks, located just below the ridgeline, noticed a puff of smoke from an Italian artillery position across the valley floor. '*Diese Teppen* – those dummies,' he said to the man puffing on a curved wooden pipe, who also happened to be his next-door neighbour from the village down in the valley. '*Auf was schiassn's?* What are they shooting at?' Soon they heard the high-pitched whistle as a shell sailed over the mountain crest and into the beyond. Another puff across the valley and this time the shell struck a snowfield some two hundred metres below the Austrian observation post. 'They're getting close,' said the farmer, who was now a soldier in His Majesty's Imperial Austrian Army. His greatest worry was not a direct hit, but the deadly shrapnel, those whirling pieces of splintered rock whenever a shell stuck a solid cliff face. More people had been killed from flying rock than from enemy bullets.

Down in the battalion's main position, the men had also heard the explosion and stared up the steep mountain side hanging above their heads. They too saw a white puff as the shell exploded harmlessly in the deep snow, before they went back to their shovel work. Then came the third round. The men at the top didn't see it and the men on the bottom didn't look up. Suddenly the ground began to tremble and the whole mountain began to move.

Those who have observed the spectacle of an avalanche, and survived, will say that they have witnessed the end of the world. The unimaginable force of snow masses bearing down from the high mountain slopes, tearing, crushing, burying. So it was in this winter war among Europe's highest peaks.

The snow layers just below the summit's crest broke into small tablets, sliding, slowly at first, until the entire slope began to move. The mass gathered speed, the pressure increased and the thin powder snow fluffed up in a cloud . . . more powder whirled up into the air . . . the cloud quickly grew into a boiling wave, 200 metres high, gathering momentum until it reached 300 kilometres an hour. The enormous air pressure, which preceded the snow mass, was the lethal factor; its tremendous pressure wave acted with the might of an exploding bomb[1] – trenchlines were flattened, artillery pieces hurled through the air, shelters bowled over . . . most men died immediately, crushed by the enormous pressure, some died from shock or cold, others died shortly afterwards, choked by the fine, powdery snow. Few were those who survived. They were called 'the miraculous ones'.

On 13 December 1916, 274 officers and men of the *1st Battalion of the Kaiserschützen* were buried under a million cubic metres of snow. Another 63 went missing, their bodies were never found.[2] They were the first to die, that day. But not the last.

When Italy declared war on Austria, it didn't count on two factors. First was the unshakeable resolution of the Tyrolean peasant to defend his homestead. And the second was the weather. Nothing is quite as fickle as mountain weather. It can dump three feet of snow in a single night in the middle

---

[1] The pressure wave of a large avalanche exceeds five tons per square metre.
[2] Even today, well-preserved bodies in WW1 uniforms are spilled forth from the Marmolada glacier.

of August, icy storms whip unchecked across glaciers and rocky slopes, lightning is attracted to anything metallic, and fog shrouds peaks and mountainsides, which makes people lose their way and fall over cliffs. In the summer, the greatest danger comes from rockslides set off by rainfalls, while the winter brings snow, and with it deadly avalanches.

At the start of the First World War in 1914, Italy was the ally of Austria and Germany. Acting in line with their principle of *'sacro egoismo'*, they switched camp when being offered territorial gains by the Allies. Especially in the Austrian mountain provinces of Carinthia, Salzburg and Tyrol, this betrayal brought forth a fury which combined with a *'vaterländisches Gefühl'* of deep love for the fatherland.

'In diesem Lager Österreich!' ('Austria in this camp!') became once again the century-old war cry. The male population of the alpine provinces – those not already called up and facing the Russians, thousands of miles from Tyrol – from the fifteen-year-old schoolboy to the seventy-year-old veteran, took up arms to defend their homes and villages. They proudly wore their peak cap with the *Spielhahn*-feather and the *Edelweiss*; their elected officers bore on their collar tabs a Tyrolean eagle. Still, the situation seemed hopeless: 17,000 men of Austria's remaining army reserves, plus 24,000 militarily untrained peasants who had banded into forty-five *Standschützenbattalione* (home guard battalions), were called on to defend a mountain frontier of 350 kilometres and face 800,000 fresh Italian troops.[3]

The Italian *supremo*, General Cadorna, was aware that

---

[3] The exact Austrian manpower along the Tyrolean theatre: two Czech and seven Slovenian reserve battalions, one battalion each of Austrian Kaiserjäger and Kaiserschützen, plus the Infantry Regiments 14 and 59, altogether 17,000 men for a 350 km frontline. On 19, May 1915, this force was boosted by 24,000 irregulars of the forty-five Landschützen Battalions.

the irregulars wouldn't give up Tyrol without a struggle, and that he had to expect some desperate rearguard action at every point of his planned thrust into the heart of Austria. But he wasn't overly concerned, his troops outnumbered the enemy twenty to one and outgunned them ten to one. He decided to attack along two fronts: along the Isonzo River to liberate the *mare nostro* (our sea) – the Adriatic – and to press a simultaneous thrust along the Eisack Valley up the Brenner Pass and across to Innsbruck. Even his critics had to admit that his plan held obvious advantages. Cadorna knew that taking Innsbruck would be his masterstroke, both psychologically and strategically, while Austria could count only on the irregulars to stop his advancing armies. If he thought that his invasion would be a walkover, the *Tyrolean Standschützen* had a surprise in store. The old and the young, whose grandfathers had successfully repulsed a Napoleonic army along these valleys and mountains in 1809, were determined to do the same to the *Welschen*. They did just that.

Each village banded into a company, then they elected their captain, normally the local innkeeper or village mayor. They took their rifles, which they used in peacetime to poach game, and marched off to war, singing their *Landesschützen Song*:

'*Und will der Feind ins Land herein, und solls der Teufel selber sein,
Dann ruhen uns're Stutzen nicht, bis dass das Auge bricht . . .*'

('And should the enemy come into our land, even the devil himself,
Our rifles will not rest, until we're all dead . . .')

In the first months of the war, the troops were vulnerable

to the great peril of the mountains, the weather. Without adequate trenches, without shelters against the fury of the elements, the guard posts had to spend weeks exposed on the highest peaks. But the *Tyrolean Wall* held, the heroism was indescribable, and the *'Tirolesi'* couldn't be pushed an inch. It didn't need a general to tell a Tyrolean to stand and fight, he sat up on the ridge while down in the next valley were his wife, his children, his farm. He stood and he fought and he died. But he didn't budge. There are endless stories of extreme bravery. The famous Austrian mountain guide, Sepp Innerkofler, led a group of climbers up a vertical rock chimney of the Tofana to silence an Italian machine-gun position. The first in line, he reached the top, lobbed a grenade at the Italian position, and was then struck by a bullet. The chimney was so tight that his fall would have taken with him the entire rope party; instead he threw himself backward from the cliff and thus saved their lives.

Fighting under these conditions was harsh. The paths leading to the individual positions were often across bouncing tree trunks, anchored with ropes to vertical cliffs; or through cracks, studded with metal spikes which they could climb like chimney sweeps; those on guard duty roped themselves to boulders so as not to crash a thousand metres to their death; others lowered themselves by rope onto narrow ridges, piled up a few rocks for protection, then used their nest for some sharp-shooting; spotters sat on the summits in gusts of icy wind, with their teeth chattering, to keep an eye on the enemy's movement. But neither storm nor danger would move them from their sacred duty, and their faces became as hard as the rock that surrounded them. 'A front line in rock and ice' was how historians would refer to the mountain warfare in later years. Pasubio, Paternkofel, Ortler, Marmolada, Rauchkofel, Tofana, Sexten, Innichen, Moos, and Sillian. One of the deadliest struggles was for the Col di Lana, which the Italians soon baptised the Col di Sangue, *the Blood Mountain.*

Why the Italians picked on this 2,462 metre high mountain for their breakthrough attempt is even today a mystery. It would have been so much easier to bypass it, but perhaps some Italian general looked for a symbolic monument. If he did, he certainly found one. Col di Lana, a mystic name, mountain of much useless suffering. In the beginning, the summit was defended by a mere dozen Tyrolean border guards until a local *Kaiserschützen* company rushed to their support. Throughout 1915, the Italian high command sent in battalion after battalion of their élite mountain corps, the *Alpini.* By late October 1915, twenty-four *Alpini* battalions had been engaged to take a mountain top of dubious strategic value. With their cries of '*Avanti Savoia*', they clambered up the steep slopes. The *Kaiserschützen,* who had somehow survived the furious artillery bombardment, looked over the parapet of their slit trench for worthwhile targets and fired to the accompaniment of vile curses against all things Italian. Medical orderlies rushed along the trenchline, slapping bandages over holes while the profusely bleeding wounded kept on shooting, dedicated to the grim task of killing at close range. Those of the enemy who were hit rolled down the steep slope to come to a halt in a wire entanglement. In a heroic final charge, the *Alpini* kept moving upwards before they got hung up on the final barbed wire, only 20 metres from the Austrians' defence below the summit.

So far as the *Kaiserschützen* company under *Hauptmann* Konstantin Valentin was concerned, the summit of the Col di Lana was their exclusive property. They had tunnelled shelters into the rockface and installed themselves 'for the duration of the war'. On Sundays, the battalion priest visited them to deliver the Holy Sacrament. Afterwards, they held hands and sang: *Zu Mantua in Banden* . . . Tyrol's anthem about their country's greatest hero, Andreas Hofer, who had stood up against the might of Napoleon. It gave them courage and confidence.

While the war continued unabated for the possession of the summits, life continued down in the valley. The women folk took over farm chores, mowed the grass, cut the wood, brought in the hay. On Sundays, the wives and daughters of the soldiers fighting in lofty heights congregated around the ancient chapel *Zur allerseligsten Jungfrau der Verteidigung* (Our Lady of Defence), which the Italians called '*Alla beata vergine della difesa*'. According to legend, the ferocious Langobards had invaded the valley. Villages were sacked, and all seemed lost when the Madonna sent thick fog down from the mountains. The Langobards attacked, and when the fog lifted, the people of the Montaneler Valley discovered that the brutal warriors had slaughtered each other. And now they recited the same prayer. '*Heilige Jungfrau, steh uns bei . . .*' ('Holy Virgin, stand by us . . .'). And the Madonna gave them a sign of her compassion; up on the high pastures and mountain tops it began to snow in July, and this brought the fighting to a temporary halt. Some of the men came down into the valley to spend a night with their families. Holy Madonna, stand by us.

The Tyroleans had used the summer months to haul up timber with which they constructed the weirdest shelters, anchored directly into the precipice. This work was done early in the morning, when clouds clung to the mountainsides and obscured the view of the Italian artillery spotters. Some of these shelters had running water, gushing from the glacier over the cliffs and, sometimes, into their bunks. To protect themselves from shells and the unstable mountain weather, they began to tunnel into the mountain. They scooped out the rock and installed wooden benches, tables, rifle racks and bunks, and then sat in there, playing cards or spooning their thin soup or mending their ripped trousers, while outside the shells burst against the rock and the deadly ricochet whizzed through the air. Storage rooms were packed with barbed wire, ammo boxes, mountaineer ropes, candles, beans, lard, felt boots with wooden soles and heavy sheepskin coats for those on guard duty. Because it could freeze outside of the winter months, mountain weather would suddenly take a turn for the worse in July, August or September.

It took many more men to bring up provisions than to fight the enemy. The work of the porters was wrought with mortal danger. On open slopes, they became the easy target of sharpshooters that hid in the cliffs. Below the summits, porters stared up at the thousands of boulders hanging precariously above their heads. They made the sign of the cross, 'Holy Mother stand by me', and then climbed past the danger. Some made it and some didn't. Those who didn't became a military statistic: 15 August, Gran Langazuoi, 4 porters, rockslide.[4]

They hacked passages into vertical rockfaces; they groped their way across, hand-over-hand, on ropes anchored in cliffs, with their feet dangling in the air and a sixty-pound load on their backs. They strung cables from cliff to cliff, and winched up the loads by hand, or installed motors in a regular network of cable elevators. Whatever the system, the provisions had to get through. And the wounded had to get down. Pain shot through the bodies of stretcher cases as their sweating bearers stumbled downhill. Yet nothing was like the horror of being lashed to an open freight platform, then lowered by cable across a yawning 1000-metre emptiness. The walking casualties, those with arms in slings and hastily bandaged heads, were sent down by foot and told to come back up the following day, carrying provisions.

[4] There are thousands of such statistics in the Austrian military archives.

General Cantore,[5] the commander of the *Alpini*, ordered a concentrated artillery bombardment of the Col di Lana. On *Stützpunkt 2,250* (Fortified position 2,250, the altitude in metres), the first line of defence, located some 200 metres below the summit, the Austrian officer commanding lost control when a direct hit crushed the cavern and killed his entire troop, including his two brothers. He jumped onto the parapet, waved his arms, and was instantly felled by a sniper. The rain of shells of all sizes was so dense that, by the evening of 22 October, only three men were still alive. That night, the Italians moved into this crucial position, and the fate of the Austrian defenders on the summit became a foregone conclusion.[6]

7 November 1915 was a bad day on the Col di Lana. The Italian artillery poured its concentrated barrage onto the summit, causing great casualties from splintering rock that whizzed through the trench. At noon the artillery suddenly stopped, and an Italian *Alpini* battalion came climbing like cats through the cracks in the cliffs. The few Austrians who had survived the artillery barrage put up a gallant fight with bullets, bayonets, rifle butts, shovels and bare fists. By 3 pm, it was all over and the last of the defenders scrambled down the opposite slope. Those in the valley saw an Italian flag waving from the summit.

'*Der Italiener ischt ob'n*' ('The Italian is on top'). Everyone knew what would happen should the Italians be allowed to remain on the high ground: the valley would become a death trap. *Hauptmann* (Captain) Konstantin Valentini of the *Kaiserschützen* rallied all those who could still walk and hold a rifle. In the fading light of the evening, they swarmed up the almost sheer slope, dashing from boulder to boulder, braving

---

[5] Cantore, a good general, was killed on the Fontana.
[6] Many of these stories come from the author's father, an officer in one of the *Kaiserschützen* battalions from 1915 to 1918. Wounded near the Col di Lana, he spent the remainder of the war on the Marmolada.

withering fire from the Italians on the summit. There were many acts of gallantry that terrible night. A fourteen-year-old boy threw himself on a grenade and sacrificed his life to save that of his comrades. A seventy-two-year-old farmer, whom everyone said was too old to milk a cow, heaved himself from rock to rock and hurled a grenade into a machine-gun nest. Under the cover of darkness, *Hauptmann* Valentini led some thirty men in a bayonet charge. His yelling horde threw the *Alpini* from the top. At 10 pm the Austrian flag flew again from the summit of the Col di Lana. On 26 November the *Alpini* gave it another try. This time, the Austrians had learned their lesson; they had replaced the rock barriers with sandbags, which absorbed some of the shell fire and stopped any ricocheting. When the *Alpini* came up the slope, the *Kaiserschützen* played dead and let them approach to within ten metres before they subjected them to a rain of hand-grenades. Those who were hit fell forward and remained still on the white limestone blackened by the explosion, the rest slid down the hillside on the loose rocks. From that day on, the Italians called the Col di Lana the Col di Sangue, the Blood Mountain.

The pile of martyred *Alpinis* in front of the summit trenches grew higher from day to day. On 16 December, Major Grandolfi led the *Alpini Battalion Belluno* in their biggest effort to storm the summit. The attack was thrown back with horrendous losses. Cries of 'O *dio mio, Ajuto!*' by the wounded, caught in the strands of barbed wire, could be heard well into the night. There was little the Austrians could do to lessen their suffering. The year was coming to its end and the first snows hid the mangled corpses under its white blanket. Snow covered the horror that had torn up the peak and flanks of a sacred mountain.

The official count of Italian casualties for this one mountain in the six months of 1915 were given as: officers wounded 199, killed 104, plus 14 missing in action; soldiers wounded 5,160, killed 1,050, plus 435 missing in action. The question must be asked, how could soldiers be 'missing in action' on a single mountain? The answer to this is quite clear: buried by avalanche.

It snowed from the Swiss border to the Dolomites, it snowed from the Eisack (Adige) to the Isonzo. Every mountain, every trench was buried under powdery snow, every pole carried a white hat. Men on guard duty were covered in white, and since they had to remain immobile to escape the watchful eye of the enemy sharpshooters, they resembled snowmen. Only puffs of pipe smoke showed that the snowmen were alive. The main occupation of the soldiers along the chain of Alps, *Alpini* and *Standschützen* alike, was to shovel snow. Paths, trenches, ladders, artillery positions, everything was covered by masses of snow. Getting provisions was turning into a major problem. The porters could no longer fight their way through the snowdrifts, and a climb that normally took a day in good weather, now needed three. Columns bringing up vital provisions, wading through hip-deep snow, had to change their leader every ten metres. Clumps of ice hung on communication wires and men had to climb ice-covered cliffs to repair the inevitable breaks. On the vast glaciers of the Ortler and Marmolada regions, crampons were as vital as boots. Thin snow bridges which covered bottomless crevasses gave way under the weight of mules and men, hurtling them to their destruction.

With the heavy snowfalls and bad visibility the mountain war ground to a halt. It led to minor actions. One happened to a *Kaiserschützen* patrol of *Fähnrich* (Ensign) Mikosch. His dozen men had lost their bearings in a blizzard. For hours they had forced their way through snowdrifts sometimes higher than a man and had reached the end of their endurance when they came upon a cluster of huts. Completely exhausted, they stumbled through the door of the nearest hut where they heard the heavy breathing of sleeping men. That was when the *Fähnrich* noticed a greatcoat of the Italian *62nd Infantry Regiment*. They had inadvertently walked into the middle of an entire enemy reserve battalion! A guard spotted them and gave the alarm. The Austrians released a number of grenades into the huts, and made their getaway down the steep slopes.

By February 1916 the weather had improved sufficiently to resume the attack. On the approaches to the Col di Lana, an *Alpini* battalion was stretched out in a long line when a soldier looked up and saw a dark cloud near the top, like that of a heavy summer storm. He yelled a warning. A grey-blue mass came thundering down, whistling and howling . . . then everything was silent, deathly silent: 341 Italian soldiers lay buried under twenty metres of hard-pressed snow. Nature had had the last word, the attack on the Col di Lana ceased for a month.

After a year of bitter fighting, very often hand-to-hand at altitudes of over 3,000 metres, the *Schützenbattalions* were steadfastly hanging on to the mountain frontline and the Italians hadn't advanced a foot into their Tyrolean Holy Land. With spring about to melt the snow in the valleys, the Italians began a new type of mountain warfare. When they failed to take the summit by storm, they started to tunnel into the mountain beneath the Austrian positions.

Colonel Tarditi, commander of the two *Alpini* batallions engaged in the Col di Lana sector, ordered Lieutenant-Colonel Peppino Garibaldi to begin work on a mineshaft leading up to the summit. For two months, the Austrians on top of the Col heard drilling noises under their feet. The Italians had installed a heavy compressor under an overhang, and drilled a shaft into the mountain. Once they had reached a position below the summit, they branched out into several small shafts with chambers at their ends. By 12 April the Italians had finished their tunnelling operations. In a single night, 15/16 April, the chambers were packed with 5,000 kg of *nitrogelatine.*[7]

That same night, Captain Adalbert Homa's exhausted 5th Company of the *2nd Kaiserjäger Regiment* was replaced by the same regiment's 6th Company under *Oberleutnant* Anton von Tschurtschenthaler.

17 April 1916. A grey dawn broke over the Alps. Suddenly all hell broke loose: 150 heavy guns fired on the summit of the Col di Lana. At 14.27 pm, *Oberleutnant* Anton von Tschurtschenthaler dispatched the following report:

'TO THE K & K BATTALION COMMANDER FROM COM-MANDER COL DI LANA. FROM 5 AM TO 9 AM LIGHT ARTIL-LERY, AFTER 9 AM HEAVY ARTILLERY ON OUR POSITION. TRENCHLINE IS COMPLETELY SHOT UP, AS IS OUR FALL-BACK POSITION. COMPANY SHELTER HAS RECEIVED DIRECT HIT. UNDERGROUND SHELTERS UNUSABLE DUE HEAVY SULPHUR CLOUD. SITUATION DESPERATE, CAN FIND NO SOLUTION. IN CASE OF ENEMY ATTACK WE WILL DO OUR UTMOST. NEED MEDICINE AND STRETCHER BEARERS, URGENT. THIS REPORT IS NOT DISPATCHED IN PANIC BUT STATES THE FACTS. I ASK FOR IMMEDIATE ASSISTANCE. TSCHURTSCHENTHALER, OBERLEUTNANT.'

As suddenly as it had begun, the murderous bombardment faded away. At 10.30 pm, the summit was suddenly illumi-nated by powerful searchlights placed on the surrounding peaks. 'Something's going on,' yelled Tschurtschenthalen: *'alle Mann in Deckung* . . . all men take cover.'

At 11.30 pm, explosions rocked the region. People in the valley stared in horror at three giant flames that reached for the sky. The summit of the Col di Lana disintegrated and thousands of tons of rock flew through the air, setting off many rockslides, of which one caught a supply mule

---

[7] The biggest mine of the war was set off by the Austrians on the Col di Pasubio on 13 March 1918. It contained 55,000 kg of dynamite. The Italians fired a mine of 35,000 kg nitrogelatine on the Castelletto.

train. The summit was gone, replaced by a 100-metre wide crater. 150 *Kaiserjäger* died in the explosion; only one of those in the trench had a lucky escape. The force of the blast catapulted him through the air and he landed several hundred metres further down in the branches of a tree. For two days he crawled with a broken leg. Those who found him, bleeding and in tatters, thought they had come upon a ghost.

It was a miracle that any of the *Kaiserjägers* survived. Tschurtschenthaler and some of his men had been inside a rock cave on a secondary peak, with its exit facing away from the blast. But a fall of rocks now blocked their escape. With no light and slowly suffocating from the dense sulphur fumes, their bleeding hands tore at the rocks to open a passage. After several hours they managed to break through, only to find themselves staring into the rifle barrels of an *Alpini* commando who had finally taken possession of the Col di Lana. If nothing else, this victory showed up the senselessness of the war in the high mountains.

With the fight for the Col di Lana over, the focal point of the battle in the mountains now shifted to the Ortler region, where Austrians held the Cima di Campo (3,480 m) and the Königspitze (3,800 m). Summer 1916 was dry and hot, ideal weather to bring supplies up the rugged, barren mountain slopes to the summit positions and to strengthen the artillery disposal. The problems of resupply were multiple; it took ten porters for every fighting man to bring up his food and ammunition. On the steep, rocky paths only mules and muscle power could carry the gun tubes and crates of shells, barbed wire, bullets, provisions. Moving across bare glacier offered no chance for concealment from the enemy's guns, while oxygen starvation turned every step into a lung-busting torture. Added to it was solar radiation, which caused a high degree of sunburn and temporary snow blindness. But the greatest danger came from falling stone.

On 14 August, under a leaden sky, a long column of *Alpini* and their mule train, piled high with the tubes and carriages of mountain guns, ascended the Falzarego Pass. Seen from the top, they looked like ants crawling up the path that wound up like a snake. The progress of the column was hampered by the heavy loads which the mules had to carry, and by the roughness of the terrain. The weather changed, the sun dipped behind a black cloud and it began to rain. The downpour made the path slippery and progress for the animals became difficult. Before long, the path had turned into a regular torrent. The column halted, the men relieved the animals of their burdens and sat down. Finally, the downpour ended and a radiant sun made its appearance. '*Andiamo* – Let's go!' ordered their *capitano*.

But the rain had done something else. The downpour had washed out the thin layer of earth from underneath the rocks, piled up in the long, steep corridors that led to the summit. A single shell exploded near the summit crest. A few bouncing rocks set off more, and in no time, a long slope of rocks and boulders was set in motion. The world collapsed for the men of the column . . . an entire mountainside bounced down on the hapless soldiers, with their mouths open in a desperate shout that was drowned by a mighty roar, as boulders the size of a house smashed into mules and men: 258 men and fourteen cannons were carried into the valley, their mangled bodies buried for all eternity under a million tons of rocks.

Marmolada region, autumn 1916. Austrian units had honeycombed this 3,344-metre mountain, famous for its giant glacier, into a regular underground ice-city. They had carved a labyrinth of gangways, artillery positions, hospital facilities, observation posts, and storage depots. There were sleeping quarters for companies, a field kitchen and a telephone switchboard. Wooden planks were laid over crevasses, smaller cracks in the glacier's smooth surface were fortified as machine-gun positions. But many fell victim to the treacherous hidden snow bridges, and even today, eighty years later, the giant glacier is still spitting out its victims. Above the steep snowfields, just below the summit, were the artillery spotters. A complicated system of baskets on cables, known as flying coffins, supplied them with the necessities of life on the lofty heights. The daily artillery duels had little impact on the men inside the ice caverns, and any attack across the polished glacier into the mouth of fixed machine guns would have amounted to suicide.

By the middle of November 1916, it began to snow. Avalanches came down like waterfalls on the valley positions around Schluderbach. It was much worse for the supply caravans. Day after day the porters had to go up the tortuous paths, into a witch's cauldron of storms and snow slides. There is no account of the number who died – frozen, crushed, buried under the masses of snow. By early December 1916, the snow lay so thick that any further resupply of the summit positions became impossible. Fortunately, the storerooms were full and ammunition plentiful. Those who had no need to be out on the open glacier took shelter in the dozen wooden huts which had been built during the summer months, well protected from the enemy's bombardment, but never safe from avalanches.

It was the day of St Lucia, 13 December 1916. The men of 2nd Company had been shovelling snow all day long. It had made them wet and tired, and they had stripped off their clothes and crawled into the bunks in the huts on the slope leading up to the ridgeline. Father Martin Metschik, the priest of the 1st Battalion, *3. Kaiserschützen Regiment*, told what happened next:

'I was in the company of my good friend Hercules in a shelter near the cliff. It had begun to snow in November, which brought down the avalanches that caused more victims than the war. On this particular morning, around 5.30 am, we heard the growling sound of an avalanche. It surprised our men in their sleep inside the huts on the slope of the Gran Poz. The cries of the injured made us realise that a drama had taken place. The first shelter we got to, that of our commander, Rudolf Schmid, the one directly against the cliff, was covered by a thick layer of pressed snow hard as concrete. It took seven hours to dig him out. Yet he was one of the lucky ones. Nothing was left of the huts of the 2nd Company, only a swathe of raw ice showed where the avalanche had passed on its destructive way. The air pressure had turned another series of huts, just off the direct path of the monster avalanche, into a mass of splintered, crushed rubble that stuck from the mountains of snow mixed with lumps of ice and big rocks. We worked for four days, shovelling and digging, always in danger of more avalanches. We found only broken bodies with blue faces. On the fourth day, we dug one last hole and ended up in a natural ice cave where seven soldiers had found refuge; one was dead, one was half frozen, but five were well. But they had lost all measure of time. One told me he thought that he had been under the snow for only twenty-four hours.'[8]

The enemy, holding the opposing slopes, was no better off. The story of Lieutenant Tullio Minghetti of the *7th Alpini Battalion* was similar to that of the Austrian priest.

'It was the night of St Lucia [13 December] and my thoughts were with my family back home. We were thirteen in a lean-to that housed the motor for our cablelift. As fortune had it, I found myself on the southside of the narrow hut, which was anchored by two steel cables in the solid rock of the precipice that dropped vertically into the Val Ciampi d'Arei. Suddenly, I felt a terrible pressure

[8] From an account by Father Metschik, on 14 December 1956 of the survivors of the Marmolada war, and written up in *Die Marmolata*, Kaiserschützenbund Wien, 1972.

in my ears and I thought that my head would burst. The candles went out. Next came a hellish crash which shook the hut and I clearly heard one anchor cable snap. "It's all over, now we're falling," was my first thought. But we didn't. Snow filled the room and my back was pushed against the wall. Air – I was frantic for air. I dug with my hands until they were raw, but I still managed to open a small passage. I managed to stick my head out when, to my shock, I discovered that half of our hut was missing, and it was dangling at a crazy angle over the abyss. Far below, where the monster avalanche had ended its devilish ride, I noticed a great mound of piled-up snow, the tomb of my company . . .[9]

On that fatal 13 December 1916, countless Italian and Austrian soldiers died, all victims of monster avalanches.[10] In dusty archives, one can find a dry statistic, written down with a cruel pen. A list of thousands of names, buried under millions of tons of rock and snow.

There is something to be learned from this struggle for possession of the 'high ground'. Both sides were determined to shun the lessons learned by mountaineers who had passed there before them; and yet, for all of their shortcomings, both *Schützen* and *Alpini* did rather well. In a conflict fought at such altitudes, it was impossible to make a distinction between a winner and a loser. In the end, three years of suffering and bloodletting came to nothing. The territorial gains were zero. Nature had thus decided.

Italians as well as Austrians counted without the mountain. In all, two-thirds of the casualties during this murderous mountain war were inflicted by the elements. Man can be victorious against fellow man; but when confronted by the unleashed forces of nature, he stands powerless. Among

[9] Tullio Minghetti, *I figli dei Monti Pallidi*, Legione Trentina.
[10] According to an account in the Österreichisched Heeresmuseum (Austrian War Institute).

mountain peaks, all men are equal. Man is always exposed to the whims of nature.

Only the mountain decides who is to live and who to die.

The week the panzers froze

5 December 1941

> '*Our sergeant had told us that winter was coming. But who thought it would be that bad?*'
>
> Letter of a German soldier from the
> Eastern Front, December 1941

Obergefreiter Otto Schiele, 4. *Kompanie, 3. Batallion, Infantrie Division 31*, reaches into his pocket and takes out a page from the *Völkischer Beobachter*. It is several months old.

'*Und was hat unser fescher Herr Hitler heute für uns* – What does our handsome Herr Hitler have for us today?' asks *Soldat* Hans Wallner, a boy from Vienna, sitting in a corner in his undershirt, catching fleas. After six months in Russia he doesn't think much of his Führer. As a matter of fact, the others share his views, crouching close to the open fire inside the only shelter left standing in the scorched village.

Otto Schiele unfolds the page with the headline 'Propaganda Minister Joseph Goebbel's Stirring Speech' splashed across: '*Kampf bis zum letzten Mann und der letzten Kugel* . . . Fight to the last man and the last bullet!' Carefully

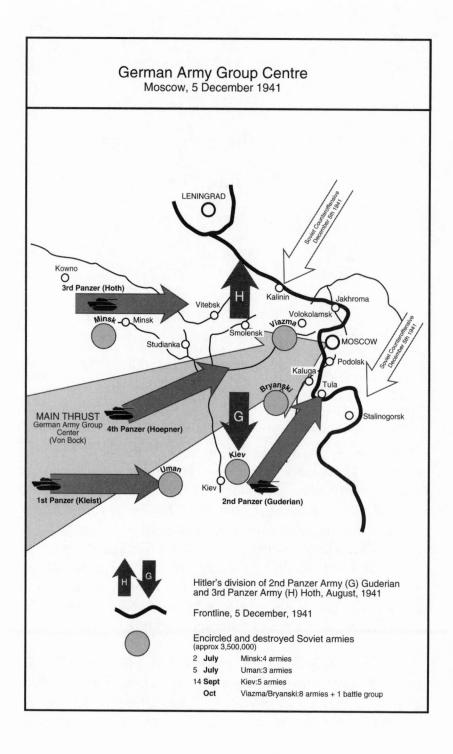

German Army Group Centre
Moscow, 5 December 1941

LENINGRAD

Soviet Counteroffensive December 5th 1941

Kowno
3rd Panzer (Hoth)

Vitebsk

H

Kalinin

Jakhroma

Volokolamsk

Minsk Minsk

Smolensk

Viazma

MOSCOW

Studianka

Podolsk

Soviet Counteroffensive December 5th 1941

Kaluga

Bryanski

Tula

MAIN THRUST
German Army Group
Center
(Von Bock)

4th Panzer (Hoepner)

G

Stalinogorsk

Uman

Kiev

Kiev

1st Panzer (Kleist)

2nd Panzer (Guderian)

H **G**

Hitler's division of 2nd Panzer Army (G) Guderian
and 3rd Panzer Army (H) Hoth, August, 1941

Frontline, 5 December, 1941

Encircled and destroyed Soviet armies
(approx 3,500,000)

2	**July**	Minsk:4 armies
5	**July**	Uman:3 armies
14	**Sept**	Kiev:5 armies
	Oct	Viazma/Bryanski:8 armies + 1 battle group

he tears off a small piece, down to the line commencing: '*Kampf* . . .' From another pocket he produces a pinch of *machorka* (Russian tobacco), which is mixed with hay to last longer, and rolls himself a cigarette. He sucks the smoke deep into his lungs before he passes the stub around. A blast of icy wind fans the fire on the ground. The door is slammed shut by a soldier with a steel helmet and overcoat sugar-coated with a fine layer of frost. Icicles stick to his unshaven face. '*Scheisse*,' comes from between quivering white lips; 'freezin' tonight.'

'So what else is new?' asks *Soldat* Wallner.

'*Wachtablösung*, change the fuckin' guard, that's wot!'

'I've heard you,' gripes Wallner, reaching for his clothes. 'I think I'll quit this job and take a long vacation. I'll even accept one without pay.' He piles on layer upon layer of socks and sweaters. 'Keep me breakfast. *Heisser Kaffee, Butterbrot mit Honig, ein weiches Ei.*' He spits it out with a sad grin, grabs his rifle and stumbles out into the night. The temperature is down to minus 42°C. When they find him next morning he is stiff as a board. He probably didn't suffer much, he just fell asleep and froze to death.

It can be accurately stated that 5 December 1941 will go down in the annals of modern warfare as the day of the sacrifice of German infantry. That day, the *31st Infantry Division* showed a sense of duty that can favorably compare with Ney's heroic charge at Waterloo or Pickett's men at Gettysburg.

It was a change in weather that decided the course of events. By one o'clock, during a full moon, the temperature was down to a numbing minus 46°C. The men wore two or three pairs of long underwear or women's knitted bloomers, and anything else they could pile onto their bodies. Some wore padded outer garments they had stripped off their fallen foe. Felt boots were at a special premium, but only

dead Russians had them. The nerve-racking wait, and having
to stand out in the freezing conditions, put the tempers of
the men on edge. From beyond the moonlit forest came the
throaty rumble of idling tank engines.

'Not ours, theirs!' an elderly corporal remarked dryly.

'Don't they ever run out of gas!' cursed a newcomer, his
nerves frayed by the sound.

'They've got so much *sprit* they can fry their asses.'

Finally, their wait was over. A red-striper, sitting inside
his heated radio truck at the back of the line, had made up
his mind what would happen to their battalion within the
next hour. To a German soldier within shouting distance of
Moscow, anything was better than freezing solid and falling
over as an icicle. Sergeants bawled: '*Auf marsch-marsch!*
Move out', the men grabbed their rifles and began to
advance through the snow. Unfed, with clothes and weapons
unsuitable for the Russian winter, lacking artillery support,
German infantry slugged forward through waist-deep snow,
their breath freezing as it escaped from their mouths. Then
the enemy opened fire; the men clutched their rifles harder
and continued straight into the flickering muzzle-flashes.
Their advance was a ripple of stumbling, falling, and getting
up – those who still could, that is. Sergeants yelled encour-
agement their men couldn't hear over the howling wind and
the zinging of bullets. Men moved at different speeds, keeping
their heads well down as if that could protect them. Despite
the numbing chill, they began to sweat from sheer effort,
exhaustion, and fear. They cursed their rifles and banged
with their fists on the frozen locks to open the breeches.
They cursed Ivan and his winterised guns which obviously
didn't jam. Everyone got caught up in the madness of yelling
and dying. They had to keep on going . . . those who fell
would be frozen stiff within minutes. What happened next
was a screaming rush of energy and sudden death. Gaps
appeared everywhere, men were simply swallowed up in

the endless white. The whole world was dying. But they kept on going.

At mid-morning, the leaden sky was swept away like the curtain being drawn back on a Greek drama. The dying continued, and the soldiers of the *31st* displayed a bravery that went way beyond the call of duty. At the moment when all the technical innovations which science had put at the disposal of a modern fighting force broke down, the foot soldier carried on by his will to survive. The *31st Infantry Division* broke through the enemy line and came to within eight kilometres of their goal.

Then it was over, they could move no more.

THE BULK OF THE RUSSIAN ARMY STATIONED IN WESTERN RUSSIA IS TO BE DESTROYED IN A SERIES OF DARING OPERATIONS SPEARHEADED BY ARMOURED THRUSTS. THE ORGANIZED WITHDRAWAL OF INTACT UNITS INTO THE VASTNESS OF INTERIOR RUSSIA IS TO BE PREVENTED.

This was Hitler's directive, *Führer Befehl No. 21*, dictated on 18 December 1940, which called for the destruction of the Soviet Union. The German onslaught, code-named *Fall Barbarossa*, which began before dawn on 22 June 1941, was brought on by an irresolvable conflict between the fanatical concept of racial supremacy and the order for a world revolution by the working classes.

Hitler misjudged the fighting abilities of Russia's poorly trained reserves and, furthermore, the political solidity of Stalin's despotism.[1] On the other hand, Stalin's belief that Hitler would not act irrationally by starting one war before

---

[1] One month after the campaign begun, Hitler's chief-of-staff, Halder, wrote: 'The whole situation makes it increasingly plain that we have underestimated the Russian colossus.'

finishing another was a capital error. The Red Czar was aware of Germany's capabilities, but not its immediate plans; and yet, on 5 May 1941, a month before the assault, he addressed the graduates of Russia's military academy thus: 'A German attack sometime in the future cannot be ruled out. Be prepared to deal with any surprises.'

When it happened, that 22 June 1941, the entire Soviet defence machine was shockingly unprepared. Despite the advice for caution by Russia's super spies, Dr Richard Sorge and Kim Philby, as well as the head of the Military Intelligence Directorate, Golikoff, Stalin chose to disregard their warning, he simply couldn't believe it; he even accused Sorge of being a double agent working for the Germans. By noon of that first day – after the Germans had destroyed hundreds of tanks and occupied many Russian border towns – Marshal Timoshenko transmitted Stalin's specific order to his forward unit commander, General Boldin:

NO ACTION IS TO BE TAKEN AGAINST THE GERMANS WITHOUT OUR KNOWLEDGE. COMRADE STALIN HAS FORBIDDEN THE OPENING OF ARTILLERY FIRE AGAINST THE GERMANS.

Against such confused muddling, even the might of the Russian colossus stood no chance, since a modern war of attack, like a nineteenth-century cavalry charge, was won by those who got there 'fustest with the mostest'. Stalin had more tanks, more planes, and certainly more men than his opponent, but the Red Divisions were untrained and scattered from Outer Mongolia to the Polish border. Prudent military thinkers, such as Marshal Tukachevsky, had tried to alert Stalin of the inherent dangers, but their voices had been cruelly silenced during the bloody army purges of 1937.

Hitler, the opportunist, realising the Red Czar's predicament, now committed a strategic blunder. Rather than follow

Napoleon's stratagem and concentrate his forces into one single thrust, he divided his forces into three prongs. North to Leningrad, centre to Moscow, and south towards the Ukraine grain reservoir and the vital Caspian oil fields, which he needed to fuel his voracious war machine. For an operation of this scale, he had neither the men nor the machines. Yet, for five months it worked. Nothing seemed to be able to stop Hitler's panzers. Nothing short of a miracle.

The summer of 1941 was hot and dry, temperatures soared way above 40°C, something the German armies were unused to. Russia's roads were covered by fine dust which clogged radiators and air filters, overheated tank engines, and blistered the paint on the panzers. As in every war throughout the ages, the foot soldiers were the ones who suffered most, with blisters on their feet, and the insides of their thighs rubbed raw from sweat. Everything was covered with a fine layer of dust whirled up by the motorised units. The sweaty faces of the troops were caked with red dust and their mouths tasted as if they were chewing mashed potatoes. In the shade of the forests their bare arms were attacked by swarms of blood-sucking insects. Drinking water became a serious problem. The retreating Russians had dumped dead animals down the well shafts to contaminate the wells. This acute water shortage made it imperative to ration their water supply, and fuel transporters for the advancing panzers were converted into water carriers. The medical corps had issued strict orders not to drink non-boiled water, but heat, dust and the cordite fumes made many disregard the danger. When thirst got the upper hand, they drank contaminated well water, with the result that many became ill – an offence which frequently led to court-martial.

The heat had other consequences, which were to prove of significant importance in the months ahead. Heavily loaded with all the paraphernalia of warfare – ammunition belts, machine guns and mortar tubes, medical supplies – any additional weight slowed up the foot soldier. Many dumped their cumbersome uniform greatcoats or heavy field jackets and advanced in shirtsleeves. Why shouldn't they? Their *Führer* had promised them quick victory – they would be home long before Christmas.

Russia was nothing like France, that delightful country with its gentle contours and cattle, its perfect roads which could be followed with the help of excellent Michelin tourist maps; France could be reached over an excellent rail network from Cologne and Koblenz. This was Russia! Everything took on different proportions, distances had to be multiplied by ten, the rail gauge was wider[2] and German rolling stock was useless. Partisans blew up rail lines and bridges along the vast distances which separated Berlin and Leipzig from Smolensk and Kiev. And then there was the weather, always the weather, boiling hot in the summer, wet in the autumn. They didn't know about the winter. Not yet. Most had heard about the Russian winter but nobody had ever lived through one.

The first phase of *Fall Barbarossa* had gone according to plan. By the middle of July 1941, two-thirds of the distance to Moscow had been crossed by Hoth's, Hoepner's, and Guderian's panzer armies. The Soviet Union suffered losses on a scale never before witnessed in global warfare. Three million Russians had been made prisoner and 17,000 tanks had been captured or destroyed. Yet the key to the collapse of Bolshevism was not to be found in military action, but in politics. That's where Hitler failed. A good case in hand was the Ukraine, with its rural population depleted by Stalin's bloody purges. Germany's political aim, to turn the

---

[2] By orders of the Czar, to isolate Russia from the rest of Europe and to forestall any military ambitions by his cousin, the German Kaiser.

people of this rich granary against the Bolshevik dictatorship, was thwarted by the *SS*'s ruthless behaviour towards the civilian population. Reports of widespread executions in the conquered territories and of the many thousands dying of neglect in German prison camps spread through the rest of Russia.

On 19 July, at the height of the battle for Smolensk, Hitler issued his *Führer Befehl* * 33. It was to prove his greatest strategic blunder. While Hoth's panzers were sent north to help out at the assault on Leningrad, Guderian's motorised formations were pulled away from their march on Moscow and instead dispatched south to encircle a huge Russian force holding Kiev. There, Hitler could take another million prisoners, a feat which would put his military genius into the record book of world conquests. In order to achieve a spectacular, yet meaningless, victory, he overlooked the three vital factors that had brought down Napoleon: *space, time, and weather.*

Despite the protestations by Hitler's generals, such as Heinz Guderian, the ablest of his panzer generals, who tried in vain to persuade his *Führer* to cancel this mad scheme which had to lead invariably to a winter campaign, the 'greatest military genius since Julius Caesar' wouldn't listen to his prophet.

'Moscow? Only ossified brains, absorbed by ideas of the past, will see any worthwhile objective in taking Moscow,' he upbraided the battle-hardened general. He also refused to listen to his own Commander-in-Chief, General Halder, who noted in his diary: 'He [Hitler] cannot be bothered by strength ratios. To him, the prisoner-of-war figures are conclusive proof of Germany's superiority.' With Hitler's obsession with taking the greatest number of prisoners, the main objective of *Fall Barbarossa*, a concentrated push by three panzer armies on Moscow, was put on hold. Four priceless weeks were wasted in focusing on secondary objectives.

With the Germans' attention withdrawn from the central sector, Marshal Timoshenko had successfully extricated over half a million men and their equipment from the trap around Smolensk. He now used them to strengthen the defensive perimeter around Moscow. Instead of a projected 200 Soviet divisions, the next German attack would run into 360 divisions, enough to upset Hitler's *Blitzkrieg* strategy.

The final phase of Hitler's plan called for seizing overall control of European Russia. To achieve this goal, the political keep of the Soviet system had to be taken – Moscow. The attack on the Russian capital was to be spearheaded by a simultaneous advance of three panzer armies. What could have been achieved in dry July was doubtful in wet October. Germany could deploy a respectable force, but with poor logistical support. The aggressors had learned nothing from their easy victories, and greatly underestimated the effect of guerrilla warfare or the influence of the weather. Russian partisans defended their homeland with skill and fanatical savagery. To the Germans' consternation, armed civilians without previous military experience mounted deadly attacks on rail lines, bridges and supply depots. Fuel and ammunition were slow in reaching the front units. All it would now take was a change in the weather to worsen this situation, and the planned German push would be severely handicapped. Hitler disregarded all possible pitfalls and ordered the drive on Moscow to be resumed on 2 October 1941 – almost to the day that Napoleon decided *to retreat* from that city to escape the oncoming winter.

It was night and quite warm for the time of the year. The men were stretched out along the edge of the forest, resting on their groundsheets. Some stared at the sky, some smoked, their cigarettes hidden in their fist. Nobody spoke. The young tank driver nervously checked his wristwatch. 04.20. Another forty minutes to go. He looked for assurance to his company sergeant, a veteran of tank battles from Sedan to Smolensk, who chewed on a hard-tack biscuit.

'*Herr Feldwebel*, what about a decent meal on Red Square, with schnapps and caviar, in about a month?' The sergeant, who had seen and heard it all before, only shrugged his shoulders. Poor kid, don't you realise?

The unit's captain, *Hauptmann* Detlef von Wagenburg, who had joined up in 1939 and gone to war for '*Führer und Vaterland*', wiped the tiredness from his eyes. He had to get his tanks ready. It wasn't just for fun that he had learned how to use them. There was this thing that nagged at his mind. In the French campaign they had rolled on concrete highways in a dry, mild summer, and were getting resupplied over a sophisticated rail network. In this immense landmass, their quartermasters were confronted with an exaggerated supply problem. And his tanks had to advance along a road which was indicated on a strategic map drawn up in Berlin, but which didn't exist, or had to be built first. On top of that he had to deal with that party asshole of a narcissistic colonel, who saluted everyone with a *Heil Hitler*, and did the rounds to assure the unit commanders that the *Reichskommissar* for Moscow was already on stand-by (in Koblenez on the Rhine!); that the *Wehrmacht* had the greatest military commanders (true); and, most important of all, they could always count on the most brilliant organiser in history, their inspired *Führer*, whose genius had thought of everything and organised all down to the last detail. *He* (as if *He* were God) had ordered to put the total productive resources of *Gross Deutschland*[3] at the troops' disposal. They would lack nothing; his panzers would have all the ammunition and fuel it took to push right through to Moscow. *Heil Hitler!*

The enemy shoreline was no longer bluish, nor was it a

[3] Great Germany, ever since Austria's annexation in March 1938.

shapeless mass. *Hauptmann* Detlef von Wagenburg looked across the river and saw only open country. He snuffed out the end of his cigarette and looked at his watch. '*Erste Kompanie*, ready to go?'

'Ready.'

'*Zweite Kompanie* . . .' The tank engines sprung into life.

Like the crack of doom, the whole front exploded. The oily smoke of bursting shells, fiery showers of earth spurted into the sky. The ground trembled. The artillery lifted to more distant targets. The tanks moved out. In the tower of the lead tank stood the *Hauptmann*, a map-case in his hand. But a map was not really necessary, for everyone in his squadron knew the direction: East, towards the rising sun – and Moscow! His tanks flattened the fields of rye and oats. The first village they came to had been flattened. Nothing was left standing. The tanks didn't stop, there was nothing anyone could do. The whole thing went on its own.

The simultaneous advance by three panzer armies pierced Moscow's outer defence perimeter. Four hundred miles of front line were ablaze, while thousands of panzers scrambled into action. General Guderian's *Second Panzer Army* blasted their way through Marshal Yeremenko's *Bryansk Front*. They quickly overcame the minefields and drove through the masses of Soviet infantry.

The *Hauptmann* stood erect in the open turret of his Mark IV panzer. He was the German vanguard to silence Russian artillery. He was looking at the burning village, when waves of Russian infantry emerged from the wood. Behind them followed a few tanks, monstrous affairs from an age well past retirement. From the long-barrelled gun of a German panzer came a huge orange flame. It scored a direct hit and shrapnel spilled into the limbs and ribs of the tank-riding infantry. The German tanks swivelled their mounted machine-gun, tracers streamed into the mass of Russians, bowling them over. Those inside the panzers could hear the shrill sound of whistles as the Bolshevik commissars drove their soldiers into the barrels of the German armoured force. From somewhere on their flank, an anti-tank gun opened up. A panzer burst into flames, while another tipped forward into a shell crater. Both sides were taking serious casualties. While the Russians seemed to have an unlimited reservoir of manpower, the Germans could ill afford their heavy losses. The battle raged for forty minutes before the Russian attack dissolved.

All along the outer Moscow perimeter the picture was similar. Suicidal wave attacks and fanatical last stands took place before the Russian line was smashed. A group of Soviet stragglers were hiding out in a wood near the village. They didn't know the name of the village, nor did they care. They had thrown away their rifles and been on the run ever since, anything to get away from the steel that rained down on them and had wiped out their regiment. Everywhere lay the dead and dying. A German horse patrol had almost caught them out in the open and the sabre-swinging cavalry had cut down a number of them. From a company of one hundred and twenty, only five were left. Between them they shared a piece of hard bread and an onion.

Through the trees they could see shadows emerging into a clearing in the woods. 'Get down,' hissed their self-appointed leader. One of the shadows stopped and pointed with his gun in the direction of their hideout. Holy Mother of Russia, they prayed, let it not be the Germans. 'They're ours! They're ours!' yelled one of the stragglers. He jumped up and waved frantically with his arms. That's when the bullets picked him out and smashed him into the nearest tree. Those were Russians, no doubt about it! They ran towards the remaining four lined them up, and shot them. Yes, those were Russians all right, but of a special kind. An *NKVD*[4] killer squad to stop deserters.

---

[4] NKVD, the dreaded Soviet State Police.

Panic! Major-General K. F. Telegin, the chief of *Moscow Defence District* and the one directly responsible for advising Stalin on the military situation near the capital, had focused on Guderian's sudden breakthrough in the south. What happened next came as a shock: on 5 October, two pilots returned from a reconnaissance sortie and reported that they had spotted enemy columns advancing along the Warsaw Chaussee (highway) on Maloyaroslavets, the historic battlefield of 1812. This seemed impossible. Checking his battle map, Guderian's panzers were reported 125 miles from Kaluga, not Maloyaroslavets, and headed in the direction of Orel. General Telegin called the commander of the Moscow District Air Force to order up another sortie by scout planes. When these returned, German panzers had already reached the Ugra River near Yukhnov, less than a hundred miles from the centre of Moscow. Telegin didn't dare call Stalin directly, he knew only too well that he who brought bad news was banished to a suicide battalion – if he was lucky. But he had to tell someone. He called up Marshal Shaposhnikov, who was similarly doubtful about the report. A few minutes later, Stalin's personal secretary Poskrebichev called Telegin, and then Stalin himself came on the line.

'So, Telegin, what's that all about?'

'Comrade Generalissimo, advance Nazi units are on the Ugra.'

'Confirmed?'

'Yes, Comrade Generalissimo.'

'Hmm,' grunted Stalin, and the line went dead. Telegin shivered. His phone rang again. This time it was Stalin's henchman, the much feared Lavrenti Beria. He screamed and ranted, calling the general a provocateur and rumourmonger. When Telegin defended himself, stressing that the Air Force District commander, Colonel Sbytov, had confirmed the sighting, Beria's men arrested Sbytov. While the entire Moscow Front verged on collapse, the general commanding the *Moscow Defence District* had to spend his time and energy saving an air force colonel from the firing squad.

What had happened was simple enough. Hoth's *Third Panzers* and Hoepner's *Fourth Panzers* had smashed their way through Koniev's *West Front* and their tank columns were racing along the Mozhaisk and Warsaw Chaussees in a pincer movement around Viazma. They had reached a position way beyond Koniev's main force and were threatening Marshal Budenny's *Reserve Front*, the ultimate defence position around Moscow.

On a Warsaw Chaussee bridge, jammed with fleeing women and children, sappers were busily attaching satchel charges. With a mighty roar, one charge was set off prematurely. The centre span lifted up and sent hundreds of refugees to heaven. The blown bridge would delay the German advance for perhaps twelve hours, but it most assuredly stranded Russian tanks and guns on the opposite shore.

After only seven days of fierce fighting, the battle culminated in the great enveloping movement around Viazma and Bryansk. After a murderous assault Guderian's tanks stormed into Orel. When General Yeremenko ordered a counter-attack, it ended up as a desperate attempt to break out in the direction of Moscow. Even that failed, and the *Soviet Bryansk Army* was doomed.

On 7 October, Hoepner's and Hoth's panzers met and the trap was complete. Caught inside the pocket were six Russian armies, 55 divisions, 663,000 men, 1,242 tanks and 5,412 guns. Endless columns of prisoners snaked across the muddy roads into captivity.

The last hundred miles on the road to Moscow were jammed with refugees. The *Luftwaffe* had also been there. The fugitives had to climb around bomb craters, smashed tanks, dead horses, a still smouldering supply column with the charred corpses of the drivers slumped over their wheels. Sometimes the fleeing masses were held up at

NKVD roadblocks where they had to show their papers; those who didn't have bona fide travelling permits were taken away to dig anti-tank ditches – if they were women, that is. The men were shot on the spot.

General G. V. Balushin had seen some of the heaviest fighting since early in July. Before Smolensk, he had led his division in a heroic charge to halt two panzer divisions and give his corps a chance to retire to a new defensive position. For this, Marshal Budenny had decorated him in person. Now Balushin's *Guard Division* held the sector north of Spas-Demensk. On the morning of 5 October, a panzer formation appeared suddenly from the mist. The panzers split into two prongs, squirmed forward like a fire-breathing dragon and had soon outflanked Balushin's line. The roof of his HQ hut burst into flames and his telephone line was cut. Without communications and through heavy smoke it was impossible to tell what was going on. His forward positions had been enfiladed, his main line breached. German infantry, following on the heels of the panzers, had squeezed Balushin's units into several pockets from which there would be no escape – unless he acted immediately and called for an instant withdrawal to the next river line. For this he had not been given the authority but, without a retreat, all his men plus their valuable equipment would be lost. Ignoring the objection of his political commissar, Balushin issued the order to withdraw. His division fell back. Before they had reached the Ugra line, near Yukhnov, his car was stopped at a roadblock manned by the *NKVD*. A car drove up, an *NKVD* captain jumped out; and from his map-case he took out a paper: 'General Balushin, by order of the *Moscow Defence Committee* you are hereby relieved of your command.'

The general didn't seem to understand. The *NKVD* captain stared down the officer who outranked him. 'Balushin, you are no longer a general. Hand over your pistol.' He motioned to his two guards who levelled their machine pistols at the general's chest.

'Grigori Balushin is herewith condemned to death for cowardice in face of the enemy. Sentence to be carried out immediately.'

At once! Such was life – yesterday a hero, today a traitor. 'May I smoke a cigarette?' The *NKVD* captain nodded, though he knew that this was not normally permitted. But Balushin was a hero, his name had been mentioned in dispatches. The general lit his cigarette, took one drag, and threw it away; the end would taste bitter. The guards took Balushin to the side of the road . . .

Despite the imminent danger, Stalin retained his outward calm. The day they shot Balushin, he took two decisions. The first was to call up General Zhukov, who had blunted the German advance on Leningrad, and order him to Moscow. When the general's plane touched down, he was rushed directly to Stalin, who was laid up with the flu in his *dacha* near Moscow.

'Our *West Front* is in serious difficulties. I want you to review the situation and report to me.' And he added: 'You have full authority.'

It was a grey dawn with some snow flurries when Zhukov set off in an unmarked staff car. He had been up all night and was so tired that he had to order his driver to stop from time to time to run a few steps alongside the vehicle to stay awake. His first stop was at Budenny's *Reserve Front HQ*, but there nobody seemed to have the slightest idea where to find Budenny. From the HQ, Zhukov drove to the town of Yukhnov, which he knew well, because this was where he had been born. Near the Ugra Bridge he finally met up with a shaken Marshal Budenny. Zhukov, though a mere general, ordered the marshal to defend the Warsaw Chaussee with all he had left. Then he sought out the other front commanders, Koniev, Bulganin,[5] and Sokolovski. They informed him that the front-line 'was fluid', an analog for 'in complete disarray', and that they had 'no conclusive information about the present location of the Germans' positions.' Zhukov did the next best thing: he decided to find out for himself. What he discovered was not reassuring. The entire Moscow ring of defences looked like a sieve, with holes everywhere. During the night of 8 October, Zhukov called Stalin. In plain words he gave him the truth. Koniev's *16th, 19th* and *20th Armies*, as well as the *Boldin Attack Group*, were encircled, as was Budenny's *24th* and *32nd Armies*. 650,000 men and thousands of tanks and guns were gone. On 11 October, Stalin appointed Zhukov commander-in-chief of the new *Moscow Front*.

'Your advice, General?'

'Forget Koniev, Yeremeko, and Budenny, let them try to fight their own way out. We must concentrate everything on an inner defence line around the capital, Comrade Stalin.'

'What do you need?' asked Stalin.

'One hundred divisions and two hundred tanks.'

Stalin nodded, and Zhukov couldn't help wondering from where Stalin would get his one hundred divisions and two hundred tanks.

That was Stalin's second decision of that fateful day. He had one more ace up his sleeve, a super spy in the person of Dr Richard Sorge, Tokyo correspondent of the German *Frankfurter Zeitung*. In late August, when the situation had become critical, Stalin needed an answer to a vital question: could he risk pulling out his reserves from Siberia and thereby open the door to a Japanese invasion. On his orders, *Moscow Centre* cabled Dr Sorge:

IN CONNECTION WITH THE GERMAN-RUSSIAN WAR, WHAT

---

[5] Who became Khrushchev's prime minister.

DECISION HAS THE JAPANESE GOVERNMENT MADE ABOUT
OUR MOTHERLAND?'

Sorge put his *apparat* [6] to work. His final confirmation
came during a private dinner with the German Ambassador
Ott, who confided to Sorge that 'those damned Japs won't
hear of standing by our treaty and attacking the Soviet Union.
Their warplans are for maritime control over the Pacific.'

On 4 October 1941, Dr Sorge ordered his radio operator,
Max Clausen, to dispatch a coded message to *Moscow
Centre*, which was immediately passed on to Stalin.[7] It
stated that the Japanese did not regard themselves bound
by the terms of the *Tripartite Pact* (the Berlin-Rome-Tokyo
axis signed in September 1940):

UNDER NO CIRCUMSTANCES WILL JAPAN DENOUNCE
THEIR NON-AGGRESSION PACT WITH THE SOVIET UNION.
THEIR STRATEGIC PLANNING ENVISAGES AN ADVANCE
INTO THE SOUTH PACIFIC, NOTHING MORE. THE SOVIET
FAR EAST MAY BE CONSIDERED GUARANTEED AGAINST
JAPANESE ATTACK AT LEAST TILL THE END OF WINTER
THERE CAN BE NO DOUBT ABOUT THIS . . .[8]

Based on a single telegram from Tokyo[9], Stalin took a
gamble. While German panzers were approaching the gates
of Moscow, the suspicious dictator entrusted the fate of his

[6] *Apparat* is a spy network. Sorge had informers in some Japanese state councils,
as well as in the organising committee of the Manchurian Railway, main supply
line for any invasion force.
[7] It was to be Sorge's last message, he was arrested by the Japanese secret police
the following day.
[8] The Neutrality Pact between Japan and Russia was signed in April 1941, and
Hitler's attack on the Soviet Union that June surprised the Japanese as much as
it had the Russians. That's why they never informed Berlin about their planned
attack on the USA.
[9] This information was eventually confirmed by Russia's spy in London,
Kim Philby.

country to an encrypted message from an agent. Stalin's order went out:

THE FAR EASTERN ARMY. ALL TROOPS FROM SIBERIA, FROM THE REPUBLICS OF CENTRAL ASIA, UNITS FROM TRAINING CAMPS IN KAZAKHSTAN AND UZBEKISTAN ARE TO BE DISPATCHED TO MOSCOW WITH THE UTMOST SPEED, USING ALL AVAILABLE LOCOMOTIVES AND ROLL-ING STOCK AND REGARDLESS OF ALL SAFETY MEASURES ON THE RAILWAYS . . .

With this order, Stalin stripped his Far Eastern border of all defensive forces. It started off the biggest rail movement of all times. Trains shunted out of stations, lost in clouds of steam and billowing snow. From railheads along the borders of China, Mongolia, and Siberia, trains converged on the Trans-Siberian main track, all headed West, sometimes travelling so close to each other that the engine drivers navigated by the red lights of the last carriage from the train in front. Fifty, sixty, a hundred trains a day, all headed for the same destination: Moscow. They brought guns and tanks; they brought men, masses of men. Eighty divisions. A million soldiers, élite formations, well equipped and used to the rough Siberian winter conditions. They wore white uniforms, had white guns and rode on white tanks – the brand-new *T-34*, a machine more powerful than anything the Germans could muster.[10]

By 11 October, the day General Zhukov was handed overall command of the central sector, two more Russian armies were encircled, feeding Hitler's obsession with pris-oners: another 660,000.

During the night of 12 October it began to rain . . . and it rained and it rained . . .

[10] From E. Durschmied's *The Hinge Factor*.

The Russian capital had become the front line. 100,000 Muscovites were called to arms; 40,000 boys and girls below the age of seventeen helped half a million women and old men dig an anti-tank trench, 98 kilometres long. Many died of exposure, wearing only the clothes they had on when dragged from their homes. Anti-aircraft balloons were inflated outside the Bolshoi Theatre and on Red Square, major thorough-fares grew into obstacle courses with sandbag barricades and welded rail hedgehogs on every intersection. The river embankment and Gorky Park were studded with anti-aircraft batteries. Men were pulled from their workbenches and put into 'voluntary worker battalions', and each man handed a rifle and five bullets, and told to stand and die. Marshal law was declared; 'enemies of order' were executed without trial. It was never specified what the word 'order' really referred to.

The city was in the grip of panic. By 17 October, the capital was being evacuated of its 'socially important elements'. Only the Kasan Station to Gorki and the Ural Mountains was still operational.[11] The square fronting the station was jammed with thousands of refugees. The 'socially important' party members sat patiently on their bundles and suitcases, while the ordinary people of Moscow watched in silence as fleets of cars containing high officials sped from the city. Anyone attempting to flee without an official permit was shot on the spot by roaming *NKVD* squads. Those were not the only ones who died during those days by the hands of *NKVD* execution squads. Special commandos emptied the jails of their prisoners. They were led into the courtyard and shot, and when there was no room for more corpses the prisoners were shot in their cells. Party cards were hastily burned, shops looted. Lenin's coffin was removed from its catafalque and whisked from the city.[12] Shots rang out in the

[11] Most troop movements from Siberia stopped at the outskirts to protect the secret.
[12] A. M. Samsonov, official Soviet chronicler.

streets. Isolated patrols of the feared *NKVD* were killed and their arms used to kill more of the hated police. Members of the *NKVD* ripped off their insignias and tried to hide, only to be caught by their colleagues and shot.

The night skies over the monumental towers of the Kremlin were criss-crossed by anti-aircraft volleys, the city centre was covered under a pall of smoke from exploding bombs of German dive-bombers. Women and children jammed into the Majokovski subway station for shelter. The diplomatic corps was evacuated to Kuibyshev and the Kremlin abandoned. All that remained in its splendid reception rooms beneath the golden cupolas were Marshal Shaposhnikov's situation maps pinned to the wall. It is not certain whether Stalin ever left the capital. In late October (date unknown), he was photographed visiting the wounded General Yeremenko in a Moscow hospital.

And it continued to rain . . . From Smolensk to Orel, from Viazma to Kalinin, it rained. The Oka and Ugra Rivers turned into raging torrents, and the dusty country roads became rivers of gooey, sticky, axle-deep mud, the bane of conquering armies throughout history. The Germans' wheeled infantry transporters sank down to their axles in the bog, horses disappeared down to their bellies, and the *Landsers* (foot soldiers) had to slog on by foot. Every single step became a struggle, the mud sucking at their jackboots and sapping their strength.

Still, the German momentum was irresistible, and the quagmire did not entirely stop the tracked German panzers. But their 'rush on Moscow' had turned into a 'crawling forward'. The only solid roads, the Mozhaisk and Warsaw Chaussees, broke down under the weight of German armour. Guderian's panzers stormed Kaluga on 13 October, Reinhardt's panzers took Kalinin on 16 October, and the final defence line at Mozhaisk was overrun by Hoepner's panzers on 18 October. But their advance was at a much reduced pace. This wasn't due to a tighter organised Russian resistance; it was that damned rain and that damned mud.

General Stumme's *40th Panzer Corps* advanced towards Ruza. Their objective was to envelop Moscow from the north-west. That damned quagmire – and the continued screaming at the front commander from up high at *Führer HQ* didn't help – his panzers were stuck, and he had to put an entire infantry regiment to no better use than chopping down a forest to build a log-dam across the mud so that he could ferry supplies of desperately needed fuel and ammunition to his advance units – by ox-cart and *Panje* (horse) wagon!

'One more week . . . just one more week of clement weather,' prayed the German panzer commanders. Hitler's decision in July to opt for a large bag of prisoners in the Ukraine plus the delay this had caused, now proved very costly.

It rained. *Hauptmann* Detlef von Wagenburg stood on top of the turret of his *Mark IV*, shaking off the rain from his black tanker's cap and studying the town before him through his glasses. Mozhaisk was supposed to be a key in the Soviet defence perimeter, and yet the town looked quite abandoned. Wagenburg studied some serial photographs, taken a week before. Two bridges, almost side by side, one for the road, and one for the railway. It was vital to capture at least one of these bridges intact. The *Hauptmann* raised his arm and pointed forward. The panzers, two abreast, entered the abandoned city and groped their way through the unfamiliar streets with its signposts all torn down. They were met by uncanny silence. The houses were abandoned, the church tower had been decapitated by a direct hit. In the main square they drove around the standard monument to socialism, a girl wielding a sickle and a worker holding a flag. Next to it was a tablet, recalling the great battle Napoleon had fought here on 26 October

1812. It was almost the same date that Napoleon had been *on his way back*, trying to escape the onslaught of the Russian winter. What must the German soldiers have thought of it, riding on tanks, soaking wet from the incessant rain and with the main street under a foot of water? The German vanguard encountered no resistance until they reached an unmanned barrier of welded iron rails. And there, in front, was the bridge, still up! Foot troops cleared a passageway and four panzers raced across the undamaged road bridge to form a bridgehead on the far shore.

'Commander of advance unit to regiment. Bridge intact and in our hands, repeat, bridge intact.'

'What bridge are you referring to?'

'The Mozhaisk road bridge.'

'What . . . what bridge?' followed by a moment of stunned silence. An incredulous voice came over the speaker. 'Repeat, what bridge is in your hands?'

'The Mozhaisk road bridge. Request support.'

'Congratulations, *Herr Hauptmann*. Stay where you are. The regiment will follow immediately.'

That's when the lead tank saw the three Russian staff cars approaching the river at high speed. Whatever were the Russians up to? Only then did it dawn on the German captain why the town was not defended and everything had been so quiet. Not only was his own HQ surprised by their lightning advance, but the Russians were totally unaware of the collapse of their front line. That's why the bridge had not been blown up! The driver of the Soviet lead car must have discovered something unusual, because he slammed on the brakes and bounced across the central reservation. Three tank guns barked out and three vehicles were no more.

In front of the four panzers lay a highway that stretched away into the distance. German panzers were sixty-five miles from Moscow. That's where they were ordered to stay.

It was a relatively clement October, with only that cursed mud. For the moment the quagmire, plus the sorry state of the equipment, had brought the German war machine to a standstill. The fine dust of the summer and the immense distances had played havoc with the material. The tank engines were worn and the gun barrels burnt out. For every five tanks that set off, four broke down. Tyres on supply trucks were bald and spun on muddy roads. There were no spare parts, there was no ammunition. Most of all, there was no fuel. But war wasn't only about tanks and guns, war was about soldiers, living, breathing human beings. And humans, when their body engines were worn down, couldn't be repaired with nuts and bolts, or replaced from some industrial assembly line. General Guderian had sent an urgent request for reserves. Hitler agreed. He would release five hundred men – five hundred to replace the hundreds of thousands who were lying buried in Russia's earth!

On 19 October, while Stalin met with members of the Politburo and the State Defence Council to determine if they should continue the defence – or abandon the capital – General von Kluge's *Central Army Group* finally ground to a halt in the quagmire. The German Central Group commander had no idea of the jinni he called up when he had to advise the *OKW* (Oberkommando der Wehrmacht, Hitler's HQ):

HAVE TO WAIT FOR FROST TO SOLIDIFY ROADS SO THAT MY PANZERS CAN MOVE.

Hitler threw a fit. Stop now? A three-day ride from Moscow. That amounted to high treason. He ordered an immediate advance. In one final push, the *3rd Panzer Division* and the *258th Infantry Division* advanced along the still viable Rosslavi Chaussee and forded the Nara River near Naro-Fominsk. From there they quickly spread out behind the main Russian defence line. Now Moscow was also threatened from the south-west. In a last stand attempt to stem the Germans, the Soviet commanders threw hastily assembled workers' militia units against the aggressors. The militia was annihilated, those who weren't killed threw away their arms and surrendered. '*Voyna kapuut* – *Krieg kapuut!* – Motherland finished – war finished.' Luckily for Russia, such a defeatist attitude did not carry across the entire front line.

And the German *Landser* slogged on; like another foot soldier, 130 years before him, he went hungry. His field kitchen was somewhere in the rear, axle-deep in mud, his uniform wet and stiff. '*Vorwärts, immer vorwärts! Auf nach Moskau!*' was the order of the day, and the next, and the day after that.

War has its highs and its lows, and for the invincible German *Wehrmacht*, the crucial point was about to be met. Just as the attempt of a breakthrough failed north of the capital, an attempt to carry the important industrial centre of Tula in the south was stopped cold. The battle was fierce. For the first time the Soviets employed the massed firepower of *katjusha rocket* launchers.[13]

The German plan was for a surprise attack to be mounted on Tula on 29 October. But military plans, as von Clausewitz had readily explained in his epic on warfare, rarely survived contact with the enemy. Tula, an industrial town of smokestacks and workers' flats, was situated astride the main southern approach to Moscow. The attack was

---

[13] Known as the Stalin organ, it was a truck-launched, fiercely deadly, if not accurate, weapon. Fired in clusters, it obliterated a wide area.

led by Guderian's *Second Panzer Army*, which had been engaged in time-consuming actions and had been slowed up by road conditions and failing logistics. Therefore, the initial attack was given to the infantry. Its epicentre was around Lieutenant von Oppen's *2nd Company*. They had reached a field some 300 metres wide, pitted with water-filled shell holes. They tried to make a dash, but the mud dragging on their boots made this virtually impossible. Soon they were pinned down by heavy machine-gun fire from a large workers' apartment building and had to dive headlong for cover into shell holes. There they lay, up to their necks in freezing water.

Corporal Wichmann pointed towards the great redbrick structure which blocked their way. '*Verdammte Scheisse*, we've got to silence that building or the whole company will get wiped out – *der ganzen Kompanie wird der Arsch weggeblasen*.' Miraculously they made it halfway across where they found an anti-tank trench in which to take temporary shelter from the withering small-arms fire. Bullets zoomed over their heads and sizzled into mud and water. Grenades were lobbed from the upper storey windows of the workers' flats, but none reached their trench. One of the men pitched onto his face and moved no more. He had taken shrapnel from a mortar grenade in his neck. They could not sit there all day long, waiting to be killed. It was to be the moment of glory for Corporal Wichmann, the big redhead, who liked fat sausages and buxom blondes, and once had been Germany's Olympic sprinter hope. He grabbed a bundle of stick-grenades, flung himself over the lip of the trench and sprinted towards the redbrick building, which flickered like a fire-spitting dragon. He made it almost to the side of the building when he slid on the mud, causing him to stumble. Though he was up in a flash, it still proved fatal. A burst of crossfire nailed him and he staggered on to the ground just beneath an opening occupied by a machine-gun. With a super-human effort, he raised himself to his knees, pulled the pins, and lobbed the grenades through the window. The entire floor heaved with flame and the Soviet gunners, plus their machine-gun, came sailing out through the hole that had been a window, before a burst from another building slammed Wichmann back to the ground. Two of his comrades raced to their fallen leader and pulled him back by his blood-soaked tunic. It was a miracle that they made it there and back, but there was no way they would have left their corporal lying out there. Wichmann died minutes later. He was awarded the *Ritterkreuz* (knight's cross) posthumously.

Inside the town life was fierce. Tula had been bombed and strafed for days, weeks. The warehouses had burned and food rations had shrunk from day to day. Soon people fought over a potato, a rat, a mouse. Bread was made from a mixture of bone flour and sawdust. The trees in the parks were stripped of their bark which was boiled. Despite the rain of shells and bombs, women cowered around the burst water mains or went down to the river to fill up their buckets. In underground shelters, by flickering candlelight, people lived, worked, and died. More and more front-line casualties were brought downstairs. Women wailed over their dead while small tots stared at the horror they failed to understand. A woman sat on her haunches near a corpse. Her eyes were swollen but dry, for she had no more tears to shed. The wounded lay sullenly on the ground, waiting for help, or just waiting for death to take them away. And all the while the ground shook, machine-guns chattered and shells exploded, while from the uniformly redbrick flats which fronted the giant steel mill, worker battalions fought panzers with grenades and rifles. They had to stop them. Their only hope for survival lay in keeping open the narrow corridor to Moscow. The bridges were down, but soon the river would freeze over, their last hope to get food across.[14]

The attack by German panzers fared no better than that of the infantry. The attempt to take Tula by surprise had failed. They were ordered to dig in and hold until the offensive was to be continued or until hell froze over. From that moment on, the panzer genius and inventor of the modern *Blitzkrieg*, Colonel-General Heinz Guderian, had to fight his attacks on horseback as his ammunition and fuel transporter were held up 50 kilometres in the rear of his front units, up to their axles in mud. Mud, mud, always that cursed mud. Effectively, he was left with only 35 per cent of his tank force to fight with, the rest lay belly-up in the quagmire. His artillery support became erratic as most shells got buried in the mud without detonating. Humiliatingly, a hastily organised, untrained workers' militia had stopped the attack of his élite infantry. One thing became abundantly clear. The change in weather had done it. That, and the soldiers' fatigue. After six months of incessant fighting, after suffering horrendous casualties, those who were left no longer had the punch to carry the offensive to its final success. The push on Moscow from the south was over. *Yes, mein Fuehrer, you've got us into this mess.* Not enough tanks, not enough shells, not enough men. And the weather! *We had read Napoleon's book, but you, you wouldn't listen when we warned you about the weather . . . jetzt sitzen wir in der Scheisse . . .*

Stalin insisted on going ahead with the traditional 7 November parade on Red Square. It was intended as a morale booster. He called Zhukov to make certain that on this particular day no German dive-bomber would disturb the ceremonies. Zhukov gave him his assurance. The troops,

[14] As in besieged Leningrad, where all supplies were brought across the frozen Lake Ladoga.

which paraded across Red Square in a driving blizzard, didn't cheer, but they gave the Muscovite something to cheer about. What was the mood really like on the Russian front line? Lieutenant Vladimir Sobel, a Russian company commander, wrote in the beginning of November. 'We have crossed the Orel-Tula Chaussee. Eighty per cent of my unit has deserted. Everyone says that the war is lost. Unless the winter comes soon, we're done for.' Lieutenant Sobel was killed on 12 November outside Tula.

The commanding general of Germany's Central Army Group, General von Bock, had prayed for frost. But frost meant much more than solid ground for a panzer attack. Frost meant winter of the Russian kind. It called for protective clothing and special materials to keep the war machine running. That, the Germans didn't have. Whether by sheer oversight or from some divine inspiration by their genial *Führer* that the lack of winter supplies would have been the spur to hasten his armies towards comfortable winter quarters in Moscow, is debatable. The fact is Hitler disregarded Napoleon's terrifying experience: but then, Hitler was never strong on history. Assured of a lightning victory by the easy successes during the early summer campaign, he had instructed the Quartermaster-General to provide winter clothing for a mere sixty divisions which would be required for occupation duties after the collapse of the Bolshevik state. Furthermore, there was the question of a special oil for winter use. Anything mechanised, from tank engines to gun recoils, from a truck's axle to a soldier's rifle, all needed the kind of oil that could withstand sub-zero temperatures. When under attack, it was no good hoping that the machine-gun would work.

All of a sudden, Berlin was beset by panic. 'What if we cannot take Moscow before the cold sets in? What if . . . ?' Suddenly party leaders woke up to the unthinkable, and how unprepared their soldiers really were to sustain a winter campaign in Russia. In a last-minute effort, Propaganda Minister Joseph Goebbels called on the German population for an ultimate sacrifice to give up their own winter clothing. It was called *Aktion Winterhilfe fuer das Ostheer*. Germany emptied its closets and millions of gloves, sweaters and greatcoats were brought to the collection centres in cities across Germany[15] – and that's where they stayed, because the distribution network had broken down. Road traffic into Russia was blocked by mud, partisans blew up rail bridges, and the available rolling stock was insufficient to supply the fighting men with ammunition and winter clothes. The German army was headed unprepared for a Russian winter. And then suddenly it was too late.

In the second week of November, winter arrived with a vengeance. On 12 November, the temperature dropped to minus 15°C, next day it was down to minus 20°C. It caught the Germans by surprise. With the cold, something else arrived: eighty fresh divisions from Siberia, and hundreds of the new *T-34* battle tanks, vastly superior to anything the Germans could field. This was something the Germans never suspected. On 17 November on a dark, overcast morning, they got their first taste of Siberian courage. In a further escalation of horror, two regiments of the *44th Mongolian Cavalry Division* attacked across frozen fields. The German *107th Infantry Division* fired over open ground. Not a single attacker made it, every single one of the 2,000 riders and 2,000 horses died in what was probably the last major cavalry charge in history. Tactically it was a senseless operation, but it proved an overwhelming psychological success. Not only did it point to Stalin's utter ruthlessness in sacrificing his troops to gain even the slightest advantage, it showed his

[15] Recorded on film by Goebbel's propaganda ministry.

vast human reserves. This no-pardon bloodbath gave birth to the tale of 'Stalin's hordes' and became the German trench-talk.

On 13 November, Hitler's Chief of Staff, Halder, convened a meeting of army group commanders during which he outlined Hitler's plan for the final attack. One commander dared to object to the *Führer*'s orders. General Heinz Guderian decided that this time the *Wehrmacht* had run out of luck, and that they had to stop before Hitler's madness destroyed them all. He knew from experience that any attack this late in the year was bound to end in disaster. The *Wehrmacht* could ill afford to lose thousands of men and much valuable equipment.[16]

'How to expect us to crank up a tank engine at minus 20°C? The pistons are frozen, the transmission oil is a solid block of ice, and the recoils on our guns are stuck. Keep your red wine and send my boys some padded winter coats instead.' Guderian was referring to a shipment of French wine, dispatched by a quartermaster in France as a good-will gesture for the coming Christmas; it arrived at the *Ostfront* as lumps of red ice. Hitler berated the hero of France for his defeatist attitude. Guderian's argument was pushed aside and the attack on Moscow was set for 15 November.

Since the element of surprise had gone, the Germans had to counter much stiffer resistance, with bridges blown and roads mined. Throughout the night, tank crews had kept fires going under their crankcases so that the motors would start in the morning. 'What's our target today, *Herr Hauptmann*?' The captain was well aware that his men had reached the limit of endurance and were about to break. He had to instill some courage. '*Der Rote Platz*, and the dining room of *Herr* Stalin,' he said grimly, 'and they can't stop us now!'

---

[16] In fact, their ill-advised offensive was to cost them 155,000 men, 800 panzers and 300 guns.

Along 1,000 kilometres of front line, engines roared into life – not all, only those whose crews had maintained fires beneath the engines of their steel beetles. The twelve *Mark IVs* of *Hauptmann* Detlef von Wagenburg's unit moved out. Their immediate objective was the next river-line, the Nara, and then on to Podolsk, 34 kilometres from the centre of Moscow. 'Take the bridges, and hold them,' came the order from division.

'Always the same, take the bridges, form a bridgehead, what's in a name? Yesterday the Protva, today the Nara, tomorrow, who knows? And what about some infantry support for my tanks,' thought the *Hauptmann*; 'as long as we are on the move, that's fine, but the bridges call for putting my tanks across the road in a blocking pattern. Then we won't be on the move and anyone can climb up and shove a grenade down the hatch.'

The lead tank crested the hill and there right in front of them was the bridge – not blown up, as they had feared. 'Go, go . . .' the captain yelled into his microphone. That's as far as he got before the ground around him exploded. All the guns in the world seemed pointed at his pitifully insufficient squadron. And this time, the shells weren't from popguns, but came out of the barrels of deadly 76-mm anti-tank cannons. Fortunately, their aim was lousy. Probably raw recruits, thrown into the fray without training as their shots zinged high over the tanks. Machine-gun fire swept his tank. The *Hauptmann* pulled in his head and closed the hatch.

'Go, go – for the bridge,' he yelled. His panzers raced downhill, the cleats sliding on the ice. 'Fire!' The tank guns barked, scoring hits. 'Keep going and keep firing.' Fountains of earth exploded in front of his lead tank, his third-in-line received a direct hit and slewed off the road, but the rest kept going, fire-spitting steel monsters racing towards a bridge. Figures were hanging in the girders, attaching fuses to satchel charges. A burst from the turret machine-gun and the figures tumbled into space to crash onto the ice. There they lay, dark specks on a frozen river. The psychological shock effect of the madly charging tanks, more than their firepower, decided the battle. The enemy's anti-tank fire thinned out before it stopped altogether as the first tank rumbled across the wide metal span. The tanks came to a stop and trained their guns on the battery of 76-mm guns, but found it abandoned. 'Green recruits, they ran,' grinned the driver.

'Green today, but they'll learn. Then what?' replied the grisly company sergeant. He jumped from his panzer. 'Hurry and put out the flag before our own *Luftwaffe* zaps us.' A red flag with a swastika was spread out on the snow. Their tank squadron was now Germany's nearest presence to the Russian capital, no further than the flight of a heavy shell from Podolsk. The *Hauptmann* studied the situation. They were without ground support and night was coming on fast. An attack by Russian foot troops after darkness, and his tank force would be wiped out. What a mad rush! His fuel tanks were nearly dry, perhaps good for only another ten kilometres, his shell racks almost empty. If he advanced without shells his tanks would be blown to smithereens. There was but one positive aspect: between him and the Kremlin, there were no more bridges to cross . . .

Every war has its story of a 'final stand'; Sparta had Leonidas and his three hundred, Custer's was at Little Big Horn, and now came the moment of glory for 'Panfilov's twenty-eight'. All had been quiet in this north-western sector of the front and that's why the Soviet High Command had only put up the minimal defences to block the Volokolamsk – Moscow road. But suddenly the flank was pierced and the entire line began to collapse. Infantry units retreated, the artillery abandoned their batteries, and everyone ran as hard as he could, all to get away from the terrible panzers. The last line dissolved. In the dying light of the day, troops streamed towards an assembly point in the rear, where they would be reformed into some kind of fighting unit. To achieve this, their commanders needed time. The fleeing troops hardly noticed the small holding unit at the Volokolamsk road intersection.

The night had been cold, it had snowed a few inches and the ground was frozen. Ideal weather for a panzer attack. The twenty-eight Russians huddled behind walls and in houses, trying to peer through the frozen mist, knowing that soon the enemy would come. The orders from division HQ had been explicit: 'Hold, and don't retreat!' In any case, they couldn't surrender. The story had it that the Germans were hanging the commissars and stripping the men of their clothes to let them die in the cold. Twenty-eight men – some too young to shave, others beyond the age of retirement, all that was left from an entire battalion of Major-General Panfilov's Division – had been placed to defend the vital road junction at Volokolamsk. For that they had been provided with one small anti-tank gun the Germans called a 'polite doorknocker', seven shells, three dozen hand-grenades and a hundred beer bottles filled with gasoline and a piece of rag stuffed into the bottle-neck to act as a touch paper: the weapon of the partisans, the 'Molotov cocktail'. Before long they heard an ominous rumble, announcing the arrival of a column of tanks. The first Mark III's broke through the mist. They did not appear to be expecting opposition and barely bothered to adopt a tactical formation, so sure were they of the collapse of the Russian front line. The gap had narrowed to two hundred metres before the two lead tanks deployed and fired a few shells at the derelict building at the intersection. The small, camouflaged anti-tank gun fired from point-blank range, and the two lead tanks were knocked out before a direct hit turned it into twisted metal. The engines of the panzers growled angrily as they pushed on with a clatter of tracks, snapping trees and hurling loose turf behind them, impervious to rifle and machine-gun fire. Five tanks were now trying to outflank the defending position, but the defenders held one advantage: their own speed. Two men dashed forward and hurled a handful of Molotov cocktails at a tank before they were mown down. The first tank had reached the ruin when more flaming beer bottles rained from a shell hole in the brick wall. The liquid trickled into the tank's slightly open turret, and a flame shot up. Another tank was stopped and the crews jumped from their burning vehicles. Before they hit the ground they were cut down by rifle bullets. '*Za Rodinu . . . Za Stalina . . .* Long live the Motherland . . . Long live Stalin . . .' More men rose and rushed forward, their petrol bottles breaking with a tinkle, and another tank was wrapped in a ball of fire. '*Za Rodinu,*' yelled Yuri and sprinted across and died. And after him, it was Pjotr's turn. And another Yuri took his place. Before he could hurl his petrol bomb, it was smashed in his hand by a bullet and he stumbled forward, a blazing human torch. With a final effort, he hoisted himself onto a tank, pulled the pin on a grenade, and shoved it down the stubby gun barrel of the Mark III. '*Za Rodinu . . .*' Altogether fourteen panzers were destroyed that way before 'Panfilov's Heroic Twenty-Eight' were silenced. The last to die was their leader, who slid with a bundle of grenades under a panzer, then blew himself and the panzer to hell.

In Moscow, hundreds of trains arrived from Siberia, and ever more white-clad soldiers disembarked from coaches and cattle-cars. Not all were élite troops. Some badly trained Mongolian divisions were given a shot of vodka, then sent directly to the front and ordered to clear a path through the minefields for the better-trained, well-equipped Siberian units. The Mongols attacked and died. But so did a lot of Germans, and not all of them from enemy bullets. On 27 November, the thermometer read minus 40°C. The forward positions had to be manned, day and night. The Germans had neither fur-lined coats nor felt boots. The Russians had both; their boots were loose fitting, which allowed them to pad them with straw or newspaper. The Germans wore *Knobelbecher*, hobnailed and tight, and the surest way to get frozen feet. The German soldier wore a dark-grey uniform, which stood out in the white winterscape. A Russian could lie in his padded white suit for hours in the snow, without freezing and without being spotted. The Russians were equipped with fur mittens, the Germans wore wool gloves which made their fingers too stiff to pull a trigger – if their rifles or machine-guns worked! Their weapons had not been winterised, and frequently the bolt action slide froze solid. Most vehicles suffered from blocked fuel lines, the oil froze in crank-cases and transmission boxes cracked open. Recoil springs on heavy guns snapped like brittle icicles. That same 27 November, the German Chief-of-Staff, General Halder, wrote: '*Wir sind am Ende unserer personellen und materiellen Kräfte* – We've reached the end of our personal and material force.'[17]

Burzevo, 55 kilometres from Moscow. A company of the *258th Infantry Division* had found shelter in a bunker on a military practice ground. Before the Germans arrived, local farmers had used it to keep their chickens. The chickens were gone, but the fleas were still there. Whenever the soldiers were not on guard duty they slept like sardines in the one coop still up. They put bricks on the fire. At each change of the watch, they took the hot bricks, wrapped rags around them and put them over the recoil of their machine-guns. It was the only way to keep the weapons from seizing up. Thirty men of the company were suffering from severe frostbite.

Those on guard had just come in from the cold and

[17] Halder, Tagebuch of 27 November 1941.

removed their hobnailed boots to warm their feet when the
Russians attacked across the field with a squadron of *T-34*s.
The German anti-tank shells bounced off their head plates
without making the slightest dent on the rapidly approaching
steel monsters. The huge tanks crashed through hedges and
fences and raced down the main street. Behind every ruin lay
a German, waiting for the Russian infantry, never far behind
the tanks. White figures came running through the snow. A
burst from three machine-guns dispatched the Russian foot
troops into eternity. But the tanks continued, unstoppable,
before coming to a halt at the main square. Like a deadly
porcupine, gun barrels stuck out in every direction. The
tank commander had probably realised that he had no
further infantry protection, and was thus vulnerable to
ground attacks. A group of *Landsers*, led by a sergeant,
trying to sneak up on the tanks, was caught in the open
by a turret-mounted machine-gun. Lieutenant Bossert, the
company commander, and a group of soldiers, dragging
heavy Russian anti-tank mines they had dug up only the
day before along the road, crawled up behind a couple of
tanks. They slid the mines under their cleats. Two tanks
moved, two fountains of fire followed and no survivors.
The tanks kept burning fiercely while the remainder of the
*T-34*s beat a hasty retreat. The attack had been stopped, but
the Germans had also suffered heavy casualties. Seventy of
them lay lined up on the ice-covered floor of a potato cellar.
A corpsman injected morphine, which he had to carry in
his pants pocket to prevent it from freezing. There were so
many serious casualties that he ran out of the painkilling
drug. The lieutenant decided to have the wounded loaded
on to two sleds and pulled back to the regimental field
hospital. He appointed twelve men for each sled, six to
pull and six to keep their eyes open for partisans. The dead
had to be left behind without burial. What happened was a
Napoleonic retreat. Not far from the huts, the leading sled

was ambushed by a band of partisans, and the twelve who manned the sled were shot and the throats of the wounded cut. The partisans were surprised by the second sled party which killed ten and captured the rest. The Germans wrapped field-telephone wires around their prisoners' necks and strung them up on the nearest tree. That too was the winter war in Russia.

Despite snow and ice, lack of fuel and food, the Germans stormed on. Colonel Rodt, commander of the *2nd Infantry Brigade*, took Pushki and advanced towards Katjushki. The colonel could see clouds of smoke rising from high-rises in the big city.

On 27 November, units of the *Third Panzer Army* under Colonel von Manteuffel took the bridge of Jachroma across the Moscow–Volga Canal, only 70 kilometres north-east of Moscow, and also took its main power station. The Germans had captured the light switch for the Kremlin.

The same day, Major Reichmann of the *2nd Battalion, 304th Infantry Regiment*, reached Gorki, 20 kilometres from Moscow.

On 30 November, parts of the *2nd Panzer Division* drove into Chimki, a mere 8 kilometres from Moscow's outer city limits. The news raced through the city: 'The Germans are at Chimki!'

And, finally, an armed patrol of the *38th Pioneer Battalion* got even closer. They took the bus station of the Moscow city line at Lobnija, 17 kilometres from the Kremlin. 'Let's take the bus and visit *Väterchen* Stalin . . .' they joked. They waited, but the bus didn't come. Something else did.

The afternoon a German unit was within 17 kilometres from the heart of Russia, the weather turned. An icy storm whipped snow across the land. All features disappeared, there were no more houses and no more trees, only snowdrifts. By next morning the fields were covered with small snow mounds. Underneath were the Germans, either frozen dead or unable to move a limb. The thermometer dropped to minus 48°C before it dipped further to an incredible minus 52°C. Exhalation froze the moment it left a soldier's mouth. Guards huddled together and puffed on their final cigarette. The next time they were attacked by Mongolian hordes, their machine-guns jammed.

The Germans gave it one last try. Aerial reconnaissance had shown that most of Tula town was intact and could be used as winter quarters. The deciding factor was to get hold of the huge coal and fuel deposits at the Tula Iron Works, massive enough to see the entire *Second Panzer Army* throughout the harsh winter months. Tula simply had to be taken!

The sacrifice of the *31st Infantry Division* to cut through the Tula salient from the north came too late. It changed nothing; it may have delayed the decision by a few days, but the final outcome could no longer be altered. The order, to throw unprotected infantry into a frontal assault, could have been written by General Haig in 1916; it didn't work then and it wouldn't work now. This futile order, given by the German High Command on 4 December, was based on a simplistic conclusion. 'Experience gathered during the "mud period" which has stopped any rapid advance by our motorised units, has shown that the only dependable force in the presence of an adverse weather front is foot-marched infantry.'[18]

In other words, 'Yes,' said the generals, 'our tanks are stuck, their engines have seized up, but infantry can march and fight in any temperature.' In a complete reversal of well-tried strategy – tanks spearheading infantry assaults – infantry was to be used to attack without supporting mobile

[18] General Halder's *Memoires*.

armour. Napoleon's technique of *attaque à l'outrance*. But this was 1941, not 1799.

The plan was set, the *31st Infantry Division* was to break through the defence perimeter of the Tula salient, link up with the *4th Panzer Division*, still immobilised by lack of fuel at Kostrowa, and so close the ring around Tula. Such was the plan. But the order came too late, two days too late. What might have been achieved across frozen earth could not be done after forty-eight hours of heavy snowfall. With four feet of soft snow, and drifts of up to fifteen feet, not even foot soldiers could move. But an order was an order and on they went, 'into the breach'. On 5 December, the *3rd Battalion, Infantry Regiment 82, 31st Infantry Division*, made their way through three kilometres of deep snow to reach their starting position. This march, and the bitter cold, sapped most of their strength. Their target was a small town, Novaja Shisnij. 'We attacked from the south. There was some heavy resistance and many of our rifles wouldn't fire, but we stormed the village, took some prisoners, some weapons, and five trucks loaded with heavy Russian winter gear. What a catch!' wrote a jubilant soldier in his diary. No wonder, it must have saved many a limb.

'Will it never end,' yelled the *Stabsarzt*, amputating another man's leg. Frostbite! Sentry duty in such temperatures was equal to a death sentence. Frostbite, followed by gangrene. It was the gangrene that killed, not the bullet. By candlelight, his staff of doctors worked overtime, cutting off fingers and toes, arms and legs. '*Unser ganzes Heer besteht nur mehr aus Krüpplen* – Our entire army is made up of cripples.' Cut, cut, and don't think. Outside the dressing station, medical helpers stacked gangrened limbs like firewood.

There is a description of the attack on Ketri, a small village held by a Russian battalion, which was launched for no other reason than to obtain shelter from the elements, and which tells us more than all the dry statistics from official battle reports. During the first wave assault, the divisional Catholic priest, Dr Scheidt, received a mortal wound. His place was taken by the Protestant pastor, *Pfarrer* Heinrich Link, who described what was perhaps the last frontal assault of the Moscow campaign, the attack by the *Infantry Regiment 17, 31st Infantry Division*:

'Just before nightfall of 4 December, I joined our forward units to provide them with spiritual support. I found the condition of our troops appalling. Having been under fire for a continuous twelve days, their faces were haggard and drawn, and they were exhausted beyond description; those on guard duty were sleeping with their eyes open. During two weeks of heavy fighting around Tula, the battalion had suffered severe casualties. Many of their comrades lay buried under the masses of snow which had fallen over the last two days; it lay so deep that even the shortest trip became a tiring effort. I spoke with them, tried to give them courage, but very few replied. One told me that they hadn't had a warm meal in over a month. Two days before, they had been given half a loaf of bread to be shared out between five, and each soldier had received one ounce of fat. When I gathered them for a field Mass, even those who'd never been to church gathered around me with their eyes closed, their hands folded, and prayed.

'Then it was night, a night as cold as none before. By around eleven o'clock, the temperature dropped to minus 35°C. Most of our men wore only the regulation issue overcoats, ear muffs made from burlap bags wrapped around their faces, with their steel helmets riding on top. They had layers of ice clinging to their beards. They were not protected like the enemy, waiting for us across the snowy moonscape in their heavily padded uniforms with fur gloves and sheepskin coats. Despite plenty of available wood, they couldn't light fires as it would bring Russian artillery down on us. I had a greatcoat, but still I froze so much that I thought I wouldn't survive the night. It soon became clear to me that, more than any fear of the forthcoming assault, it was the cold that sapped our men's strength; their movements had become slow, their gestures lethargic. Twenty minutes before the attack, everybody was ordered to move out into the open and check their weapons. The temperature had dropped another five degrees and stood at minus 40°C. The men stomped their feet and clamped their hands around their bodies.

'The attack was set for 01.00 hours that night, to take advantage of a full moon. When we moved ahead, I don't know how we did it, but everybody seemed happy to move his stiff limbs. Those poor souls were so frozen that they almost couldn't hold their rifles. When we reached a frozen riverbed, we couldn't lift ourselves over the top on the opposite side, our fingers were too stiff. Some made it over the bank, and stormed towards a tree-line. The enemy's machine-guns barked, and our first attack was thrown back with heavy casualties. Then a sergeant found a path leading up the riverbank. Since they couldn't work their rifle bolts, they planted their bayonets and stormed forward ... a great number slid around with their hobnailed jackboots on the ice before the bullets hit them ...

'Whether the battalion managed to take Ketri I cannot say with accuracy, as by that time my mind was concentrated on dispensing the last communion to the many I recalled having prayed with me only hours before. At regiment HQ at Iswolje, the ground outside the dressing station was covered with soldiers suffering from wounds and frostbite. It was impossible to help the great number of casualties, and most were left lying outside, exposed to the mercy of the elements, at temperatures well below minus 35°C.[19] To evacuate most of the wounded was out of the question; there were simply too many. The carthorses had died long ago, or had been slaughtered for food, and the engines of the trucks were frozen. Those who were operated on, amputated or patched up, and were lucky enough to be given a ride back, had to huddle on the back of open sleds or carts all the way to the rail head at Kaluga. Many died during the transportation. Others, even those not seriously wounded and who could have been saved, just closed their eyes and fell asleep, forever. The will to hang on had left them. I cannot tell how many were lying there, dead and frozen – too many to count. That day we lost more to the terrible cold than during all the fierce battles for Tula.'

That day the fighting spirit evaporated from the brave *31st Infantry Division*. As a military unit, with its spine shattered, it ceased to exist as a fighting force. But the Russians too no longer had the energy to continue. Bleary-eyed, they stared at small groups of German survivors stumbling past them, less than 100 metres from their own positions. They too no longer had the strength to counter their enemy's retreat.[20] Shortly before midnight, on 5 December, the *31st* divisional commander, Major-General Berthold, had to order *IR 17* and *IR 82* to withdraw with all haste to its outgoing position, or face being cut off by a large Russian counter-offensive which was building up along the Moscow front, and informed them that they could count neither on air support nor artillery. They would have to fight their way back. They did.

All their sacrifice had been for nothing. After the last unit had stumbled into a new defensive position, a head count was taken. What had been a division, twenty-four hours before, had shrunk to less than a battalion. In the *17th* and

[19] The coldest temperature ever recorded by the *Wehrmacht* was in Rzhev, west of Moscow, in January 1942: minus 52°C (–63°F).
[20] From a Soviet front-line report.

82nd Infantrie Regiments, the average fighting strength per company was 1 subaltern, 3 corporals and 14 men, without ammunition, without food, and still without winter clothing. The latter, somebody in Berlin had forgotten to provide for the fighting men of Germany. The survivors felt dejected and abandoned.[21]

At dawn the Russian divisions struck. On 6 December 1941, a million white-clad soldiers, riding on hundreds of white painted *T-34* tanks, smashed through the German lines. Stalin was alone when his personal secretary, Poskrebichev, rushed in, waving a telegram. News had just come in that the German lines had been broken.

Stalin leaned back in his chair and closed his eyes.

The reports reaching *OKW* (German High Command) were alarming. It became clear that at a dozen points, the enemy was developing a high degree of field superiority against the exhausted German troops, and that he would press any advantage with the utmost vigour and complete disregard for casualties. A concentration of massed battle tanks and waves of Siberian infantry maintained this momentum. Counter-attacks were not possible, most units were reeling under massive ground and air attacks, while panzers were out of fuel and shells. Thereby, enemy penetration was inevitable, and entire armies faced the danger of getting cut off.

Hauptmann von Wagenburg, bearer of the *Ritterkreuz* for bravery, stood erect in the turret of his panzer, bundled up in his anorak. His tank was stuck. His whole unit was stuck. Their engines were frozen, dead, *kaput*. In helpless fury he banged his fist on the cold metal of his tank. 'The most glorious day of the *Deutsche Wehrmacht*,' he called out in irony, 'twenty kilometres from Moscow and out of *sprit* (fuel). And for what? For *Fuehrer und Vaterland*.'

Across the field came the sound of a shot. Snow puffed up

[21] One army alone, the 4th, suffered 14,236 casualties owing to frostbite.

by Wagenburg's side. He ignored it. The next bullet struck the tank. It gave off the sound of a bell, a funeral bell. He never heard the third shot. The *Hauptmann* slumped forward, struck in the chest.

The behest of Hitler to carry out his divine destiny became the tragic destiny of the German army.

The white fields before Moscow were criss-crossed by thousands of cleat-tracks, the snow blackened by the impact of shells. White-clad soldiers climbed from a *T-34* tank, agitated by their success and the nearness of death. The tank crew joined them, sweaty faces blackened by gunpowder. They filled their lungs with the cold air, happy to be out of the stink of gasoline fumes and burnt cordite. The sweat froze instantly on their faces, but they laughed and wiped it off. One of them reached into his pocket and took out a piece of fat sausage. He handed it around and everyone took a bite. Another produced a bottle. For a long time he looked at it. '*Karasho gospodin*,' he said to no one in particular, 'I've kept this for a special occasion.' The cold had made the vodka thick and oily, and it burned his throat. But it tasted great.

Victory always has a great taste.

A grey-clad soldier, his jaw slack and his eyes glassy, lay in a foxhole. Next to him, with the coat pulled over his head, was another figure. Both were dead. Not shot, but frozen. The tanker sergeant and his young driver would never drink schnapps in the Kremlin ballroom.

A *T-34* braked to a halt next to the carcass of a *Mark IV* panzer. The body of an officer hung frozen from its turret. A Russian tank commander slipped the *Knight's Cross* from the dead German's neck and put it in his pocket. From far off came the thunder of heavy cannons. The engine of the *T-34* roared into gear and was swallowed up by the dense snow cloud it whirled up on the road leading away from Moscow.

'The attack on Moscow has failed. We have suffered a severe setback,' dared to state General Guderian. On 25 December, Hitler relieved Germany's foremost tank general of his command. At the beginning of the war, when German generals were pursuing their own strategy, they won every battle. Once Hitler took command, German soldiers were sacrificed for no gains whatsoever. Hitler's armies lay scattered in graves all over Russia.

The battle for Moscow proved that Hitler was a ruthless charlatan, who, until then, had been lucky. To take on the colossus Russia, Hitler had not enough men, not enough arms, and not enough pre-planning. His failure during the disastrous winter of 1941 left him with but one choice: total power, or total defeat. Hitler decided to play Russian roulette and lead the world to the brink of destruction.

Five days in December 1941 have a better claim than any other moment to have become the turning point in the most monstrous of human conflicts, the *Second World War*.

On 6 December, the Red Army unleashed their offensive at the gates of Moscow to halt the German war machine.

On 7 December, Germany's ally, Japan, attacked the United States at Pearl Harbor.

Within three days, Hitler was not only faced with the horrors of a winter campaign in Russia, but also with a multi-front war with the world's two economic and military giants, the Soviet Union and the United States of America.

Fall Barbarossa was based on two assumptions. That the Russian army would make its stand along their border, and that the Soviet party system was a giant with clay feet that would allow Germany to conquer Russia before the arrival of the October mud season. Hitler was wrong on both accounts. He certainly never counted on having to fight a winter war, and his postponement of a single, concerted push on Moscow in early August was a strategic blunder. The moment he overruled his military advisers and placed political goals ahead of strategic military objectives, he was inevitably headed for disaster. But his fundamental error was political. He underestimated the staying power of Stalin, and he disregarded the resolve of the Russian nation. They called it the *Great Patriotic War.*

Space, time, and the elements drained the strength and vitality of the aggressor. By invading Russia, Germany invaded a different climate, and its armies had to cope with sudden and violent seasonal changes. The German *Blitzkrieg* strategy was ill adjusted to sustain a continued operation, and the hardships of the winter of 1941 surprised the prophet of the *New Order.* When winter came, with its killing frost, more German soldiers died from bitter cold than from Russian bullets and bayonets. Yet it would be wrong to assume that Hitler's checkmate, far exceeding the losses of Napoleon's retreat from Moscow, was due only to a change in the weather. Russian sacrifices, Russian men and Russian bullets achieved that. It does not alter the conclusion that six weeks of clement weather could have made a difference in the greatest assault of all times. That, the eternal ally of Holy Mother Russia, *General Winter*, had not granted.

They say it can never happen again. That modern fighting man is insulated from the environment by modern technology. Yet nature strikes when least expected, technology tends to break down, and modern war turns into a struggle for primitive survival. Then, only the lessons of the past can serve as guidelines for future survival.

The lesson of 1941 is as valid today as it was then.

Unexpected new developments

6 June 1944

Les sanglots longs, des violons, de l'automne . . .
Paul Verlaine (1844–96), and BBC radio message (5 June 1944)

It rained. It had been raining for days. A young soldier looked up at the barrage of anti-aircraft balloons. 'Why don't they cut the cables and let the bloody island sink!'

At precisely 9.30 pm, 4 June, Lieutenant-Colonel James N. Stagg, chief meteorologist, Royal Air Force, entered the room. He saluted the generals assembled in front of a large wall map of Europe.

'Proceed, Colonel,' said the man in a tight-fitting dark-green battle jacket.

'Yessir.' The colonel opened a folder marked TOP SECRET. 'Gentlemen,' he began, 'there are *unexpected new developments* . . .'

The meteorological office had detected a weather front, rapidly moving towards the Channel, within the next few hours. It promised a temporary clearance over the region of the planned invasion. This improvement over the present weather conditions was predicted to last throughout the early morning of 6 June. After that, the weather was once more expected to deteriorate. During this 'window' of good weather, a drop in wind and clear skies was forecast.

'Thank you, Colonel.' The officer saluted and left the room.

'Gentlemen, your opinion?' he asked the six men around the baize table.[1]

The officer in a turtleneck sweater spoke out. 'I say let's go!'

The air force chief had reservations. 'To provide adequate air support, we need an absolute assurance of clear skies.'

The supreme commander was on his own. His decision would decide the fate of nations. He stared at the rain-streaked windowpanes. He had already postponed it once, he couldn't do it again.

'I am convinced that we have to give the order for attack. I don't like it, but we have no other choice.'

Based on a forecast that promised an improvement in atmospheric conditions, General of the Army Dwight David Eisenhower launched three million men on the biggest and most ambitious military invasion in the history of mankind: *Operation Overlord*, the assault on Fortress Europe.

The weather was the determining factor.

---

[1] Lieutenant-General Walter Bedell Smith, Air Marshall Sir Arthur Tedder, Admiral Sir Bertram Ramsay, Air Marshal Sir Trafford Leigh-Mallory, Field Marshal Sir Bernard Montgomery, General Omar Bradley.

For those in peril on the sea

18 December 1944

Eternal Father, strong to save,
Whose arm doth bind the restless wave,
Who bid'st the mighty ocean deep,
Its own appointed limits keep.
Oh hear us when we cry to Thee.
For those in peril on the sea.
                    Traditional mariners hymn.

They were in enemy waters. The sun was high, there was no breeze, and the heat was intense. Below deck the situation was hardly better. For the off-duty crews, those who had been on deck for a great part of the night, sleep was impossible. The interior of the ship was lifeless and without air. Stifling hot, where breathing became torture and sweat soaked the sheets. The only noise was the constant hum and vibration of the big engines pushing the ship along.

Captain Raymond Calhoun, US Navy, commander of the USS *Dewey*, a *Farragut*-class destroyer of 2,255 tons, had to report home to his wife about the first serious casualty on board, a hole in his toilet bowl, after a plumber had inadvertently dropped his heavy wrench; but 'other than that

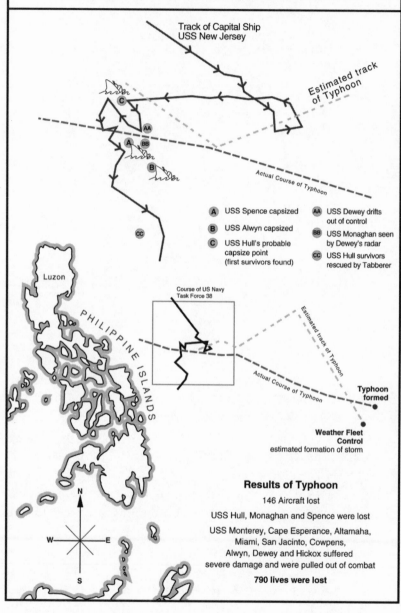

US Navy task force 38, December 1944
Chronological summery of events from 00.00hrs 17 Dec to 24.00hrs 18 Dec 1944

Track of Capital Ship
USS New Jersey

Estimated track
of Typhoon

Actual Course of Typhoon

Luzon

PHILIPPINE ISLANDS

Ⓐ USS Spence capsized

Ⓑ USS Alwyn capsized

Ⓒ USS Hull's probable
capsize point
(first survivors found)

ⒶⒶ USS Dewey drifts
out of control

ⒷⒷ USS Monaghan seen
by Dewey's radar

ⒸⒸ USS Hull survivors
rescued by Tabberer

Course of US Navy
Task Force 38

Estimated track of Typhoon

Actual Course of Typhoon

Typhoon
formed

Weather Fleet
Control
estimated formation of storm

N
W—E
S

Results of Typhoon

146 Aircraft lost

USS Hull, Monaghan and Spence were lost

USS Monterey, Cape Esperance, Altamaha,
Miami, San Jacinto, Cowpens,
Alwyn, Dewey and Hickox suffered
severe damage and were pulled out of combat

790 lives were lost

things are quiet'. So much for assurance. He was nursing a cup of navy coffee on the bridge, a man beset by worries; his vessel had been made top-heavy by the recently installed array of antennae and radar masts and might prove sluggish in heavy weather. Neither he nor his fellow officers had much experience of what to do in case of a real storm. As a matter of fact, very few American skippers had any idea what a typhoon was, other than reading up on it in Knight's *Modern Seamanship*.

However, if there was the danger of a big storm, Calhoun would apply 'Singer's Law', as he had called it following his conversation, two years back, with another naval officer, Watson Singer, who had lived through a Pacific storm and had put it in so many words: 'When the barometer drops .10 of an inch or more over the next three hours, you're in the path of a typhoon, and you'd better haul ass.'

'You bet your sweet patootee,' mused Calhoun, who, on this sunny day in mid-December 1944 was staring straight ahead at the oily sea; 'that's precisely what I will do.' Haul ass and get the hell outta there. That was, of course, if he was operating on his own. He was convinced that bad weather conditions would hardly concern his ship if he was on operation in conjunction with the fleet. In the lee of the big battle-wagons he would be well protected from the 'blow'. Like so many others, he had no clue about the destructiveness of a typhoon.

The *Dewey*, and another destroyer, the USS *Spence*, steamed alongside each other to join up with US Navy Task Force 38 (TF 38) of Admiral 'Bull' Halsey. They had left Pearl Harbor on 25 October and had made a brief refuelling stop at Eniwetok Atoll. While near Ulithi, a deepwater port in the Carolines, they had received a storm warning, Typhoon Condition II, but this turned out to be a false alarm.

US Task Force 38, a huge armada in support of General Douglas MacArthur's landings on the main Philippine island of Luzon, was made up of four separate task groups, each with a number of big attack carriers and battleships. Altogether, some ninety capital ships, surrounded by a defensive screen of destroyers. By early morning of 17 December, the barometer began to fall and fleet command decided to begin refuelling operations immediately for its escorts, so that these could ride out a period of foul weather safely. The USS *Spence*, lowest on fuel, was called alongside the massive battleship USS *New Jersey*, flagship of Admiral 'Bull' Halsey.

Typhoons feed on hot and humid air and tropical ocean waters. Evaporated seawater converts thermal energy into storm power on a truly awesome scale. From a few wispy clouds typhoons can grow into howling giants, some as wide as five hundred kilometres across. They bring with them destruction unmatched by military technology. Anything, from pleasure cruiser to huge battleship, is vulnerable and lucky are those who live to tell about it. Heavy rains obscure visibility between ships. Perhaps capital ships can survive the forceful gusts, but ships have to reckon on the storm surges, giant waves battering their sides and crumpling steel plating like aluminium foil.

In the middle of December 1944, between Ulithi and Guam, a storm was born in the waters that bred many of the tropical disturbances. The clouds' rotating motion accelerated and sent a dense mass on its unstoppable path of destruction. The monster of nature was alive. A *kamikaze*, 'the divine wind', was on its way, like the one that had protected the sacrosanct islands of Japan and sunk the armada of the Great Mongol Khan in 1281.

132 vessels of the *US Third Fleet*, presently at 14° 59′ N, 130° 08′ E, or some three hundred miles to the east of Luzon in the Philippines, were headed on a collision course with one of the worst typhoons in recorded history.

Commander George F. Kosco in the meteorological centre aboard the battleship USS *New Jersey* had received reports from the Admiralty Islands and Leyte, as well as being kept informed by weather planes out of Guam, Saipan or Peleliu, and other recently conquered Pacific atolls. Fleet Weather Central in Pearl Harbor added its own estimates four times daily. From the *New Jersey*, the weather forecast was relayed to the smaller fleet units whose only means to predict disturbances was by intuition and common sense, aided by such simple means as barometer and thermometer.

'This message has just come in, sir.' An old sailor, who had travelled on tramps in the China Sea before the war, thrust a sheet from a teletype at the met officer who handed it over to the admiral for study: DEPRESSION OF 998 MILLIBARS DEEPENING AND STORM OR VIOLENT STORM CONDITIONS TO BE EXPECTED.

Even if they could get a break, avoid the worst, there'd still be a hell of a sea running. The admiral shook his head and looked enquiringly at his met officer.

'What do you make of it?'

'Well, Admiral,' he said, in his cool voice, 'if this depression gets as bad as they say it'll get, and we get hit, then everythin' goes, 'n the decks'll be swept clean.'

The weather report was as black as the sky. Heavy weather was building up. The ether waves were alive with crackling static and panicky babble. Some were quite clear, others only a distant noise. But one thing was clear, from Hawaii to Hong Kong: anyone who could was running for shelter. A depression was moving in, and moving fast, heading straight for the present location of the entire fleet. If the depression didn't change course, God only knew what could happen . . .

The admiral was beset by a dilemma. Should he divert an entire invasion and support fleet, a hundred ships and thousands of men, and upset the intricately worked out and precisely timed operational schedule? The boys on land depended on the support from bombing runs by his air fleets. The landing options were interlinked with tide charts. Call it off? All because of one radio signal of a storm warning? Or ride out a strong gale, because that was all the weather forecast promised? Granted, a lot of the crew and soldiers would be violently seasick, but such was life at sea. No, Admiral Halsey decided not to divert.

'. . . DEEP DEPRESSION OF 956 MILLIBARS MOVING IN FROM PACIFIC RIDGE. THIS DEPRESSION STILL DEEPENING AND VIO-LENT STORM CONDITIONS CAN BE EXPECTED . . .' came the follow-up advisory over the meteorological teletype.

Then, for the next hours, the depression didn't shift. It just hung there, threatening, but stationary. In front of the command bridge, the sea was choppy, streaks of foam streaming out along the direction of the breeze. But certainly nothing to worry about. (Of course, a battleship provided a much steadier platform than those small destroyers, bobbing around on the swells.) At present convoy speed, the aircraft carriers, supply ships, troop transporters and their numerous watchdogs, those lethal destroyers and anti-submarine frig-ates, would have enough time to get past the danger zone.

Early on 17 December, the barometer reading on the *Dewey* read 29.70, with winds up to 20 knots, while some 30 miles to the north, aboard the *New Jersey*, they still read 29.85 with winds at 25 knots. Twenty-five knots was nothing special in the open Pacific. On some of the destroyers, a critical fuel situation had developed. Depleted tanks added considerably to the instability of the vessels, since it made them ride high on the water. To overcome this handicap, skippers topped up their empty fuel tanks with seawater, a most unpopular measure with the engineers as there was always the danger of contamination of the remaining fuel stocks.

By 11.07 am, the destroyer USS *Spence*, down to a mere 15 per cent of its fuel capacity, was the first to berth alongside the *New Jersey* to tank. Hoses were strung across and the refuelling began. In the meantime, the wind was freshening up to 45 knots and the operation became outright hazardous. Owing to a constant roll by the smaller destroyer, there was the acute danger of collision. Refuelling on other destroyers and escort vessels fared no better and was suspended.

By 14.00 pm, as the barometer dipped to 29.58, the outer destroyer screen advised TF 38 command that they believed they had entered the outer fringe of a tropical cyclone. Taking the only available tables at the time, it was calculated that the storm centre was some 250 miles to the south-west. That calculation was badly amiss, because the eye of the typhoon was only 120 miles distant.

'What's the latest forecast?' asked the admiral.

'It's movin' in faster than expected, Admiral. 1,006 milibars, 'n dropping like a stone, sir.'

'Direction?'

'Roughly parallel to the task force, sir.'

'What is your suggestion?'

'A south-westerly course, sir.'

'All right.' He turned to his communication officer. 'Send out a signal to batten down all hatches and secure everything above decks.'

Deck crews were ordered to secure lifelines, remove any loose gear, and stash ready ammunition, with special attention to the racks of the lethal depth-charges.

By late afternoon of 17 December, the storm suddenly veered west. If it continued in this general direction, it would cut across the path of the armada. But cyclones can be erratic, they change their path continuously. Soon the 'blow' was building up to a regular gale. The meteorological staff aboard the battleship USS *New Jersey* worked on charts and timetables. The latest news from the central met office was not encouraging: 940 millibars, and dropping.

The sky had turned into a black of swirling clouds, torn asunder by violet and orange flashes like a distant fire in the heavens. The sea had melted into the blackness. Suddenly, from out of this blackness, a thin white line bore at the outer destroyer screen, stretching as far as the eye could see, with the sea behind it a cauldron of boiling water. To the sailors on deck duty, with their eyes half shut against wind and driven spray, it was as beautiful as it was frightening. From the bowels of the ship came the first strange noises as the hull plates worked under the pressure of the seas.

The possibility of riding into a full-blown gale at first became apparent to those aboard the smaller vessels on screen duty, buffeted by high winds. The barometer had dropped a worrisome .07 of an inch in ten minutes. Within the hour it had gone from 1,006 mb to lower than 900 mb! A hell of a lot more than 'Singer's Law' to haul ass. The tannoy bells shrilled, off-duty sailors stumbled from their hammocks, grabbed for their lifesavers, and hauled themselves up the ladders.

The sea was a series of shaggy combers, some twenty feet in height. Hardly noticeable on the big ships, considering their size, those huge flat-tops and battle wagons of the US Pacific battle fleet. To be on the safe side. Admiral Halsey ordered refuelling activity stopped and established a new rendezvous some 160 miles to the north for the coming morning. Lacking fuel, the destroyers *Spence*, *Hickox*, and *Maddox* were in a precarious ballast situation, and left the outer screen to remain in the lee of the big ships. The *Spence*, especially, was riding high on the water; its skipper, Lieutenant-Commander Jimmy Andrea, was ordered to counterballast his fuel tanks with water to make his ship more seaworthy. Regardless of the high risk of contamination of fuel supplies, the *Hickox* and *Maddox* complied immediately and flooded their empty tanks. Meanwhile, the weather was getting worse by the hour as destroyer captains nervously studied their barometers. A change in course was ordered to get the task force out of the path of what had now been recognised as a major tropical storm.

Commander Kosco, the meteorological officer on the *New Jersey*, revised his estimate of the storm centre to much closer than previously thought. Within the hour, this was confirmed by a weather plane from the seaplane tender *Chandeleur*, who had discovered the storm centre at 13° N, 132° E, with winds up to 60 knots. For unexplained reasons, this new correction was never dispatched from the *New Jersey* to the destroyer screen. For safety's sake Kosco did contact two outlying task groups, those of Admirals McBain and Bogan, who reported that a depression was moving north at 12 knots. Kosco relayed this information to his superior, Admiral Halsey, but it is obvious today that Halsey never did realise the real extent of the approaching danger. Thus, unaware of the rapidly shifting weather, thirteen destroyers[1] called in that they were running dangerously out of fuel, and at 05.00 am, on 18 December, Admiral Halsey once more ordered the convoy to reduce speed and to commence refuelling operations. For this it was already too late, and that delay was to prove costly.

At 06.16 am, a thirty-degree change of course was ordered, which brought the entire convoy right across the path of the cyclone! It wasn't long before lighter escort carriers, the *Nehenta Bay*, *Cape Esperance*, and *Rudyerd Bay*, reported that they were being pounded by high waves. Halsey instructed them to pick a course of their own choice.

At 08.18 am, Halsey dispatched a message to General Douglas MacArthur that he would not be able to strike land targets on Luzon for the next twenty-four hours. Actually, it would be much longer than that . . . The sea was taking on a wild look: ragged breakers stretching to the horizon, the sky a leaden mass with slashes of orange. The first rain squalls dashed against the windows of the bridge. The wind moaned through the wire rigging. The pounding of the waves against

---

[1] *Yarnall, Wedderburn, Stockham, Welles, Moore, Taussig, Colahan, Bush, Franks, Cushing, Maddox, Spence, Hickox.*

the hull increased by the second, the noise of the gale changed into a demoniacal howl.

The horizon was now a writhing black mass that enveloped heaven and sea. A wash of foam raced towards the destroyers. The line-squall hit and the ships heeled. On-duty sailors, working at their assigned chores on deck, and who moments before had been held in the grip of the fantastic spectacle, now bolted for hatch doors like a bunch of frightened rabbits. Several slithered across the sloping deck and only those remained on deck who managed to hang on to something, the rest disappeared in the dark waters. Those who made it to the hatches lurched inside, followed by a tremendous gust of wind and spray from a wave colliding with the ship's sides. The lightning, which flickered constantly, illuminated an extraordinary scene — a huge armada riding into the fury of a typhoon. The roar increased. Those on deck were shocked into stillness, clinging to whatever stanchion or ladder was close to them. And suddenly the first of the monster waves loomed out of the maelstrom of rain and spray.

The bridge floor heaved and the captain staggered like a drunkard for his elevated swivel chair. All around, the sea boiled in white foam, the glass of the bridge window obscured by sheets of water. The ship lifted and rose high on a wave, then fell forward, biting deep with her prow.

The admiral's face was tense and strained. He knew he was carrying a heavy load of responsibility.

'What do we read?'

'958 millibars and dropping like lead. Anemometer shows windforce between 50 and 60, and lots more behind it.'

'Secure all the hatches, shore up everything that is loose,' ordered the captain of the *Monterey*, reacting to a signal that had been passed from the flagship. 'Let's see if we can ride it out.' The silence below decks was shattered by three blasts from the tannoy and men tumbled from their bunks.

Early on 18 December, Admiral Halsey had to report to Pearl Harbor that his task force was entering a typhoon, its centre now clearly visible on radar a mere thirty-five miles off. Minutes later, it struck! Wave after consecutive wave washed over the armada. The depression was now down to a shattering 938 millibars. The storm roared across the decks, howling around the locked hatches, slamming into metal, tearing at gun mounts. To the men on the bridge, most of whom had lived with the sea long enough to understand its power, it was beyond anything they had ever experienced.

Worst off were the destroyers, their bridge windows smashed, the doors ripped from their hinges. To hold the wheel took two husky seamen. Suddenly another ship was right across the path of the *Hull*. 'Bring her around! yelled the captain over the crash of the waves. They turned the wheel frantically. Too late. With the sound of tearing metal the bow of the destroyer smashed into the quarterdeck section of a sister ship. Both destroyers were wounded but neither fatally. The *Hull*'s forecastle was a tangle of rigging and twisted metal, with the sea breaking over her. The ships wallowed drunkenly in the seas, climbing to the crest of giant waves only to drop down on the other slope. Water was rising inside the ships and the electric pumps were soon fighting a losing battle. The destroyer lurched under the onslaught of another gigantic wave. A heavy thud of propellers echoed up the tunnel of the propeller shaft. The propellers were running wild, thrashing air above the wave top! With a bone-jarring jolt she fell back into water. There was a screech and a sound like someone's insides being ripped out.

'Damage control, report to bridge.'

She was down by the bows and water rushed in through a tear in the plates. Water was rising with alarming speed in the forward hold.

'Will she float with that much water?'

'Probably – until one of the bulkheads goes.'

'And then?'
'Then she's gonna come apart at the seams.'

To those up on the bridge of the *Monaghan*, the weather was now so vicious and the view so impenetrable that they caught not the slightest glimpse of the rest of the huge armada. They lurched to the top of an enormous wave and suddenly saw, a mere 100 yards away, the grey prow of a warship headed straight for them.

'Rudder hard starboard,' yelled the bridge officer. Caught beamside in the waves, the ship swung around, much too slowly for those who watched it happen. 'Bring her around, for God's sake, bring her around . . .' Then followed a tremendous crash, followed by a tearing sound as steel struck steel. All throughout the ship seamen were thrown to the ground.

'Damage report,' yelled the captain, scrambling back to his feet.

A long silence followed, until a voice came over the intercom: 'Bow sheared off, but the bulkheads are holding.' Everyone gave a sigh of relief. Thank God for good old American workmanship!

The men inside the ship had no idea of the real windforce, they weren't seamen but carpenters and accountants, taxi drivers and farmers, called to arms in the defence of their country. They had never lived through an ocean gale gusting 130 knots and more, so they didn't knows what was going on outside. That was the most terrible thing, hearing but not seeing, being prisoners inside a steel coffin, unable to judge what was going on outside. The movement was sickening and whatever they clutched for support, they could feel the ship's tremor through their bodies. The howl overlaid any other sounds, as did the crash of water pounding the steel plates. The mess hall stank of vomit and fear.

From the big ships in the convoy came reports of their problems. First was the tug *Jicarilla* with engine trouble. The carrier *Independence* had a man overboard, and the carrier *Monterey* a fire in the hangar deck where an aircraft had broken loose. Still, in a message sent to Pacific Fleet HQ, Halsey did not classify it as anything more than a 'tropical disturbance'. While the *Monterey* was losing speed fighting her fire. Halsey finally realised that he was hit by a regular cyclone and directed a new change of course. By now the visibility was almost down to zero, with the huge bulk of the *Monterey* lying dead in the water, a menace to every other ship. At 10.02 am, the *New Jersey* executed a violent manoeuvre to avoid a collision with an unidentified carrier. At 10.10 am, the destroyer *Dewey* almost rammed another destroyer. Two minutes later, the *Wisconsin*, *Miami* and *Boston* lost their scout planes and fire broke out below deck on the carrier USS *Cowpens*.

Shortly before noon, Halsey ordered a new change of course, and the carrier *Cape Esperance* reported a fire on its flight deck. Further bad news came from the carrier *San Jacinto* with four fully fuelled-up planes sliding around on her hangar deck, ready to explode any moment.

Contact between the flagship and the various units, as well as from ship-to-ship, broke down. The entire armada struggled to regain station as best as they could and remain on a uniform course, but this was impossible. The *Dewey* lost steering control and, for an hour, the ship was being steered by several seamen below deck, who received their signal from the bridge over a voice-pipe and then had to position the heavy rudder by hand-cranking! The most modern battle fleet the world had ever witnessed was back to the era of the sailing ship. With all watertight doors buttoned up, this would prevent any rapid escape for the men below deck. Eventually the mechanics managed to repair the *Dewey*'s rudder control, but then the ship's radar packed up. With visibility less than 300 yards, the captain was running his ship blind in the hope that nothing lay in front of him.

That's when he saw a monster right across his path, the *Monterey!*

'Hard left rudder!' he yelled. The destroyer leaned over, and anything that wasn't screwed to the floor was smashed. She just managed to pass beneath the carrier's flight deck looming high above before she slid into a pall of black smoke from the fire on the *Monterey.* That violent manoeuvre must have broken a spar in the *Dewey*'s steering mechanism, because the destroyer was no longer responding to its rudder.

'This is *Achilles.* I'm out of control, crossing through the formation from starboard to port. Keep clear!' Captain Calhoun had to advise the convoy. The next minutes turned into a nightmare ride while the *Dewey* staggered across the path of a dozen ships.

'Suddenly a black hull loomed up in front of us. As we were lifted high on the cross swell, it seemed to me that we were going to coast right down on top of her, but as we descended into the trough, the oiler was picked up by the next crest. Towering above us now, her own momentum, plus the force of the wind and sea coming from behind her, were overpowering . . . it didn't seem possible that we could miss, or worse, being hit by one of those huge ships.'[2]

The barometer was at 28.84 and falling like a rock! At 12 noon it stood at 28.10 and the wind velocity had reached over 125 knots. The *Dewey* had taken the precaution of filling its depleted fuel tanks with sea water so that the ship would ride low in the water, and still her roll registered beyond the 60 degree danger-mark. Captain Calhoun knew that 70 degrees was the absolute maximum before she'd go down. At the worst possible moment, all bridge controls ceased to function. Just before he lost his radar, he had noticed a blip some 5,000 yards off. The operator of the *Dewey* thought this to be the destroyer *Monaghan,* since its captain, Bruce

2 Account by Captain C. R. Calhoun in *Typhoon: The Other Enemy.*

Garrett, only minutes before had reported to be drifting out of control, caught by the swell.

The pounding got worse. Soon the *Dewey* rolled at 70 degrees! Then she lurched to 75 degrees!! And everyone, from the captain down, prayed: 'Please make her come back!' She did, after part of the superstructure gave way. Everyone was convinced they were going down, and Boatswain Miller asked Calhoun: 'Captain, are we going to abandon ship?' To which Calhoun replied: 'Not if I can help it. As long as the *Dewey* doesn't abandon us, we're not going to abandon her.' As he said it, a wave tilted the ship, the depth charges broke loose and rolled overboard, luckily without striking an object to set them off. Their ordeal continued: a guide wire snapped, whipped across the deck, and the forward smokestack came crashing down, smashing the lifeboats and rupturing the steam line to the fireroom. Scalding steam escaped with a high pitched scream. Perhaps it was the collapsed smokestack that saved the *Dewey*, because immediately afterwards the vessel's roll lessened. Still they were wallowing in the mad ocean like some giant's plaything. The thudding force of gusts struck at irregular intervals. The bulkheads creaked dangerously, but held. Gone were aerials and antennae, air ducts, and smoke stacks. And yet, despite all that destruction, a spirit of 'we shall overcome' prevailed throughout the chaos.

The situation aboard the other destroyers was even worse, every monster wave tilted the ships beyond the danger mark. Bill Rogers and his men on the *Alwyn* hung on to the end, and lived through it, although the mast snapped and smashed a gaping hole in the vessel.

The *Hickox* lost all its power at 10.30 am, following a sudden manoeuvre to avoid collision with another vessel, and was wallowing in a deep trough. After struggling for hours, the *Hickox* finally managed to come through.

Not so the *Hull*. At 10.30 am she was hit by gusts of almost 200 knots; the roar of the storm drowned out any other sound, and seawater flooded the fireroom through the air intakes. In the engine room, they had heard a violent report like an explosion, when suddenly the grating beneath their feet gave a lurch, with the sound of rushing water filling the compartment. Mechanics lay sprawled on metal gratings, their senses numbed by the pounding, a dull boom that tore through the vessel. They felt the ship beginning to slide beneath them. Lights flickered, then died. Someone yelled: 'Emergency lights.' A stoker had a serious cut across his head, blood dripped onto the metal plates. He crawled on his knees to reach a vertical metal ladder. He began climbing in frenzy, followed by all those who could still move. They were oblivious to anything but escape. A solid column of water hit some and swept them from the ladder. Then the emergency lights came on. Behind them, a bulkhead creaked. A sailor knocked off the last hatchway catch and the door sprung open. Everybody rushed through the narrow, dark passage, banging into shelves and pipes.

Up in the living quarters it was not much different. Groans, screams, and the crash of equipment breaking loose and smashing into walls. A telephone was dangling from its cord. Heavy pumps crashed through sleeping quarters, catching sailors, crushing and maiming them on their journey across the width of the vessel. Men lost their footing and crawled forward on hands and knees. Another wave bounced them back, they grabbed each other by legs and belts until they reached the ladders to scramble up. They reached the mess room and found it knee-deep in water, and depending which way the ship lurched, the water sloshed over the tables. There was no way through the mess hall, its hatch was jammed by a jumble of torn-off furniture and soggy bags of flour.

Some made it on to the deck. Then the drama took place, the destroyer heeled over and stayed that way. The ship's emergency evacuation equipment had been smashed by falling debris. There was no question of taking to the boats, for that would amount to suicide. While still dangling from the davits the boats would be smashed against the steel sides. Captain Jim Marks remained on the wing of the bridge, which stood up like a tombstone, and watched his crew, making sure that everyone wore a lifejacket. A wave thundered across and anyone on deck without a lifeline was swept off. A second before the ship capsized, Jim Marks jumped into the sea. Those who managed to escape clung to any piece of flotsam they could find. But most were trapped below deck and never made it. From 263 officers and men of the *Hull*, out of those who endured another night of horror on floats in the open sea, 41 were rescued.

Bruce Garrett, skipper of the *Monaghan*, must have experienced a similar fate. Her steering motors failed and she began to pitch violently, left to the mercy of the sea. The ship lurched and groaned. Her stern jutted high into the air. Emergency crews, tethered by safety ropes to ladders so that they wouldn't be washed overboard, rigged ropes at hip-level between stanchions and hatches to be used as lifelines. All around them the superstructure was buckled and twisted, the companionways blocked by wreckage. There was another tearing sound as one of the bulkheads gave way.

A cluster of men in orange lifejackets huddled behind the wheelhouse in deceptive security, every one in silent prayer: 'Oh Lord, send thy word of command to stop the roaring sea . . .' Great sheets of dark green washed over her from stem to stern, exploding against the bridge structure with devastating force. The ship climbed up one side of a wave to swoop down into the trough with the wild, unchecked pounding of its screws as they thrashed clear of the water. The ship gave another sickening lurch and it seemed a miracle that every time she came up again.

Down in the engine room, the chief mechanic refused to panic. He turned off the wild-running turbine when he was hit by a torrent of water and pressed against the ship's side. He died alone.

There were no further reports, no calls for help, and no officer survived the loss of the *Monaghan*. According to one of only six survivors, McCrane, 'the next thing we knew we were on our side, we scrambled out and those who jumped into the sea were pounded to a pulp against the side of the ship – then I flew through the air. "Hey, Joe, grab that raft," I heard Guio[3] call out. Then the raft turned around and we had to fish everyone out. Gulo later died on that raft and we buried him at sea.'

The *Spence* capsized at around 11.00 am. A mountainous wave had curled in, and washed over the ship. When the wave was gone, so was the ship. It happened so suddenly that only twenty-four survived.

At midday on 19 December, for those battered and sick inside the ship's bellies, the thing which filtered into the recess of their minds was the sense of silence. The noise had rolled back until it was lost as a distant murmur. What had been a roaring nightmare was now still and quiet. The only thought that kept them going was of dry clothes and hot soup. With a sense of disbelief and remoteness, the survivors stumbled on deck. Bright sunlight stabbed their eyeballs. Shocked, they stared at a nightmare, and saw only what was directly in front of their feet, a scene from a battlefield. A big hole in the deck where the forward gun had been, a crane forced off its mounting, its jib sagging at a drunken angle. Dented pieces of superstructure, staved-in sides of ammunition lockers. Crates, bales, and orange life-jackets bobbed about on the water. Then they took in the rest. More sea and more damaged ships. An ocean strewn with a badly mauled invasion armada.

What the Japanese called *Kamikaze* – the divine wind – had struck, more furious and more devastating than anything

[3] Gunnen's-mate Joseph Guio, Jr.

man could think of. And they had lived through it to tell their children and loved ones about their day of terror.

On 19 December 1944, at 09.22 am, the Commander Third Fleet, Admiral Halsey, sent a top secret dispatch to Pacific Fleet Command at Pearl Harbor:

TYPHOON CENTER PASSED THIRTY MILES NORTH OF FLEET GUIDE MIDDAY 18TH. FLEET TOOK BEATING. *TABBERER* REPORTS *HULL* CAPSIZED WITH LITTLE WARNING AT 1030. ONLY TEN ENLISTED SURVIVORS. SEVERAL OTHER STRAGGLERS STILL UNREPORTED. *MATACO* TOWING DISABLED *JICARILLA* TO ULITHI. *MONTEREY, COWPENS, SAN JACINTO* BEING SENT TO ULITHI FOR REPAIRS. *DYSON, LAWS, BENHAM, HICKOX, ALWYN, DEWEY, TABBERER* WITH ASSORTED DERANGEMENTS WILL ESCORT CRIPPLES . . .

He didn't yet know about the loss of the *Monaghan* and *Spence*. Some of the major units which required emergency repairs were the carriers *Cowpen, Cabot, Lexington, Ticonderoga, Essex*, and *Langley*, and the battleship *Iowa*. These main units were lost for the forthcoming battle of the Philippines.

What the squadrons of *Kamikaze* suicide planes had failed to achieve, a divine wind had accomplished. This fact gave an enormous boost to Japanese morale; they believed that, once again like seven centuries before, a *Divine Wind* had saved their country from an invasion.

Following an investigation by a US naval board into the tragedy of the Philippine Sea, Admiral 'Bull' Halsey signed a statement,[4] which concluded:

I have no wish to avoid my proper responsibility in these

[4] Navy Endorsement No. 12 of 29 September, 1945.

circumstances; however, I also wish to state unequivocably that in both the December 1944, and June 1945, typhoons the weather warning service did not provide accurate and timely information necessary to enable me to take timely evasive action. For that inadequacy I can not accept responsibility.

W. F. Halsey

There was an amendment by the Chief of the US Navy, Admiral King, stamped and approved by the Secretary of the Navy, Forrestal.[5]

I am of the opinion that the proceedings, findings and recommendations of the courts of inquiry and of the convening authority ... are in no way altered and that primary responsibility for the storm damage and losses ... attaches to Commander Third Fleet, Admiral William F. Halsey, US Navy.

E. J. King

790 American seamen lost their lives.

Those who survived the typhoon thought of it as nothing short of a miracle.

[5] Navy Endorsement No. 14 of 23 November, 1945.

A deluge of fire

24 December 1944

'*Almighty and most merciful father, we humbly beseech
Thee, of Thy great goodness, to restrain these immoderate
rains with which we have to contend. Grant us fair weather
for Battle.*'

Army Chaplain James O'Neill, 'Patton's Prayer',
22 December 1944.

'Only nine more days to Christmas, and counting,' cheers
Davis I. James, serial number EM 37554T43-44, a young
American paratrooper from the Bronx.

'By Christmas, we'll be home,' chimes in his buddy, John
D. Ford, 016332T43-44, a private in the *101st US Airborne*,
minutes before they climb onto a truck on this 16 December 1944.

'I betcha they'll make us jump on Berlin.'

They are not headed for Berlin, but a place in a snowy
landscape they have never heard of, a small town in the
Ardennes Mountains: Bastogne.

Private D. James is killed on 20 December, and his friend
Johnny on the 21st.

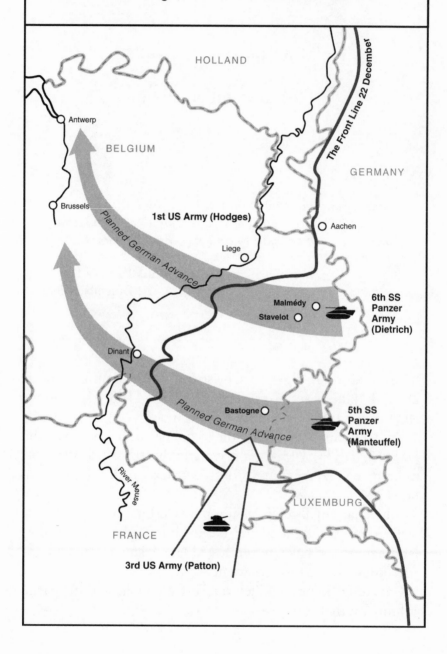

Battle of the Bulge, situation at 22 December 1944

18 December 1944. Obersturmbannfuehrer (Lieutenant-Colonel) Joachim 'Jochen' Peiper, at twenty-nine one of the youngest field commanders in the German *Waffen SS*, and his *Kampfgruppe Peiper* of the élite *SS Leibstandarte Adolf Hitler Division* (Hitler's personal guard division) have raced ahead of all other attacking units. Their objective: the capture of the rail and road bridges across the Meuse. His awesome *Tiger* and *Panther* panzers rattle through the outskirts of Stavelot.

'*Obersturmbannfuehrer*, stone bridge ahead. Must expect to be mined.'

'The hell with it, go for it!' yells Peiper, sure of victory in his grasp. His men have been specially selected for the job, all experienced in close combat. His panzers, the very best Germany can produce, flatten fences and punch their way through brick walls. They end up in the deserted Place du Marché of a small provincial town. That's where the American bazookas of a detachment under US Major Sollis open up. They cause more noise than harm. The driver of one *Tiger II*[1] is so baffled by the crash reverberating inside his steel hull that he loses control and drives into the side of a house. The whole building comes down on the tank; the 60-ton *Tiger* reverses, covered in dust and bricks. Another *Tiger* leaps forward and mashes the bazooka squad under its cleats. Machine-guns bark from tank turrets. Americans are hit and stumble; others dash into an alley, followed by a stream of tracer bullets. A GI jumps into a shell-hole to find that it is already taken by three dead buddies. Another party of Americans had placed themselves in a ditch behind a heavy machine-gun. Its bullets bounce off the steel monsters and spin into the sky with a sharp whine. A *Tiger* whips around on its axis and roars at the machine-gun. More huge *panzers* roll snarling down the main street until they come up against

---

[1] The latest version of the German main battle tank, *Panzer VI*, or *Tiger II*. It was more powerful than anything the Allies had.

their final barrier, a row of anti-tank mines. Tank-mounted infantry sprint ahead to remove the obstacle; they are caught in a deadly hail of bullets from another heavy machine-gun. Colonel Peiper's face turns to stone as he orders two of his *panzers* to explode the anti-tank mines placed across his advance. Two 60-ton *Tigers* advance. With a ball of fire, two *panzers* lie in the road, their tracks blown off. But the road is open and Peiper's steel-cleated juggernaut moves on.

The American major, acting more like a general who wants to fight it out with the entire German army, finally pulls out his men, with Peiper's *Tigers* in hot pursuit. There is something US Major Sollis knows, and the Germans do not. On the outskirts of Stavelot, well hidden under a canopy of trees, lie stacked thousands of oil drums: 13,000,000 litres of precious gasoline, the food of a *panzer*! God only knows what would happen if the Germans ever get hold of that treasure. In that event nobody could stop them. He knows what he has to do. In contrast to their German adversaries, where personal initiative is so often rewarded with a bullet in the neck, American officers frequently make decisions on the spot, without having to refer back to a superior at headquarters.

'Get a dozen drums, pour the stuff across the road, then blow that damn dump sky-high as soon as the first *Kraut* gets a smell of it,' orders Sollis. With that in mind, he places two bazooka units far enough away for their own safety, but close enough to blast a hole into the stacks of oil drums.

Fourteen *Tigers* of Spearhead Peiper are within two miles of the biggest gasoline depot on the western front. The first *Tiger* puts its blunt snout around a bend in the forest road when the tarmac in front of it bursts into flames. The column of fourteen *Tigers* comes to a sudden halt. Why run a curtain of fire if there is another road nearby? They reverse, and drive away from the burning road.

It is noon. The German *Ardennes Offensive* is fifty hours

old. Never before has an American army been caught so completely unprepared by a German assault.

'*Es muss unser absolutes Ziel sein, hier im Western die Sache offensiv zu bereinigen . . . das einzige, was diesmal night zu unserem Gunsten wirkt, ist die Luftlage. Aber gerade sie zwingt uns, unter allen Umständen jetzt das schlechte Wetter, den Winter auszunutzen.*' ('It must be our unique objective to clear up the situation in the West . . . the only thing not in our favour is the situation in the air. Therefore, we are forced to make the most of the bad weather, and the winter.')

Adolf Hitler's secret orders went out to his military commanders on 12 December 1944.[2] Ever since the encirclement of his armies at Falaise, and the Allied breakthrough at Avranches (July/August 1944), Hitler had been planning 'the ultimate and decisive offensive'. Allied armies had delivered Paris (at the end of August 1944). This was shortly followed by Montgomery's plan, code name '*Operation Market Garden*'. It called for a British group of armies to advance in one lightning thrust, assisted by parachute brigades, to take the bridge across the Rhine at Arnhem and, from there, roll into Germany through Holland. Nothing seemed to stop the Allied steam roller. Then, suddenly, their furious advance began to fade. This convinced the Allied Commander-in-Chief, General Eisenhower, on the advice of General Omar Bradley, to bring General Patton back into service to take command of the 3rd US Army. Patton was put into a holding pattern, and ordered to support the British effort at Arnhem by a diversionary push through southern Belgium. 'Market Garden' had turned into a disaster: the British and Free Polish paratroop brigades had been decimated, the attempt to break into the heart of Germany across Holland had come to nothing.

In the fall of 1944, the German High Command decided

---

[2] Warlimont, *Im HQ der Deutschen Wehrmacht*.

that the point to launch an offensive was from a geo-graphic bulge protruding from the German border into Luxemburg and Belgium, across the Ardennes Mountains, from Echternach in the south to Saint-Vith in the north. Hitler bestowed upon this forthcoming action an appropriate name, *'Die Wacht am Rhein'*[3] ('The Guard on the Rhine'[4]). This was changed in the last moment to *'Operation Herbstnebel'*, or 'Autumn fog', an appropriate name since the German thrust depended on bad weather.

Facing the Germans was a terrestrial group of armies under General Bradley: the 1st US Army of Hodges, the 9th of Simpson, and the 3rd under Patton. Even more worrisome was the huge Allied aerial armada: 4,700 fighter planes, 4,000 reconnaissance aircraft, and 6,000 medium and heavy bombers. That factor dictated a ground attack during an assured and prolonged period of bad weather.[5] German meteorologists, under the direction of a Dr Schuster, went to work. Having studied the prevailing conditions for a number of years, they settled on the beginning of December.

The impetuous General Patton was not at all happy in his supporting role; that was not his way of fighting a war. He called, pleaded with, and harangued General Eisenhower until he gave him permission to push the 3rd Army up to the Rhine before the onset of winter. Patton's XII Corps, under General Eddy, was to advance on Nancy, while the XX Corps of General Walker was to take Metz. The attack was set for 7 November. When General Eddy asked for a postponement owing to adverse weather conditions, General Patton cut him down in typical manner. 'If *you* cannot attack, kindly propose your successor.'

---

[3] Popular German song during the First World War.
[4] Poem by Max Schneckenburger 1819–49 *The Watch on the Rhine*.
[5] When warm air rises and cools to its *dewpoint temperature*, it forms into a visible accumulation of tiny water droplets or minute ice crystals, which then remain buoyant in the atmosphere. We call it a cloud, or a fog. It can hang there for a long time.

Eddy attacked on 8 November, and his tanks got bogged down in mud and minefields, while Metz held out until 22 November. Patton was furious, but this didn't solve his problem. As long as the weather didn't improve, his tanks were stopped.

On 16 November, supported by 2,500 heavy bombers, four divisions of the US 1st and 9th Armies went into action against the German border town of Aachen (Aix-la-Chapelle). The ensuing battle for the River Roer was bitter. For the first time, the Germans were with their backs against their own border. An idea of the kind of battle that would take place is provided in the struggle for Vossenach, a small crossroad village. German infantry abandoned it, then recaptured it, twenty-eight times! Their success in delaying the Allied ground superiority of eight to one in tanks set the stage for the forthcoming *Battle of the Bulge*[6]. All it took was a continuing spell of cloud cover. This was predicted for the second week of December. The offensive was postponed twice, but on 12 December, the date for the attack was set for 05.30 am, 16 December, 1944. Hitler had given specific orders to instil in the German soldier the spirit of the *Alte Fritz*. (Frederic II of Prussia) on the eve of his battle at Leuthen 2 December 1757):[7]

Soldaten der Westfront
Eure grosse Stunde hat geschlagen. Es geht ums Ganze!
(Your hour has come. All is at stake.)
Gez. (signed) Feldmarschall Gerd von Rundstedt. 16. Dezember 1944.

'Excellent, excellent,' mumbled a grim-faced Field Marshal

[6] The Germans call it *Ardenmen Offensiv*.
[7] Frederick the Great, his back to the wall, had achieved a last-minute victory over the Austrians about to invade Prussia. When the Prussian grenadiers walked into battle, singing, an officer asked the king: 'Majesty, shall I stop them?' 'Never! With such men God will assuredly grant me victory today.'

Gerd von Rundstedt, studying the latest weather report, 'the forecast is for the bad spell to continue.' Yes, bad weather was good news, because it would keep Allied air power nailed to the ground. The Germans could match tank for tank, but nothing their *Luftwaffe* could do would overcome the enemy's air superiority. Patton and his 3rd Army alone could call on 1,300 four-engined *Flying Fortresses* and *Liberator* bombers. Rundstedt knew what would happen should the Allied airfleets be able to take to the sky: they would make mincemeat of his *panzers*. Even Hitler's own operational directive specified '*to benefit from the effect of surprise and to attack during a period when weather conditions are unfavourable for the enemy's aviation*'.

Under the overall command of Field Marshal Gerd von Rundstedt, the German attack forces were made up of the Army Group B (Field Marshal Model), comprising (north-south) the 15 Army, *SS Obergruppenfuehrer* Sepp Dietrich's 6 *SS Panzer* Army (target Liege), General Hasso von Manteuffel's 5 *Panzer* Army (with target Antwerp), 7 Army, 1 Army, with Army Group H (General Blaskowitz) to secure their southern flank. The *Blitzkrieg* drive was to be conducted by the 6 *SS Panzers* and the 5 *Panzer* Army. In a final briefing at *OKW* (German High Command), it was stressed that the key to the German breakthrough was to capture intact the bridges across the Meuse, and that within forty-eight hours. This called for the speedy elimination of the Allied strongpoint of Saint-Vith and Bastogne. Once achieved, the *panzer* armies were to swing north and cut off the entire Allied forces in Belgium and Holland (Field Marshal Montgomery) in a similar enveloping movement like the one so successfully executed in June 1940. But this was no longer the German army of 1940; the *Vaterland* was in its sixth year of war, and the nation had suffered from terrible privations and irreplaceable losses. On the evening of the final briefing, all participants knew that the *Ardennes Offensive* was to be

Germany's last hurrah. If they could not reach their targets in forty-eight hours, all was lost.[8]

The *Wacht am Rhein* was ready. 250,000 German soldiers awaited the order to advance. Final preparations were completed. General Bayerlein, commander of Division '*Panzer Lehr*', ordered his supplies of precious gasoline to be stored inside a rail tunnel near the town of Cochem to keep it out of harm's way. It snowed during the night, and the countryside was sugar-dusted with a layer of pure white, which covered the horrors of the previous weeks of seesaw slaughter.

At precisely 05.30 am, on 16 December, 1944, the earth trembled under the impact of shells, while scores of *V-1 Flying Bombs* roared overhead, and a German *panzer* formation advanced across a winterscape.

The vanguard of *SS* General Dietrich's 6 *SS Panzers* raced against positions near Monschau, held by the V US Corps of General Gerow. Taken by complete surprise, Gerow threw in two battalions to bolster the hard-pressed units of his *99th Infantry Division*. In the Losheim *Graben* (Valley), units of the *Kampfgruppe Peiper* raced towards the positions of the nine hundred men of Colonel Mark Devine's *14th Cavalry Regiment* of the VIII US Corps. A small American unit under Lieutenant Bob Reppa and Sergeant John Bannister was destined to make the initial contact with Peiper's tanks. It had been a quiet week. For the first time they had taken a bath and changed their socks. Their heavy machine-gun was placed in a second storey farmhouse on the edge of the village of Krewinkel. From there, they could spray any advancing German infantry that might dare to attack again. But everyone knew the Germans were *kaput*. That was yesterday. Now they were crouched down behind their guns and fired until the barrels glowed. Lines of white-clad Germans advanced

---

[8] General Westphal, *Heer in Fesseln.*

across the open fields behind tracked vehicles. Within minutes, Bannister saw only the dead lying in the snow, and the wounded crawling back to the rear. He was sure that they had faced only a minor attack, and had successfully stopped it.

'Serge, they're turning us,' yelled one of his men.

'To hell with them. We stay.' That was before five huge *Panther* tanks made their appearance, and their shells took the village apart.

'Pull out, pull out,' yelled Reppa; 'make for Holzheim.'

Reppa established a new holding position at Holzheim. There he found to his dismay that the locals had already dumped anything that would connect them to the Americans onto a bonfire.

'Bastards,' mumbled one of Reppa's men, 'in a few minutes they're gonna hoist the Nazi flag.'

To their flank, a strong element of Manteuffel's *5 Panzer Army* was making for Saint-Vith where the *106th US Infantry Division* was in danger of being cut off, while the German main thrust was directed against Clervaux and Bastogne. This objective was handed to General Freiherr von Luttwitz and his *XLVII Panzer Korps*, consisting of the *2 Panzer Division*, the *26 Volkgrenadier Division*, and the *Panzerlehrdivision*, better known as *Panzer Lehr*.

General Fritz Bayerlein of *Panzer Lehr*[9] addressed his men: 'Our objective is the Meuse. This is the decisive battle of the entire war, and I expect from every one of you sacrifice and initiative. Let's go.' With that he jumped into the lead panzer. When his ADC tried to restrain him, he said only: 'What does it matter if I get killed today . . . ?'

In Allied GHQ, where the rapidly developing situation was anything but clear, General Bedell Smith turned to Omar

---

[9] *Panzerlehrdivision*, or tank-training division.

Bradley. 'Well, Brad, you've always asked for a counter-offensive. It seems, you've got yourself one.'

'Well yes,' replied Bradley, 'but I'll be damned if I wanted one this big.'[10]

US Brigadier-General Bruce Clarke had finally received permission to spend a few well-deserved days of rest in Paris when the phone rang. It was the division commander, Hasbruck. 'Your fun's been cancelled. By order of Brad. Get your *7th Tanks* over to Bastogne.'

'Why? What's up?'

'Don't ask me, nobody's got a clue.'

Bruce Clarke never made it to Bastogne. By order of General Middleton of VIII Corps, his tanks were redirected towards Saint-Vith. What he found there was hell.

During the night of 16–17 December 1,200 German élite paratroopers of the *Kommando von der Heydte* climbed into their JU-52 transport planes. Their objective: the crossroads of Baraque-Michel near the town of Malmédy. They were to hold it for the arrival of the *panzers* of *Kampfgruppe Peiper*. Lieutenant-Colonel Friedrich August von der Heydte dropped over the target at 03.30 am, but most of the other planes flew off-course owing to the atrocious weather conditions and an error in navigation. Fifteen JU-52s dropped their paratroopers – on Bonn! Only 200 men dropped on to the target, including their commander, who was badly wounded and captured by a US patrol near Monschau on 22 December. *Kommando von der Heydte* became a combat casualty before it even entered action.

That same day, 17 December, at around 1 pm, one of the most notorious and widely reported incidents of the entire war in the West took place. Heavy mist blanketed the snow-covered valleys, wispy clouds rose to the heights.

[10] John Toland, *Battle of the Bulge*.

Low-lying fog obscured what lay ahead in front of a vanguard from *Kampfgruppe Peiper*, rumbling along a secondary road towards the Belgian town of Malmédy. The *panzers* crawled through the mist, their guns ready to fire at anything that moved ahead of them. Tank crews stared through the tiny slits in the steel. Two open half-tracks drove as scouts ahead of the lumbering *panzers*. In the lead vehicle stood an officer, holding on to the top of the windscreen. What happened next has never been fully elucidated.

The lead half-track had just cleared a rise when suddenly, out of the fog, appeared a column of trucks belonging to an artillery spotter unit, Battery 'B' of the *285th US Field Observation Battalion*. The two German half-tracks ground to a halt, their machine-guns swivelled, and sent a stream of bullets into the truck column. The hapless Americans piled from their vehicles and stuck their hands in the air in the internationally agreed sign of surrender.

A German *SS* officer (the one in the half-track, but definitely not 'Jochen' Peiper) ordered the Americans to march into a field by the side of the road. Suddenly, several shots were fired.[11] 'The officer raised his machine pistol and fired at us,' stated a survivor, US Army Lieutenant Virgil T. Lary later. 'His first shot killed my driver. This was immediately followed by several bursts from machine-guns.'

The Americans threw themselves to the ground, but the mounted *SS* troopers kept spraying them with bullets. Many of the eighty-one Americans died right there. But not all. When the firing stopped, English speaking *SS*-men walked around the wounded and asked if they could be of help. Those who could still answer were then dispatched with pistol shots to the head. Forty-one wounded captives were thus killed. Within minutes after the shooting, the German unit revved

---

[11] According to the account given by Colonel Otto Skorzeny at his trial, Peiper, though later standing accused of the crime, was nowhere near the scene, but with another unit several miles off.

up their engines and moved out. The tanks disappeared in to the mist.

Lieutenant Lary stumbled to his feet and, with a few lucky survivors, eventually made it back to the American lines. Still in a state of shock, he gave an account of the atrocity committed. According to other accounts, some of the SS troops fired in passing at the dead and wounded, lying in the field. That random fire *after* the killing spree provided the basis for the subsequent trial of those concerned with the wilfully ordered *Massacre of Malmédy*.[12]

Of the various accounts available, not one tells the same story. The Germans claimed that the shooting started as soon as the American column – which they took to be armed – appeared out of the fog. The account by American survivors was unanimous: they jumped from their vehicles to surrender, then were ordered by an SS officer to move into the field *before* the shooting started. Once in the field, they were gunned down in cold blood. Nobody disputes the outcome. Eighty-one American soldiers died that morning.[13]

By nightfall of Day Two, *Panzer Lehr* had reached a position 16 kilometres east of Bastogne. Their advance had been handicapped by the bad condition of local farm roads. Bayerlein's problem was made worse by an infantry division, which had taken the same route and whose trucks had gridlocked vital intersections. Checking his map, General Bayerlein found that he had actually three roads to choose

---

[12] After the war, Lieutenant-Colonel Peiper and 74 of his men faced an Allied war crimes trial at Dachau. Peiper and 43 of his commandos were condemned to death. A political necessity (the Cold War) as well as legal controversy stopped the executions. Peiper was released from prison in 1956. He died during a mysterious fire in his Paris apartment in 1967.

[13] A Hollywood film showed the captives being brought to the field in German tarpaulin-covered trucks. That version has never been corroborated. The bodies, left lying in the field during the German advance, were recovered during the US counter-offensive. Pictures, taken by a US army photographer show clearly that none of the victims was armed.

from. The decision of which one to take was made during an encounter between a local peasant and a German general.

'Which road is the best to Bastogne?'

The farmer, having spent a few months in a POW camp, felt no love for anything remotely German. The moment he said: 'The one through Mageret,' he was sending them onto the worst possible route. After only two kilometres, the paving ended and the heavy advance units churned up the country lane into axle-deep mud. Support vehicles got stuck, others broke down and had to be pushed off to clear the road; the *Blitzkrieg* of *Panzer Lehr* was reduced to a crawl. It was not until 19 December that the first German units reached Mageret, two days behind schedule and still five kilometres from target. The snow and the atrocious weather conditions that kept the Allied airforces grounded had equally affected the Germans. It slowed up their *panzer* drive. Without knowing it, a peasant had saved the Allies: an unpaved country road was to be a key factor in the Americans' stand at Bastogne.

SS Colonel Peiper and US Lieutenant Reppa entered Honsfeld at about the same time, though from opposite directions. Peiper had tanks, Reppa had none. Before the Americans could slip out the back way, the *SS* knocked on the door of their hideout.

'*Ihr da drinnen, heraus mit erhobenen Händen.*'

Sergeant Lovelock, Reppa's ADC, opened the door: '*Kamerad*,' he said, with his hands clamped over his head.[14]

Without the slightest pause, Peiper pushed his tanks onward. His greatest concern was fuel for his *panzers*. A few miles from Honsfeld, Peiper's advance unit ran into a hastily erected roadblock manned by an infantry unit of the *2nd US Division*. The Americans had decided to make a stand, and

[14] Kurovski, *Von den Ardennen.*

their bazookas managed to knock out some German tracked vehicles. While this holding action was taking place, a reserve unit of the *7th US Tank Division* approached the village of Baugnetz and its *Shermans* ran into the main force of Peiper's *Tigers*. The American guns were no match for the mighty 88s of the German battle tanks that blasted their way through the village and from there took the direction of Ligneuville.

At the entrance of Ligneuville stood a lone sentry, a single *Sherman* tank. It had been left behind because one of its tracks needed repair. Gallantly, it fired once and, with a lucky hit, set the lead *Tiger* on fire, before three more *Tigers* turned their 88s on the heroic tank and pulverised it. Shortly after that brief engagement, Peiper's men captured an American officer driving past them in his jeep. After a hasty interrogation, Peiper jumped into the US colonel's own jeep and raced to his forward units, to stop them from firing. He didn't want to give advance warning to an American headquarters unit at the nearby town of Stavelot.

Peiper checked through his field-glasses. Two 57 mm anti-tank cannons were posted at either side of a stone bridge, barring his entry into town. 'Steinbatz,' he called to his second-in-command 'you take out the one on the left, I'll take the right.' Two long flames spat from the gun barrels, and two anti-tank guns were no more. The bridge was taken because there were no explosive charges attached to it. Before the Americans realised what was going on, the *Tigers* were upon them. The huge *panzers* rumbled into town. Two reached the Place du Marché when both were struck point-blank from shells of yet another 57 mm gun, put there by US Major Sollis. A *Tiger* stopped in its tracks and black smoke came from its turret. The tank crews threw themselves from their burning vehicles and rolled on the ground to douse the flames on their oily tanker's garb.

Fourteen *Tigers* of *Commando Körfken* crushed the lone-some 57 mm under their cleats, while the survivors of Major

Sollis's unit beat a hasty retreat, hotly pursued by Körfken's *Tigers*. The *panzer* swung into a forest road and reached a slight incline when, suddenly, the entire road in front of them erupted in flames. The burning gasoline barred their forward movement. Not realising it at the time, a scant five minutes and a half mile had separated the Germans from the 'big prize', the American gasoline storage depot of Stavelot holding 13,000,000 litres of fuel, more than enough to speed Hitler's *panzer* armies to Brussels and Paris.[15]

Now was the time for one of the most famous units in the American forces to cover themselves with glory. Following their night drop in Normandy on 5 June, the *101st US Airborne Division* had changed its general. Their new commander was Brigadier General Antony McAuliffe; shortly after the beginning of the German offensive, he had received a coded message to rush his division to the immediate assistance of Lieutenant-General Courtney Hodges' *1st US Army*. On the morning of 18 December, McAuliffe's 'Eleven Thousand' loaded into 380 trucks and headed 180 kilometres towards an obscure town in a wooded hill region in the south-eastern tip of Belgium: Bastogne. They were to reinforce the badly mauled *28th US Division*, under pressure from two German mobile divisions, *Panzer Lehr* and the *2nd German Panzer Division*. In a race for time, the *101st* made it into Bastogne only hours before *Panzer Lehr* was able to extricate itself from the mud at Mageret. McAuliffe ordered the *501st Regiment* commanded by Colonel Ewell to establish a defensive position along the hill-line east of Bastogne. He put his *506th Regiment* to the north and the *327th* to hold the south-east. When *Panzer Lehr* finally showed up, the Americans were well dug in. General Bayerlein had missed his rendezvous with history by one hour.

---

[15] The entire German offensive of three armies started with only 7,150,000 litres of fuel (General Jódl's diary).

It had been a night of dense ground fog when Bayerlein launched his attack at 5.30 am on 19 December, with tanks supported by infantry. The Americans had set up their machine-guns in a fixed fire-lane pattern and their crossfire peppered the mist. American shells screamed in, the sulphurous explosions turning the fog into yellow patchwork. In the confusion of their advance through dense fog, struck down by shells and bullets from the invisible American gunnery, the German *901st* and *902nd Regiments* were badly cut up. Bayerlein had to call a halt to the assault on the foothills around the city. His great worry was the weather. The German general had one eye on Bastogne and one on the sky and all was well as long as the bad weather held. Among the tank crews, one rumour had it that the Americans were ready to surrender, another that Patton's tanks were on their way. Patton or not, the power of the main German battle tanks was too overwhelming for the men of the *101st Airborne*. In a series of lightning strikes, the *panzers* outflanked the American units. By 21 December, the city was completely cut off from the rest of the Allied forces; Bastogne became a rock awash in the tide of German *panzers* and its defenders were headline news.

The mood in the crew-rooms of Allied airbases around Europe was at zero. Frustration alternated with despair. The bomber crews wanted to rush to the assistance of the beleaguered ground troops, but couldn't. For days the weathermen had promised that there was a possibility that the cloud might actually lift but at that moment there was no possibility at all of flying weather. The problem was not only clouds, but also altitude. The standard-issue altimeters were altogether inaccurate over a snowy landscape; their impulses beamed to the ground got lost in the mass of deep snow. It was virtually impossible to judge altitude or distance. To add to the problem the clouds and ground merged into a universal grey. Furthermore, radio conversations between ground scouts and aerial commanders were weak and incoherent. There was no way to tell up from down, friend from foe. They'd more than likely be bombing their own units. And thus pilots and crews sat and waited, day after day.

Enter Colonel Otto Skorzeny of the *Waffen-SS*. Six fighting years had left their mark on his face. As leader of a commando unit, he lived dangerously. But that was precisely what fate (and Hitler) had ordained him to do – Hitler's *Commando Extraordinary*. The man who had liberated Mussolini from his mountain prison, the commando leader his men called '*Der Schmissige*' (he had a gash – *schmiss* – across his cheek from a brawl in his youth), launched himself on *Operation Greif* (Griffon). Dressed as American MPs, his commandos were to infiltrate the enemy lines and make a pig's breakfast of communications and traffic. Their uniforms came from POW camps, but there they encountered a major problem: all POW uniforms had been overpainted in big letters: *KG*, for *Kriegsgefangener* (prisoner of war).

Hitler himself had sanctioned the commando operation. Skorzeny divided his men into individual combat teams and every team was provided with an American jeep. The operation started badly. On 21 December, while approaching Malmédy, a shell exploded in front of Skorzeny's command car. Shrapnel shattered the windscreen and the colonel hung from the passenger seat, his face and combat jacket covered in blood. His men pulled him out moments before the car's gas tank blew up. He looked dead, but he wasn't, and instead of allowing himself to be evacuated to a field hospital, he ordered the medic attending him to pass him a bottle of cognac, while the unit's doctor removed bone fragments and bandaged his wounds. The '*Schmissige*' had added another facial gash to his collection.

The wound didn't stop someone like Skorzeny. When he couldn't get enough American uniforms, he loaded his men into two captured American trucks, covered the backs with tarpaulin, and provided the two drivers with a 'Sammy' uniform. Off they went. The trucks, with their white stars on the cab, sped past American roadblocks and waved to heavily manned machine-gun positions. When they stopped, they cut telephone lines, turned signposts, and mined roads. Half a dozen jeeps, all that Skorzeny could get his hands on, set off to create a monster traffic jam behind the American front line. Their greatest success was with a US tank regiment. When the column of *Shermans* rolled up to an intersection, a team, dressed as MPs, redirected them, and for the next two days the headquarters of the US X Corps couldn't locate its tanks.

The end of this incredible adventure had to do with the German mania for saving material and space. Americans never put four MPs into a single jeep; hence the reason for the overcrowded jeep being stopped and its German cargo discovered. The *SS* men knew that as they were dressed in American uniforms they were destined for the firing squad as spies.

'You can shoot us,' said their leader without blinking an eyelid, 'but there are already thousands of us behind your lines.'

'Stop kidding me,' smiled the American interrogation officer. 'So, who's your valiant commander?'

'*Oberst* Skorzeny.' The smile left the American's face. That name was enough to panic the entire general staff. Special security arrangements had to be made, convoys slowed up, headquarters were given added protection,[16] roads had to be patrolled by troops needed at the front, and many more real Americans than Germans-dressed-as-Americans were arrested simply because they looked like Germans. An American captain, wearing German-type officer boots, spent a week in prison. Even a general suffered the ignominious fate of detention. 'I am General Bruce Clarke,' the general pronounced

[16] There was even a rumour that Skorzeny was out to kidnap General Eisenhower.

when his jeep was stopped at an intersection. The MP sergeant stared him in the eye. 'And I'm the Pope. Get in, you're under arrest.' Three dozen dedicated men had achieved what a division could not do.[17]

Kampfgruppe Peiper, their direct route cut by the furnace of burning fuel, had turned north, towards the hamlet of Trois-Pont, held by a small unit of American engineers with one 57 mm gun, which they placed at the entrance of the village near the only river crossing. The first *Tiger* burst into flames from a direct hit, before another tank silenced the gun. As the *panzers* advanced, the bridge disintegrated in a cloud of dust. The road was effectively cut, forcing Peiper into a further detour.

'How's our fuel situation?' he asked while studying his map.

'Critical.'

Peiper stabbed with his finger at the map. 'Stoumont. We're going through Stoumont, and by tomorrow night we're across the Meuse.'

At the *Hotel Britannica* in Spa, another man studied his map. General Courtney Hodges had to stop Peiper's shock advance.

'Collins,' he addressed his VII Corps commander, 'what have we got?'

'Nothing until tomorrow.'

'Well, let's send up a few planes.'

'In this weather?'

'Damn the weather . . .'

A few fighter-bombers of *9th Tactical Air Command* went up into the clouds. Suddenly they found a hole in the cloud cover, and there, right below them, was Peiper's column.

---

[17] From an interview by the author with Otto Skorzeny in Madrid, 1959.

They dived through the hole and set ten *Tigers* ablaze, while the rest of the *panzers* scrambled for the cover of trees. It stopped Peiper's advance until nightfall. Though only a relatively minor success, it provided a foretaste of what massive airstrikes could achieve against ground units bereft of aerial defence.

On the night of 19 December, Peiper drove his panzers towards Stoumont. They swept aside the meagre defences when an advance unit of fourteen *Shermans* and five 90 mm 'tank killers' emerged. It dawned on the Germans that these were not just some stray tanks, but the advance unit of a much larger group. Patton's army! Peiper ordered three *Tigers* to run interference. One tank hit a cluster of anti-tank mines and cartwheeled into a field where it flipped on its back, its crew killed, their necks broken by the explosion. The two tanks behind slid on the snowy field like sledges as they came to a sudden halt. Then their engines roared and turf was thrown up behind their cleats as they by-passed the mined passage and attacked.

This sudden counter-stroke, followed up by a company of *Panzergrenadiers* (foot troops), netted Peiper's men 133 soldiers of the *30th US Division*, including their leader, Major Hal McCown. Being informed of the Malmédy massacre, the American turned to the German panzer commander: 'Colonel, will you give me your word that nothing will happen to my men, according to the Geneva Convention?'

Peiper seemed taken aback by the major's demand (which is a good indication that he knew nothing of the Malmédy affair). 'I give you my word, Major,' he replied. And he certainly kept his word; he liberated all of his American captives, with the exception of Major McCown who managed to escape during the night.[18]

---

[18] McCown later stated that he had found Peiper not to be one of 'those bastard Huns'. This incident was used by the defence during the Peiper war crime trial.

Ever more American units rolled onto the field and soon the *Kampfgruppe* found themselves inside a pocket. Though Peiper still had just enough fuel to attempt a breakout, that option was denied by German HQ. His situation turned desperate. Driving in circles, his tanks soon lay out of action in the field, out of everything, gasoline and ammunition. He radioed his division commander, *SS* General Mohnke, who told him he couldn't help and that Peiper had to do with what he had left. He had nothing left, neither provisions for his men, fighting hunger and cold, nor 'Otto' (code-name for gasoline) nor 'Hermann' (ammo).

Again he tried. 'Request permission to withdraw my men.'

HQ's answer was crystal-clear: 'Denied, unless you bring back your tanks.'

Much valuable time had been wasted while a continuous stream of shells from American 155 mm howitzers decimated Peiper's *Kampftruppe*. He sent out more cries for help, but for the rest of the day, his radio remained silent. By the time Peiper decided to withdraw his men, and so risk a court-martial and a firing squad, the *82nd US Airborne* had dropped on Stavelot and reinforced the units who surrounded the remainder of *Kampfgruppe Peiper*.

'Damn those idiots,' cursed the young *panzer* commander. He turned to his radioman. 'Smash that bloody set. It is useless. Tonight we go back. By foot.' They did, after blowing up all of their *panzers*. Eight hundred men, sometimes up to their hips in snow, taking with them their wounded. When they met up with the encircling line of Americans, they shot their way out. The night was lit up by mortar flares and streaked by tracer bullets. The Germans faced dug-in artillery, heavy machine-guns, mortars, and squadrons of tanks. Despite the darkness and the confusion, soldiers forgot the danger they were in, and acted. Two *King Cobras* blocked their escape route. A *Panzerjäger* crawled up behind one, clamped a T-mine to the turret and pulled the stickpin.

A shattering explosion and the tank was a roaring mass of flames. Two men leaped out and rolled on the ground, extinguishing the flames of their tanker suits in the snow. The second tank blasted away with its gun. The trees shook from the impact of its heavy shells. The last of Peiper's 88s lined up on the tank's muzzle flashes. A tongue of flame, a direct hit and the way was cleared.

When Peiper's divisional HQ finally tried to contact him by radio, granting him permission to withdraw, their call remained unanswered. 'They're all dead, honourably dead,' thought General Mohnke. But no, they were not. They had suffered great losses, but Peiper kept control of the situation and brought his men through. On Christmas night, those left from a once proud *Kampfgruppe Peiper* finally reached the German lines, but they had nothing to celebrate.[19]

A week before, General Patton had ordered his chaplain, Captain James O'Neill, to prepare a prayer, which was transmitted to his troops by Armed Forces Radio on 22 December:

'Almighty and most merciful father, we humbly beseech Thee, of Thy great goodness, to restrain these immoderate rains with which we have to contend. *Grant us fair weather for Battle.*'

The lead vehicles of *Panzer Lehr* rumbled from the dark forest. A wide plain, covered by a thin layer of snow, swept towards them. It looked as if God had put out a shroud. During the night, the wind had obliterated the track marks of all previous passage. The German units were alone in the white world. The light was much brighter than on previous days. General Bayerlein had a worried air. His eyes were fixed on the sky. The wind had increased in strength. The cloud layer was still

---

[19] Peiper survived the war, and died in a fire, which broke out in his house in France on Bastille Day, 1967. Though foul play was established, followed by a brief investigation, the culprits were never found.

dense, but already along the higher ridges, clouds were lifted up like a great curtain.

There was no doubt, the weather was about to change.

By the afternoon of 22 December, the weather changed for an hour and the German ground troops got their first taste of Allied airpower.

A sergeant in Lieutenant Hinterholzer's unit of *Panzer Lehr* heard them first.

'Planes coming!'

'Relax, those are ours.'

'No, *Herr Lieutnant*, they're heading in from the west!' The sergeant's voice suppressed his anger. He knew as well as anyone in his group that those were not German planes. All the promises of close air support by Reichsmarschall Goering had turned out like everything else he had ever said, just empty promises. *Fat Hermann* had no more planes that could fly.

A dozen *P-47 Thunderbolt* fighter-bombers roared across their heads in a low-level attack and unloaded their deadly cargo on a nearby unit.

'Stay down, don't move. They haven't seen us.' And the lieutenant added silently: not yet. Those damn planes were there to stop them, but also to wear them down. Only when the noise had abated did they dare to move on.

General Patton paced the floor of his map room. Damn it, still no official go-ahead to put his tanks in action. Order or no order, he would open the noose the Germans were pulling ever tighter around McAuliffe and his valiant boys. Patton took a decision and launched his entire *3rd Army* into the face of a blinding snowstorm. His *4th Armoured Division* headed for Bastogne, the *26th* attacked in the direction of Witz, while the *80th* operated in a circling movement around the enemy's right flank. In the moonless night units lost contact with each other, traffic jams built up at intersections, broken-down tanks were simply pushed into the ditch to clear the roads. Patton pushed them on relentlessly. 'Head for the noise of gunfire,' he ordered his unit commanders. They could hear the distant rumble of massed German artillery pounding Bastogne. Patton didn't have to tell them, they all knew that they had to get there in a hurry; those guys of the *101st* couldn't last much longer.

The eyes of the western world were focused on a small place in the Ardennes. Could their boys hold out, those who had left their cities and farms in the United States, sailed across the stormy Atlantic, and then travelled on winter-bound roads to face the German onslaught?

22 December was a day of intense shelling and of continued explosions. Shells crashed and boomed into the positions around the city and into the houses of Bastogne. German artillery was taking no more chances and, with ruthless accuracy, pounded the town into rubble. The air was filled with the acrid stink of cordite. Bastogne became a cauldron of fragmented shells, fire, and dust, of wicked gouts of flame and singing shards of hot steel. Running through brickdust, past burning houses, company commanders found it impossible to make contact with their units. Encircled Bastogne had become a trap for the exhausted, shell-dazed boys from Minnesota, New Jersey, Iowa. The corpses of civilians and soldiers alike lay buried under its rubble. By nightfall, the city had become a wasteland of smoking timbers and charred bricks.

With his eyes fixed on his dial, and earphones clamped to his ears, the radio operator in General McAuliffe's command bunker suddenly looked up with a quizzical expression and then shouted for the general's deputy.

'Message from the Germans, sir.'

An hour later, four German officers under a flag of truce marched into Bastogne and were led to McAuliffe's headquarters. Their commander, General von Lüttwitz, demanded an immediate surrender.[20] McAuliffe took just enough time from his conference to find out what the hell this was all about.

'They're asking us to surrender, Crock.'

Without bothering to read the German document, he turned his back on the German and spoke a word that was to go down in history:

'*Nuts!*'

The swirling snow made it difficult for the boys in the trenches to distinguish friend from foe. The bad weather had strategic planners pacing the floor. 'The weather, that damned weather,' cursed the aircrews, sitting all dressed-up in their crew-rooms. The weatherman had promised them a change, but for the time being, the cloud cover was still so dense it made pigeons walk.

At first light on 23 December, despite heavy clouds and driving snow, the men in the trenches around Bastogne awoke to a terrific roar. Two hundred *P-47 Thunderbolt* fighter-bombers dropped out of the clouds and came thundering at rooftop level over the town. Their propeller wash tore the mist apart. From their bellies dropped large containers, falling gently to the ground from billowing yellow and red parachutes. Rations, fuel, and ammunition for the besieged garrison. For the Americans, it was Santa Claus coming down the chimney. For the German soldiers, suffering from a shortage of everything, this display of material abundance was an incredible spectacle. Here was a garrison, sealed off from all sides, and they were provided with all the goods the German transport system couldn't get to the front along open roads. And for the German commanders, pressure to bring matters to a conclusion was building. If *Thunderbolts* could fly under such

---

[20] General von Manteuffel was not informed of the surrender demand, and when he found out, was angry.

conditions and deliver on target, what could be expected once the skies cleared? Before that happened, Bastogne had to be taken! The *OKW* (German High Command) ordered their field commanders to launch 'an attack without retreat' and break the fortress. They fed battalion after battalion into the sector, and their final reserves of *panzers*. Fully resupplied with ammunition, McAluliffe's men stood, fought, and died.

The lonesome crew of a 57 mm anti-tank gun was dug in behind a barn. A company of *Tigers* crested a ridge and rumbled on menacingly, spreading their fire. The gun crew fired two shots before a direct hit silenced them forever. A monstrous 60 ton *Tiger II* overran the Americans' first-line defence, grinding to dust a machine-gun position. GIs threw satchel charges under the tank tracks. Explosions from petrol tanks and ammo boxes shook the ground. One sixty-tonner caught fire, but another took its place. The tanks were closely followed by a battalion of *Panzergrenadiers*, armed with flame-throwers and machine pistols. Mortar rounds fell all around them. Two *Shermans* put their noses around a house. One was immediately hit by an 88 mm shell from a *Tiger*. The other smashed into his stopped partner. American anti-tank guns blazed, their murderous crossfire taking its frightful toll. Another *Tiger* blew up. Its crew tried to get out from the turret but were cut down by shrapnel from a bazooka shell. The world had gone mad. German infantry and US paratroopers engaged in hand-to-hand combat, nobody knew any longer who was friend and who was enemy. In this individual com-bat, all leadership had ceased, and everything turned into a slaughter without plan or direction. The German waves attacked by day and they attacked by night. Bastogne held.

On Allied airbases throughout the European theatre, meteor-ologists read out their prediction for the coming morning, 24 December: 'Clear, with visibility 5 to 8 kilometres . . .' The rest was drowned under a mighty cheer from the bomber crews. Tomorrow they would fly.

'. . . *t'was the night before Christmas*' . . . Actually, it was a few nights before Christmas, December 22, when the prayer of Patton's chaplain was heard and the tired defenders of Bastogne looked up at a perfectly clear blue sky. Airfields, from the south of England to the Pas-de-Calais, from Italy and southern France sprang into action. Early that morning, people all across liberated France felt a ground-shaking thunder as swarms of Allied fighters and bombers, fuelled up and ready to take off for many days, took to the sky. There were so many clustering along the air lanes that squadrons had to fly wing to wing. All were headed for the same destination, there where the Meuse cut in a bulge through the mountains. *Lightnings, Thunderbolts, Mustangs, B-17s, Liberators*, they buried the German *panzers* under a deluge of bombs. Entire units of the feared *Waffen-SS* were frying in phosphorus. From the moment the weather cleared and the Germans were robbed of their cloud protection, vast airborne armadas strafed and bombed German ground troops.

High above the protective fighter screen flew the big, four-engined *B-17s*. Their pilots and crews watched from the corner of their eyes the strafing runs by the smaller but faster aircraft. They admired the courage of the fliers in the *Lightnings, Mustangs*, and *Thunderbolts*, pressing home their attacks through intense anti-aircraft fire. From the moment they pushed their sticks forwards when the aircrafts' noses dropped and their instrument dials whirled, it took twelve to fifteen seconds for the dive. Fifteen seconds of hell, of tracers and fragmenting steel. Until their own rockets streaked to the ground. On the edge of a forest, an entire column of vehicles disappeared in a single massive explosion.

A squadron of *P-51 Mustangs* buzzed the treeline, its pilots ready to strafe the moment the Germans gave away their position by anti-aircraft fire. Beyond the fighters came a big formation, black dots in a blue sky. The four-engined bombers could not be heard, but their first bombs began to strike the hillsides, followed by a storm of explosion, saturating the valley floor. General Bayerlein sat in his command *panzer* and looked on helplessly as clusters of 500-lb bombs burst among his men. The carpet of explosions flung trees and shattered vehicles into the air. At the receiving end were veterans of the heroic tank battles of the Kursk salient in the summer of '43; there they had bravely faced the hordes of Soviet *T-34*s, but against this mass assault from the skies they were without defence.

Every morning, they had stared at the sky and wondered: when will the clouds give way to a clear sky and our lives become snuffed out by a rain of fire. For the men of Germany's *panzer* divisions it was an unequal contest against the world's mightiest airforce. German anti-aircraft gunners attempted to lock on to their fast-approaching targets, while men and vehicles scrambled for the cover of trees. They never made it. The planes were simply too fast and their rockets too deadly. It was turning into a nightmare. Allied planes were within hearing all day long. Sometimes they were quite near, the cacophony of their engines howling above the treeline, two, three hundred feet up. At other times, it was just a distant rumble of bombs. Most unnerving for those on the ground was the uncertainty of a far-off engine noise coming nearer. Would they be the next targets?

'*Jetzt sitzen wir in der Scheisse* – They're gonna drop that shit on us . . .' jabbered a pimply-faced soldier, covering his head with his arms, as if that could stop a bomb.

'*Deckung!*' screamed Karli Prinz, a grizzled sergeant in *Panzer Lehr*, and pointed towards the head-on speck of a plane, racing towards their position. With a high-pitched roar the fighter swept over them.

'*Deck . . .*' An ear-splitting explosion cut off the rest of the shout. For the illusion of safety, he hugged the ground, a cloud of dust swept over him. From somewhere inside the red dust cloud came a slaughter-house din, the terrible mixture of shrieks ending in a thin wailing. The bomb had dropped onto the clearing where the wounded waited for evacuation.

General Bayerlein was to write in his report: 'The air bombardments continued without interruption. The Allies bombed everything without making the slightest distinction. Near Barriére and Champlon, vehicles of the division burned until next morning. Through my glasses, I could see enemy cargo-gliders coming in by the dozen and landing inside the Bastogne perimeter. In the beginning, my troops were spared, but not my supply columns. Our heaviest losses occurred when bombs obliterated two mobile tank repair units. As all our fuel stocks were far from us, at Troisdorf, on the long road to the front we've already lost over thirty petrol transporters. When we asked for aerial support to defend our vital supply columns, not a single *Luftwaffe* fighter showed up.'

It is true, the *Luftwaffe* was almost non-existent. On the rare occasion when some *Messerschmitts* or *Focke-Wulffs* turned up, they were outmanoeuvred and outgunned by swarms of *Mustangs* and *Thunderbolts* pouncing on them. The attrition rate was rising, and it took a special kind of courage for a German fighter pilot to come back for more. *Ritterkreuzträger* (Knight's Cross) Hauptmann Karl Kretschmann was one of them. He flew a war-weary *Messerschmitt BF 109*. When he had joined the *Luftwaffe* as a young pilot, this was the best flying machine in the war. Its nose-cannon had made it a fearful weapon. That was back in 1940, in another war altogether, or, as one of the captured 'Sammy' pilots had put it: 'Another ballgame'. Five years on and he was still flying the same obsolete fighter. But he had taught them a lesson. Minutes ago, he had downed two *P-51 Mustangs*. Must have been raw recruits. He had lined up behind the duo, his machine shuddering as the shells poured out. They smashed into the American planes, exploding in their fuselage. His wingman, a young kid just out of training school, was chased by a couple of *Thunderbolts*. A flame escaped from the engine canopy; the slipstream fanned it on until the fire engulfed the fighter. Then its dive steepened before it disappeared beneath the trees.

Kretschmann stared at the ball of fire and, for an instant, forgot to check his own tail. He caught a glimpse of sun flashing on metal, and that's what saved him. A *Mustang* was hanging on his tail. With the instinct of the seasoned flyer, he pushed his stick forward into a suicidal dive, then pulled up at the very last moment and skimmed full throttle a mere ten feet over the trees. The *Mustang*'s pilot misjudged his own move and its wing clipped a pine. The plane exploded in a ball of fire, its burning wreckage skipping across treetops before it disappeared into the woods. Kretschmann advanced the stick, and the sole presence of the German *Luftwaffe* climbed skyward.

The sound of shelling and bombing had become a steady, echoless rumble. The men of the *Waffen-SS* and the *Panzergrenadiere* stared at the sky overhead and saw contrails criss-crossing the blue. If it hadn't been war, the delicate lines would have been beautiful. But death was never beautiful. And those up there were American bombers with clusters of bombs in their fat bellies, ready to drop. For ground commanders like Sepp Dietrich and Hasso von Manteuffel, the next hours and days turned into a muddied, bloodied Armageddon.

Von Manteuffel called German High Command. He asked permission to turn north to achieve at least a partial success. General Jodl, chief of *OKW*, came on the line. 'The *Führer* forbids you to withdraw a single metre. *Vorwärts – niemals zurück.*'

General von Manteuffel knew that it was hopeless to argue his point. He did however change his divisions around Bastogne from an aggressive into a holding pattern.

About the same time, the advance units of Patton's tank units approached Bastogne. First in line was the *37th Tank*

Battalion of Colonel Creighton Abrams. Reaching the heights, with Bastogne before him, he radioed Patton's HQ from his command tank; *Thunderbolt IV.* 'Request permission to go straight for Bastogne.'

'Hold it, Creigh,' came the reply from one of Patton's ADCs, 'I'm going to ask the boss.' He did. When Patton learned of Abrams' request, he growled: 'Do I want to? *Let's go!*'

Abrams stood up in his tank. 'Everybody ready? All right, batten down the hatches and let's go! Today we'll be in Bastogne.' While Abrams' tanks raced for the German ring, American artillery from Bastogne opened up and annihilated the village of Assenois, only a mile from the city limit and heavily held by Germans. Abrams' tanks were getting close to the deadly artillery bombardment. 'Colonel, we're gonna get hit by that *shiiiit* from our own guns,' came a voice over the radio. It was the commander of a tank unit of forty-ton *King Cobras.*

'Go! Go!' yelled Abrams. And his nine *King Cobras* raced at top speed for the village, on into the village, and out on the other side. In a motorised re-enactment of the Charge of the Light Brigade, Abrams' tanks crushed anything in their way under their cleats or shot it to pieces. Once a hole had been punched through the German perimeter, infantry of the *80th US Division* poured through it. The lead tanks raced towards a forest. A forester's house was blasted into dust by a tank shell. In front of them, the ground was covered with coloured parachutes. Theirs? Ours? The tank gunners were so excited that they were prepared to fire on anything that moved, when, over the lip of a trench, a helmet appeared, followed by a face and the figure of a soldier in olive green, madly waving his arms while he stumbled through knee-deep snow towards the lead *King Cobra.* It was Lieutenant Webster of the *101st Airborne.* 'God, am I glad to see you guys.'

Patton's men had done their job. The siege of Bastogne was over.

The *Battle of the Bulge* was not over, but its outcome could no longer be reversed – the bombs and bullets of thousands of Allied aircraft made sure of it. Fire fell from the sky. The German road traffic, stretching bumper-to-bumper from the border, was strafed, bombed, annihilated. *Panzer Lehr* was a division only in name. During their retreat, they had skirted villages and avoided main roads by keeping mainly to the forest tracks. And still those cursed planes had found them. The division had performed their final death dance in an inferno of bombs.

The field in front of a tired General Bayerlein was devoid of life. The moonlight illuminated the snowscape, dotted with ugly black holes where the explosions had churned up the earth. Bombed and strafed, tanks and vehicles sprawled awkwardly, pieces of metal twisted into grotesque angles – crushed and flattened by a rain of bombs. Cold gun barrels pointed blindly at the moon. Scenes of destruction, proof of what hundreds of bombers could do to a *panzer* division.

Bayerlein rubbed his eyes; his division lay out there on the field, flattened and shattered. How many of his men had paid for their courage in that brief moment, when the forest disintegrated, when trees and men flew skywards, when the world ended. His world.[21] *Panzer Lehr*, the division that had come so close to achieving the breakthrough, and had marched into battle with 100 tanks and 11,000 men, ended the year 1944 with 10 tanks and 400 men. As a division, *Panzer Lehr* was finished.

Losses were great on both sides. Americans casualties were given as 75,600 soldiers, 733 tanks and 1,200 vehicles. Germany lost over 110,000 — killed, wounded, or taken prisoner, and most of its precious armour. Five hundred and fifty tanks were destroyed, many of them *Tigers* and *Panthers*;

[21] General Bayerlein ended the war as a Corps Commander.

5,000 other vehicles were left behind or bombed to bits, and 1,280 planes were shot down. The German *Luftwaffe* tried one more sortie. Air Marshal Goering ordered *Operation Grosser Schlag*. Early on 1 January 1945, 1,100 German fighter planes took off from their bases. Their order: destroy the Allied airpower, their airfields, their bases. *Focke Wulffs* and *Messerschmitts, Junkers* and *Dorniers*, anything that could fly took to the sky. A fatal error in planning put many squadrons into the well-established launch corridors of the *V-1 Flying Bombs* and directly into the most concentrated anti-aircraft curtain anywhere in the European theatre. Despite this defence, the Germans annihilated twenty-seven Allied airbases. But their sortie proved to be a pyrrhic victory. Three hundred and four German planes were shot down that morning, and the German *Luftwaffe* suffered their Waterloo.

On 3 January 1945, the Allies began a vast counter-offensive. The planes of US Airforce General Hap Arnold 'isolated the battle front' by carpet bombing and low-level strafing runs. It stopped supplies from reaching German front units. Out of fuel and ammunition, the Germans began to dynamite their equipment. On 13 January, the Soviets began their end-run for Berlin. The Germans had nothing left to put up against them, their *panzers* lay smashed and broken in the hills of the Ardennes. Hitler struggled to push pieces into a war puzzle where they were most needed. Only, he had no pieces left.

At 9.05 am, 16 January, advance elements of the *1st and 3rd US Armies* met near Houffalize. The *Battle of the Bulge* was over.

The *Ardennen Offensive* was the last major clash fought on the Western Front, with thousands of tanks and planes and a million men caught up in its horror. Perhaps the German soldiers believed in victory, but certainly not in their generals. They knew the truth.

In 1968, Hasso von Manteuffel, former army commander, summed it up:

'On 24 December, the weather changed. Allied forces had such aerial superiority that all movement by our units became impossible and supplies and fuel could no longer be brought up to the front. The idea to gain time in the West, by stopping the Americans, proved an ill-fated illusion. The only ones who profited were the Russians.'

Hitler may well have acted from a political afterthought when he ordered his last reserves to make a stand along the Ardennes. The way he looked at it (and in that respect, he was correct in his assessment), the Western powers could hardly want the Soviets to occupy all of Germany. Evidence for this comes from a recorded conversation between Hitler and Goering which took place at Hitler's HQ on 27 January 1945.[22]

Hitler: 'Do you really imagine that the British are enthused about the Soviet advance?'

Goering: 'They've entered the war to stop us from going east [i.e. Poland 1939], but not to allow the east to reach the shores of the Atlantic.'

If Hitler could halt the Western Allies long enough, their delay would create such panic in Washington and London that Germany might achieve a '*Separatfrieden*', a separate peace, with the Western powers.

The bitter truth was different. Those who still clung to the desperate hope for a 'final victory' were sadly disillusioned. The *Battle of the Bulge* became the funeral pyre of the once proud German *Wehrmacht*. Two land armies had been thrown senselessly into the fray against the mightiest assembly of planes the world had ever seen.

The day heaven's gate opened, Hitler's armies thundered into the inferno.

---

[22] Frederick Gilbert, *Hitler Directs the War*, Oxford 1950.

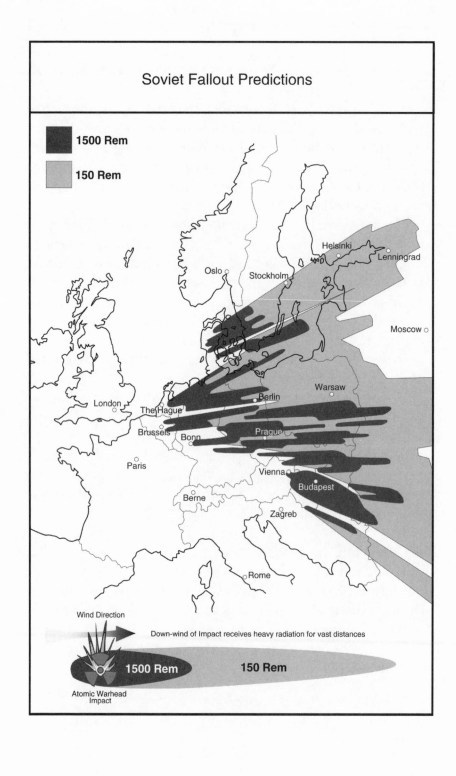

The wind factor

1945–1970

'The story is like the wind,' the bushman said,
'it comes from a far-off place, and we feel it.'
Laurens van der Post, *A Story like the Wind*

Weather has decided the destruction of a town.
The pilot of the sleek B-29 *Superfortress* knew his orders.

. . . TO DELIVER THE FIRST SPECIAL BOMB *AS SOON AS WEATHER WILL PERMIT VISUAL BOMBING* AFTER 3 AUGUST 1945, ON ONE OF THE TARGETS: KOKURA, NIIGATA, HIROSHIMA, NAGASAKI . . .

Since their take-off they have been flying over a cloud-covered Pacific. At 06.10, the clouds begin to break up, replaced by a thin veil of high-altitude cirrus clouds. At 07.00, the meteorologist observing in the US Airforce weather plane over Kokura reports heavy cloud cover over the target. A report from the weather aircraft over Niigata is similar, eight-tenths clouds. Finally, at 07.15 comes the coded message from the weather observer in the spotter plane over Hiroshima.

TWO TENTH CLOUD COVER LOWER ALTITUDE, AND TWO
TENTH AT 15,000 FEET.

'We've got a target,' announces Colonel Paul Tibbets and,
after a brief pause, he adds: 'Hiroshima.'

The flight crew slip into their bulky anti-flak suits. At
07.40, the four huge engines roar and the big siver-grey
aircraft climbs to 31,000 feet. Ten minutes later they achieve
landfall over one of the smaller Japanese home islands,
Shikoku. At 328 mph, the 'Enola Gay' heads for a city
on the horizon, sharply outlined in the morning sun. Their
precise target is the fork in the Ota River, the span of the
Aioi Bridge in the city centre.

The bomb doors open . . . a black, four-ton cylinder drops
from the gaping bomb bay . . . the arming wires are pulled
from the security latch . . . with a violent turn, Tibbets swings
the plane away from the target while below he sees three
parachutes open on a monster with a destructive force such
as the world has never before witnessed . . .

08.15, 6 August 1945. The world enters the Nuclear Age with
a searing flash. From now on, the spectre of a mushroom
cloud will hang over humanity.[1]

When Pavel Kolnikov looked up at the sky from the window
of his workers' flat in a suburb of Kiev, that night in 1962,
he didn't know how close to extinction he really was. This
was the height of a dramatic confrontation between the
two super-powers. That afternoon, the US President, John
F. Kennedy, had delivered an address to the nation in which
he made quite clear his intentions to stop the delivery of
missiles to Cuba. The Soviet Union reacted with a nuclear

---

[1] The first to react was the co-pilot, Captain Robert Lewis. 'My God, what have
we done . . . ?'

countdown. Now, Soviet *SS4* and *SS5* rockets, each armed with a two-megaton warhead, were poised to be launched on targets throughout Central Europe. Even if major cities were not primary targets, the civilian population would certainly suffer from an attack aimed at military objectives. (In military parlance, this was called a *plus bonus*.) An atomic strike was not meant to 'disrupt, degrade, and devastate,' but to 'annihilate'.

The horrifying spectre of a Soviet surprise attack, a bolt out of the blue on Central Europe, appeared time and time again, based on the idea that 'surprise is the paramount principle of war that belongs in the sphere of psychology'. Western politicians failed to mention the fact that the Soviet Union had begun to adopt a 'coexistence formula' as the determinant of its foreign policy that rested on the practical necessity of *avoiding* a thermonuclear war. They knew why.

Nuclear experts in both camps were fully aware that any Soviet nuclear strike on Central Europe would result in Russia's collective suicide. Not due to the West's nuclear retaliation, which would be unavoidable, but because of the permanently prevailing weather pattern. *The wind factor*. The dominant wind direction – west to east – in combination with the Earth's rotation, would have it that the radioactive cloud from a two-megaton bomb, if exploded over France's nuclear arsenal in the mountains of Provence, would rapidly extend to Kiev in the Ukraine. Or that a similar nuclear device, dropped on a NATO troop concentration at Germany's Fulda Gap, would irradiate Moscow within twenty-four hours.[2] Such was the equalising justice of the weather. Of course, one could expect sudden, brief changes in wind direction, but who dared to count on that?

---

[2] The Soviets rectified their miscalculation with their new *SS20* and *SS21* rockets, which carried a much smaller warhead with greater target precision. These represented a real danger, as their 'wind candle' fallout was minimal. (From studies by General Pierre Gallois, one of the foremost military strategists.)

The fact was, he who controlled the wind controlled the next nuclear war. This launched the powers into an intense research programme. Scientists suggested that to trigger large-scale reactions in the Earth's weather system was feasible. But to stimulate instabilities of climate, it would need to modify the interaction between air, land, and water. Suddenly, the world became conscious of the fragility of the environment as more diverse and sophisticated weapons were being developed. A new category of arms was on the horizon, weapons probably more pernicious and devastating than nuclear arms, designed to bring about changes in existing weather patterns and become the terror weapon of the next millennium. The avoidance of such peril was placed high on the agenda of the meeting between President Richard Nixon and his Soviet counterpart, Leonid Brezhnev, in July 1974. The key phrase appeared in the preamble to the draft resolution. 'Our two powers will undertake negotiations on ways to forestall attempts to modify the environment for military purposes that could have widespread, long-lasting and severe effects harmful to human welfare.'

The World Meteorological Organisation meeting in Washington in November 1974, issued an amplification of the statement, which included a more detailed assessment for different weather modification techniques. This led to a United Nation ban on altering weather in war, a proposal co-jointly sponsored by the United States and the Soviet Union on 3 September 1976 and signed in Geneva by the heads of twenty-five nations on 18 May 1977.[3] It called specifically for the environment's improvement and peaceful use. But how to define what is peaceful and what is military? Artificial dispersion of fog from an airport to assist the landing of civilian airliners is peaceful, but if an enemy needs to see what he bombs, dispersing fog is military and harmful. Artificial

[3] For the US, Cyrus Vance; for the USSR, Andrei Gromyko.

rain to help a 'dry country' feed its people is humane, to inundate the same country and drown it in mud, is not.

'I cannot believe that God plays dice with the universe,' said Albert Einstein.

It isn't God but man who is playing dice with the universe.

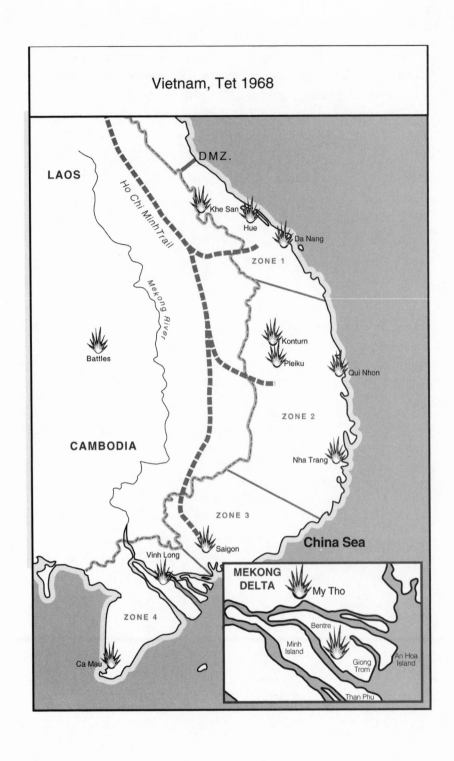

Vietnam, Tet 1968

Death in the Delta

2 August 1965

Last night, the big meteor came down and everyone went red and ugly.
An American GI, in the Mekong Delta, July 1965.

Vietnam, sultry mistress of the Mighty Mekong, pearl of South-East Asia, where the indigenous population spent a minimum of six months in the mud, and the moment it stopped monsooning or typhooning, a white sun fried their brains beneath their conical hats. Added to these joyous climactic conditions was a lush green jungle buzzing with beasties that sucked, stung, bit, or simply devoured. Under the dark canopy of lianas, thorns, rotting leaves covering a large portion of this exotic paradise could be found an abundance of red ants, black ants, orange ants, lice, fleas, hairy spiders, snakes, and that purple bag, the leech.

Those who had to live there showed a great divergence of interest, none of it healthy. There were Vietnamese regulars and Viet Cong guerrillas, CIA, KGB, Montagnards, Khmer war lords, Laotian poppy growers, Vietnamese drug dealers, Catholic missionaries, Buddhist monks, Chinese merchants,

French planters, and an army of hookers freely spreading clap, infective hepatitis, and syphilis.

There were booby traps, pungy sticks, anti-personnel mines, random artillery fire, Kalashnikovs, Agent Orange, black market bazookas, rotting bodies, and pimple-faced kids from Oklahoma and Wyoming, Indiana and New Jersey, wandering to little practical purpose across this landscape.

I spent almost ten years in Vietnam. Not as a soldier, but filming and reporting for a television network. I saw a lot of misery and a lot of death. I slugged it out through the paddies of the Delta, and crawled up vermin-infested paths in the Central Highlands. We all suffered. The bad guys like the good guys. Much had to do with the weather. Metal rusted, lenses misted up, leather mildewed, boots rotted. When it rained we were wet, and when it didn't rain we were still soaking wet from the humidity. The water we drank made us sick and the food we ate made us sick.

I stayed always with the 'good guys', because the good side is always the one you are on. I had once read a piece of wisdom by a historian, Sir Michael Howard. It was all about taking sides. 'First: do not. Second; if you do, pick a side. Third: pick the side that will win, and then make sure it does.' Well, we, the good guys, didn't. We were the heroes and they were the Charlies, Victor Charley for Viet Cong. They won.

Monsoon comes from the Arabic language and means season; it specially refers to the season when it rains. In the jungles and mountains of South-East Asia, the monsoon lasts from the beginning of April to mid-September. An important aspect of maintaining an effective fighting force is proper hygiene; mud and rain preclude this.

The French had found this out to their loss at Dien Bien Phu. They never intended to stay beyond the start of the monsoon, they were looking for a quick, decisive victory. But they had chosen their terrain badly, 300 kilometres from their Hanoi supply base, in a flat valley surrounded by high hills, covered with lush, tangled jungle. 'We cannot take these hills, so they cannot either,' was their logic. But Viet Minh General Nguyen Giap proved them wrong. Not only did he lay siege to the high ground, he then shut the gate and the French were caught in their own mousetrap. When the rains came, the Nam Youm River flooded and cut off the French camp. The rain submerged the trenches and fortifications with rivers of mud, setting off severe medical problems. Diarrhoea and typhoid became serial killers; even the lightly battle-wounded died of festering sores and gangrene. In this situation, where the operation depended entirely on its supplies and casualty evacuation on airlifts, no supplies reached the fighting units. The season had pulled a curtain over the valley, a permanent cloud cover. Artillery craters cut up the two landing strips and, in any case, the ground was too soggy to put down any large aircraft. While the besieged French had to rely entirely on modern transport, the Viet Minh used coolies to deliver material and supplies to their units. After suffering a month of continuous bombardment from Giap's artillery (every shell had to be brought in on the back of a coolie), the siege came to an end. Too ill to fight and too weak to walk, the French garrison of 7,000 men had to surrender. Not many survived their captivity.

Before any conflict, a general's job is to plan for the worst. The US generals may have heard of the French disaster at Dien Bien Phu, but they had not read the book; nor the account written by the French; nor the one written by their future nemesis, General Nguyen Giap, who had spelled it all out. But they must have heard of the jungle campaigns their own troops had to fight during World War Two in tropical regions[1] such as Burma and New Guinea. As it had there, weather was to become the Americans' biggest foe. After some

[1] By 'tropics' is generally meant the region between the Tropic of Cancer and the Tropic of Capricorn.

initial moves, and for the first time in their illustrious history, America stared at a very real possibility of humiliation. Still, they managed to land some solid punches.

When the United States stumbled blindly into the Asian quagmire, the war leaders kept telling their public one thing while knowing the actual picture to be quite different. On 8 March 1965, the first US Marines went ashore in Da Nang, in what General Westmoreland called a re-enactment of Iwo Jima. It was nothing like it. Instead of being met by bullets, local villagers stared curiously at the big, beefy men marching ashore, carrying their company flags. A Marine public relations officer, who had disembarked minutes before the main troops, distributed tiny American flags to the local kids.[2]

The crewcut boys, straight out of a boot camp somewhere in the States, were very green, naturally friendly, with the underlying seriousness of Americans, and pumped up with testerone; they brought with them frozen steaks, rock music and Coca-Cola. Around their hastily assembled camps grew regular tinsel-towns, where 'the boys' could forget all about the war in makeshift brothels. Some female radio voice, nicknamed 'Hanoi Hannah' gave joyless little propaganda chats. The Americans countered it with rock'n'roll on the American Forces Network, Veeetnaaam.

The nascent guerrilla movement, known as the Viet Cong, was anything but an efficient killing machine. In the beginning, their weapons consisted sometimes of metal tubes fixed by wire to a wooden stock, with a rubber band-and-nail firing-pin. They learned quickly and turned into masters of the ambush. Viet Cong seldom held the ground, but sought to strike, inflicting maximum casualties, only to withdraw before the enemy could react. They went around the

---

[2] The author was present, and his TV documentary 'The Mills of the Gods' was widely commented on.

countryside, lecturing the villagers on a glorious communist tomorrow and murdering some headmen who didn't want to listen. It so upset the powers in Saigon, that they sent their own goon squads to massacre some more villagers, standing accused of being Viet Cong supporters. This left more dead and more homeless, and played right into the hands of the VC. More joined the movement, until the 'communist threat to the region' began to glow on the radar screen of the White House. The State Department think-tank worried that some of their regional allies could begin to waver under red pressure. Their panic was emblematic of the problem of dealing with the cold war, as it was no secret that the Viet Cong received tacit support from the communist North. When the political pressure increased, Saigon cried for outside help and 'invited' some muscled assistance from the *Free World Forces*, i.e. the United States of America.

The US Army entered the Vietnam War as one of the best-equipped forces in the world. An innovation was their air-cavalry division, equipped with 435 helicopters.[3] Despite a relatively high state of combat readiness, the transition from peace in Texas, Michigan, or Idaho to war in the jungles of South-East Asia posed a serious problem for the army. The major weakness was the army's lack of preparation for the type of war it was about to engage in. The nuclear-war threat had made military planners forget that there existed also another kind of warfare, one fought by men on the ground, small-unit manoeuvres even to a point of hand-to-hand combat, and mainly fought under 'unfavourable meteorological conditions'. And so, the first arrivals of the huge American build-up had no experience in the type of warfare going on in Vietnam, and were given nothing but confusing last-minute

[3] Organised only three months before as an independent unit, the division disembarked in Qui Nhon on 28 September 1965.

instructions, sprinkled with a dose of 'anti-red sentiment', before leaving the States.

Within two weeks of stepping ashore, the weather changed and it began to rain. For the next months, rain was to follow the Americans everywhere. The struggle against nature took over from the fight against an elusive enemy. Faced by the force of the elements, modern technique had to surrender. Motorised transport sank into the mud. Helicopter pilots had to fly 'by the seat of their pants', slicing through cotton-candy clouds, hoping they would not fly into a mountain. 'It's a huge rush of adrenaline,' said a pilot, 'it's kind'a addictive, the faster and lower the better.' Such wasn't the case on the ground. Down in the paddies, foot patrols slogged it out in knee-deep mud, as if stomping in a bowl of molasses.

Other than a few boys from the Florida swamps, the majority of GIs were utterly unprepared for life in the tropics. Day after day they had to go out into the blinding monsoon rain. The water ran down inside their shirts, filled their boots and their pockets. The permanent dampness led to skin diseases. They swallowed pills by the handful and still got malaria, they stuffed their water bottles with water purifiers and ended up with diarrhoea, or worse. And yet, their future was not a walk in the rain; soon they would encounter the hardcore Viet Cong.

'Well, out on patrol it's quite scary, with all that rain coming down and you can't hear a thing. You get used to it after a while,' a young boy from Alabama told me.

'Have you?' I asked.

'Not exactly,' he said, with a drawn face.

I remember Master Sergeant Franklin, a tough veteran from the war in Korea and mother hen to his boys, who grieved already over possible casualties among his troops, once the 'big boys stop shadow-boxing'.

The day they were assigned to go into the Delta, he gave them a briefing. 'Every unit has a minimum of ten men, you're providing your own flanking security. We're gonna be dropped – here.' He stabbed at a red-circled spot on the map, next to a hamlet. 'Don't pay no attention to the village itself, you'll get a lot o' noise from the village – but it's a friendly village.'

Nobody ever looked forward to action in the Mekong Delta with its mud, leeches, and elusive Viet Cong. Add to that a terrain made soggy to the point of impassable by heavy monsoon rains, and the misery was complete. The boys might have heard of St Mere Eglise and Iwo Juna, but they were too young to know where these places were located. Not too young to have already tasted fire – only the day before two of their buddies had been killed while crossing a supposedly friendly village. They were learning fast never to suppose. It was hard to tell who was and who wasn't a VC.

The operational order was for a surprise airdrop on Bao, an island fringed by heavy mangroves, with a fertile plain of rice paddies, fruit trees, and coco palms. Aerial observation had indicated the presence of a sizeable troop of VC operating in the area, near Bentré. The action called for a co-ordinated operation between Vietnamese *Rangers* and Americans. Each was to protect the other's flank on a three-company movement on an S-and-D – *Search and Destroy* – or, in soldiers' slang, *Flush 'em and waste 'em*. To this purpose they carried automatic rifles, grenade throwers, bazookas, rockets tied to bamboo poles, coloured signal flares, blood plasma, and, most of them, a good-luck charm stuck in the strap on their helmets. They had blackened their rank badges with shoe polish; wristwatches and belt buckles had been turned to avoid reflection. The company lined up alongside a grassy strip. The operation was planned for 3 pm. It was now 4.30 pm. They sat, they waited, and they chased away the flies. The only active person was the battalion priest, identified by a cross on his helmet. He lifted a plastic Jesus and gave absolution to those that needed or wanted it.

Then they waited some more and listened to the chirping of crickets. One boy had his eyes wide open, a newcomer, not knowing what lay ahead. Another, the one with his eyes closed, had seen it before and suffered from baleful presentiments. One thought of his family or his sweetheart, and the one who moved his jaws thought only of his Hershey bar. Others just stared ahead, their minds already out there, in the swamps. I lay on my back, with a thick layer of anti-mosquito lotion on my face, my arms crossed behind my head, observing a pair of grey herons picking insects from the water. Idly the graceful birds ambled past us on stilt like legs. It could not have been more peaceful. Then the scene came alive to a faint hum. A swarm of flying scorpions appeared from the heat haze. Activity exploded across the field. Sergeants got their platoons in shape. That's when it began to rain, the heavy monsoon type that comes always when it's least expected, and in buckets. An inch a minute.

'C'mon you guys, lift yer asses.' We sloshed through the ankle-deep water; the whirling blades of the helicopters blasted us with rain, like grains in a sandstorm. As an 'accredited reporter', equipped with my plasticised green press card, I was assigned to a platoon in the second wave. A helicopter gunner with earphones clamped over his helmet cupped his hands and yelled to us that the first wave had taken casualties. As they approached the target, I saw Vietnamese Rangers with their brightly coloured helmets firing into a swamp. I couldn't spot the enemy, only endless green rice and splash marks where the bullets bit into the water. Before I jumped, I started the camera and locked the button so it wouldn't stop accidentally. I stayed glued to the platoon sergeant, a giant from a sand hole somewhere in Utah. We splashed through water, devoid of cover, two open targets in a flat landscape. My legs pumped, my boots were sucked into the mud. I felt I was moving in slow motion and every step became a nightmare. I cursed the VC, I cursed the war, but most of all, I cursed the goo that kept me from reaching a wall or a hole to hide. We had almost reached the edge of an irrigation channel leading to a hamlet when a stream of tracers flew at us. 'Scatter . . . scatter!' yelled the sergeant. For one of his boys, the warning came too late. He might have just made it but for the mud, which held him upright like someone caught in a vice. With a cry of agony, he staggered, his arms grasping at air, searching for support. I ducked instinctively before I hit the mud. The American lay moaning in it. One of his buddies dragged him behind a low earthen wall, which was actually a divider between rice paddies. There was no telltale muzzle flash but we knew that the snipers weren't far away. Twenty yards ahead of us was the rim of a bomb crater. I crawled towards it, hurtled over the edge and landed up to my neck in water. The platoon sergeant and the boy on his first combat mission slid down beside me.

'That's Charlie,' yelled the boy, poking his gun over the rim and sending a stream of fire at a row of reed huts.

'No kiddin',' muttered the sergeant, 'it surely ain't Santa Claus.'

With clammy fingers, I changed film rolls. I had just closed the lid when there was the most almighty bang and with it came a deluge of brown mud. A rocket-propelled grenade had slammed into the outer rim of our bomb crater. The rancid odour of cordite made my eyes smart.

One thing was sure: for once the surprise element had worked. The attack had dropped from the sky too suddenly for the hardcore Viet Cong to melt into the paddies and mangroves. Now they found themselves cornered in and around a hamlet, ready to fight it out.

'Heads down' the sergeant barked; 'lay covering fire!'

A heavy machine-gun laid tracers into the dun-coloured dam, shredding a bamboo thicket. The burst was answered by the harsh cracks from an AK-47 assault rifle.

The sergeant turned this head towards me: 'We're in the fuckin' middle o' them.'

From the top of our crater came a gurgling noise, like boots being forcibly pulled out of the mud. A Vietnamese Ranger had worked his way across from the other side of the earthen dam. Before he could reach our hole, a crack came from the end of the rice field. The Ranger threw up his arms, his knees gave way and he sank lifeless to the ground.

'Must get out o' that hole,' whispered Utah Jack. He slid up the bank like a cat. He swung himself over the low earthen dam. A second shot rang out, much closer this time. And another. A burst of machine-gun fire swept overhead, but it was too high and a rain of twigs and leaves came down on us. It was impossible to tell what was really going on and this uncertainty was becoming unbearable. Another murderous burst and the palm in front of us disintegrated. I saw two A-1 *Skyraiders* dive over us and towards a group of palms near the water's edge. The ground shook as their bombs struck. All that remained of the bamboo in front of us was a black cloud, with leaves showering down like confetti. After the dull thump of the heavy bombs, I could clearly distinguish the coughing of a heavy machine-gun. Ours? Theirs? What was it the sergeant had told me just before they went into action? 'Keep your head down. Bullets are invisible. You only hear a bullet after its no longer meant for you!'

I recalled that piece of advice as I peered over the edge of the crater. Our platoon was spread out, half submerged in the rice paddy, taking cover behind shallow paddy walls. I had just rolled away from one when another *Skyraider* raced over us with a terrifying howl at near paddy level. I ran a few steps before the ground gave from under my feet and I landed behind a dyke. Rubble and earth rained from a darkened sky. My mouth felt parched. Water – I craved for a drink. I took a quick swig from my water bottle. Helicopters raced towards the greasy cloud, their Gatling guns blazing.

'Eleven o'clock!' screamed the sergeant, and opened up with his carbine. Bang-bang – ratatat, bang, ratataaaa . . .

'What is it, sarge?' I hadn't seen a thing.

'Black pyjamas, I think we fried them muddafuckers.'

A mud-covered soldier, with his head bent low, zigzagged towards the sergeant. 'Charlie's over there' – he pointed to a set of palms – 'at two o'clock, about three hundred yards.' He tried to catch his breath. 'Them fuckers got in right between *Bravo* and us . . . they don't move so good now . . . I think we zapped them good.'

'Okay, get on the horn and tell Curly to get his ass over here and set up cover. I'm gonna take a look.'

'Check.' The soldier jumped up and doubled back to his position. A few moments later I noticed the machine-gunner signalling that he was ready. And so was the rest of the platoon, ready for the dash. I had to go with them to get what I had come for – pictures. 'What the heck,' I thought, 'let's just hope they're all dead.'

The sergeant whispered, 'Curly'd better know what he's doin'.'

He raised his arm, and pointed forward. The signal for attack.

'Let's go!' he screamed. Our machine-gun hammered as we splashed through the paddies. A black-clad figure jumped up, broke away and fell, cut in two by a burst from an automatic. I hurtled over another dyke and landed next to a black object, half submerged in the muddy water. Like some inflated inner tube, air had been trapped inside black clothing. A rifle stuck from the mud with a hand frozen on the trigger. The body lay face down.

'Sergeant,' I yelled, 'over here.'

Suddenly the body turned. I froze as Utah Jack let go with a blast. The body fell back. With his giant fist the sergeant grabbed the soggy black hair and pulled. A head rose from the water, a horrible sight, the face was gone. He let go, and the head flopped back into the mud. I shook all over my body.

'Damn close,' he said. I still had a lot to learn.

Three soldiers ran towards us and took a quick look at what a few moments ago had been a teenage boy. 'He should'na have run,' said one, blowing a balloon of bubble gum, which exploded and stuck to his lips.

'Sarge' called the radio man, '*Bravo* company is moving in, we're to cover their left and move alongside.'

'Anyone hurt?'

'Yeah, Burt's down. So is Curly and Billy-Joe.'

'How bad?'

'Dunno, they're waitin' for the medevac.' A group of men were huddled around their fallen buddies.

'All right, snap out of it, move it.' The sergeant turned towards a soldier and pointed at the corpse. 'Take this Charlie's gun, the rest of you guys follow me.'

We splashed on, then a burst from an automatic rang out. It came from an isolated cluster of huts on the edge of the hamlet. The platoon sergeant crawled on his belly along the ditch, towards the hut from where the fire had come. He poured a full magazine through the flimsy structure, then lobbed a grenade through the bead curtain. There was a sharp report and the firing ceased. The sergeant burst through the curtain to find four pyjama-clad men spread out in their blood.

'All clear,' he yelled.

The shooting had died down. It had been only ten minutes since we had piled out of the helicopter. But in these ten minutes, *Bravo* company had lost seven men. Covered with mire and soaking wet, we made our way through the knee-deep muck. Near the clump of trees we found four dead VCs and a Chinese-made heavy machine-gun. Where the bombs had struck clumps of earth and splintered bamboo had been churned into an impassable obstacle. In a tangled mess of branches, I noticed the bleeding carcass of a water buffalo impaled on the stump of a smashed palm. Napalm had left a black smear with charred forms, which could have been human. We reached the first hut of the village and found a Vietnamese Ranger who looked like a ghost. In front of him was the body of his dead comrade. Behind the hut were some more bodies, a family with faces with blue lips and eyelids that had been caught in the hail of fire. Next to the dead cowered an old woman. Her moan seemed to rise from the earth itself. The rest of the village looked abandoned.

'Sarge, something's in here.'

Inside the hut they found the body of an old man. Next to him, the wrinkled face of terror; another old woman who had never seen Americans. Her husband had bled to death. Behind the fireplace they discovered a hole, and in it a young man with a baby. Since he had been hiding it had to be assumed that he was a Viet Cong. They dragged him from the hut, clutching the baby. The sergeant pointed to the old woman: 'Give the baby to mama-san, come on, give baby to mama-san.'

The young man didn't understand or was too scared. A soldier took the screaming bundle and handed it to the old woman. Then they tied up the man's wrists and put a tag around his neck with place and time of capture.

'We'll bring back papa-san.'

The old woman fell to the ground, hanging on to the sergeant's trousers. The sergeant tried to move off, but she wouldn't let go. Two men pulled her off and carried her and the baby into the hut. 'Is this what war is all about?' I thought.

Near a palm grove stood a group of youngsters, motionless. There was little to be feared from them. Vietnamese Rangers rounded them up and prodded them with their gun barrels. An officer screamed at them and waved furiously with his pistol. One of the youngsters broke away. A shot rang out and the boy fell to the ground.

'My God, those are only simple peasant children.'

'Don't kid yerself,' mumbled the sergeant between his teeth.

'Hey, sarge, look what I found.' A soldier pointed his AR at another old woman cowering behind one of the big village rice jars, cuddling a toddler. The green young soldier, overjoyed at being alive, lifted his rifle and rummaged through his pockets. He came up with a Hershey bar. 'Mama-san, chocolate?'

The shrivelled-up crone grinned at him through betel-juice stained teeth. She put out her gnarled hand for the unexpected delicacy. Suddenly, the silence was shattered, a shot rang out and one of the Americans collapsed, holding his belly. The rest dived for cover, firing wildly at the invisible sniper. No one had paid any further attention to grandma who had dropped the bar of chocolate, and, from beneath the whimpering little boy, brought out a grenade, pulled the pin, and pitched it into the midst of the group of soldiers lying under cover behind the hut. The explosion killed the sergeant and four men. The only survivor whipped around and his burst cut the old hag in half.

It took another two hours of fighting, and the support of eight *Cobra* gunships, before the shooting finally stopped. The hamlet had been reduced to a heap of shattered, blackened rubble.[4]

The rain continued throughout the night. Next morning I felt ill. For the next ten days I was laid up in bed with high fever. I had survived the bullets, but not the parasites in the water I had so greedily swallowed to quench my thirst and calm my nerves.

In hindthought, it can be truly stated that the tropical jungle presented one of the most difficult environments for combat. Intense heat and continuous humidity broke down the built-in defences of the body. The rain bred clouds of deadly insects.

---

[4] This entire account is from the author's forthcoming book, *The Snow Owl*.

Hepatitis, malaria, typhoid fever were rampant, and minor wounds became infected by tetanus. Lockjaw, where muscles constricted, and faces froze into horrible masks.

The elements, more than the black-pyjamaed battalions, were the enemy. In the jungles and in the paddies of South-East Asia, nature was in control.

... and coming up next:

'Owning the Weather in 2025'

'The present is theirs, the future is mine.'
Nikola Tesla, electronic pioneer (1857–1943)

The dream to modify the weather is as ancient as the first primitive man who prayed for rain, or the fervent wish to bring down heaven's wrath on 'mine enemy'. In days of old, the task was left to a tribe's sorcerer or druid. Shamans shook rattles at the heavens to conjure up rain, witch doctors threw dried chicken bones into the air to end a drought, wizards mumbled sacred words and burned magic dust to make their foes die of thirst, medicine men danced around totem poles invoking magic to smite the tribe's enemy with a bolt of lightning. Even Moses had no qualms about asking God to visit upon his enemies the worst of suffering, and his God was ruthless and vengeful.

A few thousand years passed before man fired primitive bombards at clouds to explode them and bring down a flood of rain. And if that didn't work, those who sold them the guns and the powder simply said: 'Bad aim.'

Weather fronts are still as unpredictable and uncontrolled as they were during the days of Noah. Progress in the understanding of how to control the weather has been slow because of the complexity of our Earth's atmosphere, made up of different layers called 'belts'. These consist of the troposphere (from sea level to 16 kilometres above the earth's surface); the stratosphere (it contains the shielding ozone layer), which extends from 16 to 48 kilometres above the Earth; and the ionosphere (from 48 kilometres to the final barrier to protect us from cosmic rays), and the Van Allen Belt (at 3,200 kilometres distance), discovered in 1958 during the initial operation of America's first satellite, *Explorer I*.

For countless millenniums, earthman did not dare to intrude into the realm of the gods. Also, they did not have the means. This changed in 1944, when Germany launched the *V-2* rockets, designed strictly for a destructive purpose. It was said about the father of the rocket programme, Wernher von Braun, that 'he aimed for the stars, and sometimes hit London'. The interest in space research was launched following the Second World War for the delivery of guided missiles with nuclear capacity. Research into weapon technology and atmospheric research went hand in hand. This led to the discovery of the earth's different atmospheric belts.

The Cold War set the super-powers on a furious race for the control of space. Russia panicked the West with *Sputnik*, then sent Yuri Gagarin whizzing round the globe (1961). The United States launched itself on a series of 'galactic programmes.[1] *To mention a few*:

From August to September 1958, *Project Argus*, when the US Navy exploded three fission type nuclear bombs high above the South Atlantic Ocean. In addition, two hydrogen bombs were detonated over Johnston Island in the Pacific. The military called this 'the biggest scientific experiment ever

---

[1] Most of the following information comes from an article by Rosalie Bertell, PhD, who was appointed to the review panel of the *SPS* (*Solar Powered Satellite Project*). Other sources are C. L. Herzenberg, *Physics and Society*, 1994, and B. Eastlund, *Microwave News*, 1994.

undertaken'. Its purpose was to assess the impact of high-altitude nuclear explosions on radio transmissions, missile controls, and radar operations. Their next plan was to create a 'telecommunications shield' in the ionosphere. This was to be achieved by seeding a belt of orbiting copper needles in the ionospheric belt.

Project Starfish followed *Argus*. On 9 July 1962 another ionospheric experiment, the explosion of a 'one kiloton device' seriously disturbed the lower Van Allen Belt, substantially altering its shape and intensity. This experiment brought forth the protest of the Royal Astronomer, Sir Martin Ryle.

In 1968 followed the *SPS* (*Solar Powered Satellite Project*), intended to intercept solar radiation by using solar cells on satellites and transmit them in the form of energy via a microwave beam to a giant array of receiving antennae, called rectennae. The projected cost of the electricity produced was so far above that of conventional energy sources that the project was put on hold.

Although *SPS* was proposed ostensibly as an energy programme, it did carry significant military applications. As a psychological weapon, it was capable of causing general panic. By 1978, *SPS* research took a new turn when Michael J. Ozeroff pointed out the possibility of developing a satellite-borne beam weapon for anti-ballistic missile use. President Carter approved the project; however, the US Congress denied it funding. The same project, under a different name, resurfaced a few years later under Ronald Reagan, who moved it to the considerably larger budget of the Department of Defense. They called it *Star Wars*.

In 1975, the malfunction of a *Saturn V* rocket burned 'a large ionospheric hole' in the atmosphere that temporarily prevented all telecommunications over the Atlantic Ocean. This chance discovery led to a new type of research. By 1981, the NASA *Spacelab 3 Mission* of the Space Shuttle injected gases from the shuttle into the ionosphere from the Orbit

Manoeuvring System to induce 'ionospheric holes'. On 29 July 1985, a 47-second *OMS* burn produced the largest and most long-lived ionospheric hole to date. Another experiment in August 1985, lasting only six seconds at an attitude of 68 kilometres, produced a visible airglow, which covered more than 400,000 square kilometres over Connecticut.

During *Operation Desert Storm* (1991), the war against Iraq, it was reported[2] that the US deployed an *electromagnetic pulse weapon* designed to simulate the flash from a nuclear bomb. The Sandia National Laboratory had built a site on the Kirkland US Air Force Base (1989), to house the *Hermes II electron beam generator* capable of producing 20 trillion watt pulses for bursts lasting 20 billionths of a second.

In 1994, a rocket was launched from the Poker Flat Research Range, located 50 kilometres north of Fairbanks, Alaska, 'to understand chemical reactions in the atmosphere associated with global climate change'. Similar experiments have been launched from Churchill, Manitoba (Canada), such as those of March 1989, when two *Black Brant X* rockets and two *Nike Orion* rockets were launched into the skies over Canada, releasing barium at high altitudes and thereby seeding artificial clouds.

And finally came *HAARP*, (*High Frequency Active Auroral Research Program*), started on 18 October 1993 and jointly sponsored by the US Air Force and the US Navy, on a site based along the Tok Highway near Gakona, Alaska. Its task is to 'understand, simulate and control ionospheric processes that might alter the performance of communication and surveillance systems'. The project has been variously explained to the public as a non-military enterprise, a space shield against incoming weapons, or as a mechanism to repair the earth's ozone layer, *HAARP* is certainly an experiment that can be expanded, as it is closely related to fifty years of intensive

2 *Defense News*, April 1992.

studies to understand and control the upper atmosphere.

One of its research areas is into weather control or, under a military euphemism, *weather modification*. If technicians can eventually send radio signals into the Van Allen Belt, they could admittedly use Nikola Tesla's resonance effect to control global weather by triggering the release of vast energy sources over specific areas.

The modern era of weather modification began with a chance discovery. In 1946, scientists at the General Electric Corporation accidentally discovered that dry ice (frozen carbon dioxide) particles dropped in a cold chamber created ice crystals identical to those found in clouds. That launched a research intended principally for drought-stricken areas. The military speedily picked up on the idea.

During the Vietnam War US forces made the first serious application of weather modification in the pursuit of an armed conflict. In an attempt to increase rainfall, the *US Air Weather Service* used three modified *WC-130* cargo planes to release silver and lead iodine flares in order to seed clouds and precipitate rain showers over the Ho-Chi-Minh trail. This secret mission, code-named *Operation Popeye*, was to extend the regular monsoon season, drench the ground, and turn the vital supply route into impassable mud, thereby reducing the enemy's line of communication. Flying out of Udorn Airforce Base in Thailand, *Popeye* operated twelve hundred such rain-seeding sorties over North Vietnam, Cambodia, Laos, and South Vietnam. The operation was started in 1967 and continued until 1972. Reports about success or failure of the *Popeye* weather modification project varied, depending on the side that issued them.

This modification attempt, spraying salt from *C-123* cargo planes in order to suppress the morning ground fog on the runway of the beleaguered US Marines based at Khe-San, ended without positive results. (Today, the dissipation of cold fog, made up of liquid droplets at temperatures below freezing, has become routine weather-modification technology, performed at most major airports.)

In the early seventies, the American media revealed the secret weather operations,[3] and it ended in a public outcry. A congressional investigation was ordered. It led to the 1978 United Nation's treaty which banned 'environmental warfare'.

Operation Popeye showed the future potential for battle-field weather modification. The reason for the operation's failure was not only due to the limited knowledge of cloud seeding, available at the time. In 1965, at the early planning stage of the operation, the Truong San (Long Mountain) Strategic Supply Route – the Vietnamese name for the Ho Chi Minh trail – was a washed out dirt track, used by Montagnard tribes for hunting forays into the jungle. To take 'the trail' was to journey to the limits of human endurance. From September to February, at the height of the monsoon, floods washed away the man-made trails and streams turned into monstrous rivers. Knapsacks were so soaked that men broke down under their weight. The trail was passable only during the dry season, even for the famous 100,000 Uncle-Ho bicycles, pushed by hand. Even in the dry season, creeks had to be crossed on hair-raising, swaying bamboo bridges.[4] The North Vietnamese recognised the importance of a secure supply route and worked day and night to improve it.[5] The dirt track was turned into an all-weather road with a surface of crushed rock, or, where such was not feasible, a corduroyed log dam. A sophisticated drainage system ensured that the road could be used even during the heaviest monsoon

---

[3] *Operation Popeye* is not to be confused with *Agent Orange*, the defoliation programme.

[4] Wilfred Burchett, *Vietnam, Inside the Guerrilla War*, 1965.

[5] In 1979, the author met the North Vietnamese colonel in charge of the project in Hanoi, Colonel Van, who explained that bombing interfered with supplies reaching the front units, but bad weather did not.

rains. 'It was a road system of 13,000 kilometres along the South Vietnam border, doubling back and twisting around, like a car's fuel system, with North Vietnam as its filling station,' said Colonel Ha Van Lau, a Hanoi strategist. 'On it, we certainly sustained more casualties from the weather than from American bombs.'

'Wash out the trail!' was replaced with 'Zap Charlie Cong!' as the US military's key phrase. *B-52s* dumped 2,235,000 tons of bombs on the trail, but this didn't stop sixty tons of supplies from reaching the North Vietnamese units every day. Americans bombed the trail by day and Vietnamese filled the craters by night. When bombs did not do the job for them, Americans worked on *Plan Lava*, to turn the moist forest soil into slippery grease. That didn't work, nor did the homing pigeons with bomblets under their wings. They even came up with such harebrained ideas as dropping cans of Budweiser beer in order to get the enemy's truck drivers drunk. Fortunately, this never got off the drawing board.[6] 'The trail' was perhaps the last major conflict where man outwitted technology. For years, the Americans tried, and finally they had to admit that there was no way to stop traffic along the Ho Chi Minh trail.

Many other programmes were launched. Project *Prime Argus*, paid for with funds from the Defense Advanced Research Projects Agency, looked into ways of creating artificial earthquakes. The US Department of Defense sampled lightning manipulation studies in *Project Skyfire*. Another programme, *Project Stormfury*, began as a joint *US Navy* and *US Weather Bureau* experimental programme in the early sixties. It had peaceful applications, and its objective was a series of experiments on hurricanes for better understanding and prediction, and for controlling the path of these severe storms. These *stormchaser* planes, specially reinforced

[6] One of the harebrained ideas tried, according to Frank Snepp, CIA operative.

airframes, braved 150-mile winds to penetrate into the 'eye' of a hurricane. Though plane and crew were severely battered, valuable experience was gathered and not a single aircraft was lost.

By 1994 the US Air Force had revealed its *Spacecast 2020* master plan, including weather control, abiding by the UN charter that stated *'using environmental modification techniques to destroy, damage or injure another state [is] prohibited'*.

Artificially created weather patterns could not only influence enemy battlefield action, but also change behaviour and living patterns of an entire population. The thought is frightening, but it isn't new. That such effects could be achieved had been theorised a hundred years before, but nobody had the means to put it into practice and the project was put to sleep. Scientists picked up on the theories of a Yugoslav physicist, Nikola Tesla (1857–1943), who helped to discover *AC* (alternating current) and then applied his mind to the development of a viable transmission system for Hertzian waves. He expounded on the feasibility of modifying the emotional state of people.[7] Since those visionary days, tremendous progress has been made. In the far reaches of Alaska's Copper Valley stands the prototype of an ionospheric super-heater that makes a science fiction movie obsolete. Its concentrated energy from an array of forty-eight antennae, acting in concert like some focused ray gun, is beamed at a precise point in the ionosphere.[8] The emitted waves collide with the river of charged particles trapped in the ionosphere, forcing it to explode outward in a gigantic bubble, dubbed a 'plume', in an operation known as

---

[7] This can be used in a most positive manner. Dr Reijo Makela has already successfully demonstrated that certain chemicals in combination with VLF waves can alter a patient's debilitating disease. On the other hand, Dr Jose Delgado showed the disabling effects of electromagnetic waves on the human brain.

[8] The existence of the ionosphere was first discovered by Appleton and Barnet (UK scientists) in 1925.

'skybusting'. It can be used to study the effect of and, perhaps, control global warming and ozone depletion. Its end effects or applications are unknown.

A Texan physicist, Bernard J. Eastlund, filed a US Patent, No. 4,686,605: '*Method and Apparatus for Altering a Region in the Earth's Atmosphere, Ionosphere and/or Magnetosphere.*' His application was sealed for a year under a government secrecy order. According to the patent, 'large regions of the atmosphere could be lifted to a high altitude so that missiles encounter unexpected and unplanned drag forces with resultant destruction ... Weather modification is possible by altering upper atmosphere wind patterns, by constructing one or more plumes of atmospheric particles, which will act as a lens or focusing device ... molecular modifications of the atmosphere can take place so that positive *environmental effects can be achieved.*'[9] In other words, if proven successful, such technology could confuse or disrupt sophisticated guidance systems of aircraft and missiles, spray large areas of earth with electromagnetic waves, and modify our environment.

A century ago, Nikola Tesla wrote these prophetic words: 'The present is theirs, the future is mine.' He proved to be right. Today, influencing, or even modifying, weather patterns is no longer the figment of some mad scientist's imagination; it falls well within the power of the military and industrial complex of any nation that possesses advanced technology. The human being is an ideas machine, moving along at full capacity. What is today an idea, a dream, or a vision, is tomorrow's reality; ideas are funnelled into vast research programmes, which can help modify our lives and the lives of those who come after us.

A reluctance to discard conventional wisdom and embrace new ideas still persists. Many of us may welcome the projected

[9] Quoted in '*Angels don't Play this HAARP*' by Dr N. Begich and J. Manning, 1995. However, a *HAARP* project spokesman has assured this author that the experiment will have no military application.

developments as important advances in our knowledge and our ability to improve the quality of our lives; others again may consider them of questionable merit and regard them with alarm. Genetically engineered crops, alien seeds, and test tube maize for instance. There is no end to what scientists will dream up. To grow more food needs more sunshine and more water. In other words, the world needs sunshine and rain made to order for its transgenic tomatoes the size of pumpkins. Science, for all its marvels, has left humanity at a moral crossroad. Controlling the weather is one possibility. What has always been the domain of a Higher Being may soon no longer be His.

The next stage will be not *to forecast* but *to order up* the weather. By the beginning of the coming millennium, those who can master the weather will furthermore control cloud distribution, global precipitation, and with it, vegetation density. They will command global temperature and be able to stop or start desertification as well as dictate population density. This may well produce a phenomenon even more disquieting. If the present increase in the number of natural disasters can be directly linked to atmospheric overheating, a continued pursuit of man's interference with nature could bring on extreme climactic changes that could lead to dramatic consequences.[10]

In our present Age of Information, no place on earth is out of reach of spy satellites and remote sensory systems, which provide a multitude of information not only about the enemy's position, but also about developing weather patterns. Satellites and computer enhancement could turn a fog-shrouded terrain, such as the Allied airforces had to contend with during the Battle of the Bulge, into pristine clear countryside.[11] Accurate weather predictions are

[10] G. Bertz, head of ecological research, for the Munich Re Insurance Company.
[11] During the Gulf War (1991) and the Serbia conflict (1999), bombing was not hindered by dense cloud cover.

an indispensable tool for any deployment of forces, and will greatly benefit those who have them. General Eisenhower took a serious gamble when he ordered the invasion of Normandy, based entirely on an educated guess by his chief meteorologist. In the future, military planners will no longer be limited by existing weather patterns. They will be able to design the weather pattern they would like to have or wish to fall on their enemy. They will order up a storm, their technicians will turn on the rain tap and thus create an artificial mud barrier to stop the enemy's armoured columns. They will call up snowfalls, then introduce a sudden hot spell to melt the piled-up snow, and flood an entire region. They will destroy harvests with hailstorms, starve an enemy into submission by droughts, or burn down his forests with man-made thunderbolts.

As the Western world settles into an extended interwar routine,[12] it does so in an era of unprecedented change in scope of future warfare. In the coming millennium's geophysical battles, we may see warriors dressed up like space stormtroopers dispatching their thunderbolts from little black boxes at an enemy they don't even have to see in order to kill.

The military and scientists call it a new line of defence. What can the world look forward to in terms of sophisticated supertech weapons in a *geophysical conflict*?

1. Artificially launched floods.
2. Modification of ocean currents.
3. Diversion of tropical storms.
4. Opening of holes (skylights) in the atmosphere.
5. Extension of the polar icecap.
6. Artificially induced earthquakes.

America's military meteorologists believe they can win a weather war early in the next century. Their ray-antennae

---

[12] Not taking into account 'brushfire wars' or the role of 'the global gendarme'.

will heat the ionosphere to interrupt enemy communications, lasers will set off lightning to bring down attacking aircraft, unmanned planes will seed the atmosphere with microscopic black dust, creating rain and more rain. They will turn around the heavenly fan to redirect a nuclear fall-out pattern. China inundated, Europe frozen, California razed. The possibilities begin to look endless. Mine enemy of 2025, beware!

'*Weather as a Force Multiplier: Owning the Weather in 2025*', is the prophetic, if somewhat scary, title of a recent two-year study, undertaken on behalf of the US Air War College. It outlines in great detail an advanced nation's weather-modification capabilities.

'From enhancing friendly operations or disrupting those of the enemy via small-scale tailoring of natural weather patterns to complete dominance of global communications and counterspace control, weather-modification offers the war fighter a wide-range of possible options to defeat or coerce an adversary . . . *Some intervention tools exist today and others may be developed and refined in the future.*'[13] Their vision is that by 2025 the military will be able to influence weather on a gigantic scale in order to achieve favourable operational capabilities. It may also be claimed that a weather war will be less destructive than an atomic holocaust. I don't think that humanity should put it to the test.

The last time the military attempted to change weather patterns was in Vietnam. That misfired. Their next effort may well turn out differently. Tomorrow's warrior chiefs will be able to count on a weather arsenal of undreamed proportions. Supercomputers will have advanced atmosphere-monitoring and climate-manipulation down to a fine art. Weather is going to be delivered to order. To put no finer point to it, they, whoever 'they' are, will own the heavens.

---

[13] From *Weather as a Force Multiplier: Owning the Weather in 2025*, Chapter 15, Volume 3, USAF.

But so can all of mankind, especially future generations faced by a population explosion. Advanced technology can be applied in a most peaceful and beneficial manner, for instance to overcome the shortage of our drinkable water supply. A growing global population will put increasing pressure on water needs, and weather patterns could be adjusted to stimulate the growth of cereals and rain squalls could relieve droughts. While there is plenty of water on earth, it is not always in the right places, or in a drinkable condition. Chronic water shortages affect about one-third of the world's population.

By 2025, the estimated global population will reach nine billion, but only 0.26 per cent of the water on our planet is drinkable; the rest is either saline or too polluted to be fit for human consumption. According to a recent study by the *Water Research Institute*, 623 million in 26 countries no longer have access to pure drinking water. Even in Europe, only one out of every seven has 'healthy drinkwater'. In Israel, water distribution falls under 'defence security' and is controlled by the military.[14]

Since water obeys no man-made boundaries, there are often national quarrels over its use. Many of the wars in the last century were about oil, conflicts of the twenty-first century will be over water. A peaceful application of a weather-modification programme should not be expected to solve everything, but it could be a major advance in improving life in general.

Not everyone subscribes to the view that peaceful weather modification will improve our lives. Professor Thomas Malone, a meteorologist at the Holcomb Research Institute, predicted some years ago: 'The biological outcome of weather modification is apt to be a mixed bag of good and bad effects on man's artificial ecosystems.' Scientists would be well advised to let

[14] Nguyen Tien Duc, *L'humanité mourrat-elle de soif?*, Paris 1999.

the general public in on their secrets. The alternative could lead to an outcry of legitimate public concern and outlandish doomsday scenarios.

Destructive, or beneficial, the prediction of *owning the weather in 2025* may soon become a reality. Controlling the elements is a powerful symbol, linking man's awesome technological skill with his self-destructiveness. It is a massive global experiment where people and the environment are the guinea-pigs. Today's world is faced with an age-old dilemma: how to ensure that ideas which concern the modification of nature's weather forces are applied responsibly and after due thought.

Throughout the process of evolution, nature has developed over millions of years. Modifying the weather is a giant step. With it, man wants to be the orchestrator of the Promethean forces; he could well turn into a sorcerer's apprentice.

We cannot stop progress, but we all have to obey the law of nature. The 'ancient ones' blamed all evil on the Devil, and that included the weather. Naturally, nobody believes any longer that the Devil has anything to do with the weather. But some of us still derive comfort from watching a priest sprinkle holy water into the air, in the hope of assuring us that the weather during our next ski holiday – or upcoming air battle, should you happen to be a fighter pilot – will be bright and sunny.

Weather fronts are still as unpredictable as they were during the days of Noah. We must learn to live in harmony with nature. It would be folly for man to try to master the elements; there are simply too many imponderables.

There is only one certainty:

> *Man has managed to harness almost everything.*
> *But God still controls the elements.*

Bibliography

The lost legions of Varus

Bühler, J., *Deutsche Geschichte*, Leipzig 1934

Dio Cassius, second century AD, *The Reign of Augustus* (transl.), London 1987

Duenzelmann, *Der Schauplatz der Varusschlacht*, Gotha 1889

Hoops, J., *Generallexikon Germanische Altertumskunde*, Berlin 1984

Meyers Lexicon, *Arminius*, Vienna 1893

Mommsen, *Die Varusschlacht*, Berlin 1885

Secundus, Gaius Plinius, *Histori Naturalis*, AD 47.

Stieve, F., *Geschichte des Deutschen Volkes*, Munich 1943

Suetonius, Gaius Tranquillus, *Book 56*, (transl. R. Graves), London 1957

Tacitus, *Annales*.

Velleius Paterculus, AD 30

Verlag Wissenschaft, *Deutsche Geschichte*, Berlin 1965

Wais, Gerhard Julius, *Die Alamannen*, Berlin 1943

Archives, Institut Historique Allemande, Paris

The Divine Wind

Archives of Japanese Cultural Institute, Paris

Ballard, G.A., *Influence of the Sea on the Political History of Japan*, London 1921
Brinkley, F., *Japan*
Gibbon, *Mongols and Ottoman Turks*
History of Japan, *The Mongol Invasion*
Kodanasha Encycl., *The Mongol Invasion*, Tokyo 1983
Murdoch, J., *A History of Japan*, London 1903
Neumann, J., *Mongol Invasion of Japan*, American Meteorological Society, 1975
Yamada, Nakaba, *Ghenko – The Mongol Invasion of Japan*
Yule, *Marco Polo*
Illustrated books of Tosa artists, scroll paintings.

The night it rained on Paris

Aubrey, O., *La Revolution Francaise*, Paris 1945
Cabanes, Dr, *Le coup de pistolet du gendarme Merda*, Paris 1938
Caron, P., *Paris pendant le terreur*, Paris 1914
Courtois, E. B., *Rapport sur les evenements du 9 Thermidor*, 1794
Dictionnaire de la Revolution, 1880
Dulac, H. G., *Lettre en date du 7 Thermidor an III au representant du peuple*, 1795
Hamel, E., *Histoire de Robespierre et du coup d'état du 9 Thermidor*, Paris 1862
Madelin, L., *La Revolution*, Paris 1933
Mathiez, A., *le 9 Thermidor dans Autour de Robespierre*, Paris 1925
Méda, A.C., *Mémoire présenté au ministere de la guerre*, 30 Fructidor an X
Melie, E., *Les Sections de Paris*, Paris 1898
Tuetey, A., *Paris pendant la Revolution Francaise*, Paris 1890
Walter, G., *La Conjuration du 9 Thermidor*, Paris 1974
Warwick, C., *Robespierre and the French Revolution*, London 1909

Archives of the Bibliotheque de la Ville de Paris

The frozen armada

Archives, Institut Neerlandais, Paris
Archives nationales, Paris
Archives de la guerre, du 1er au 10 pluviôse, an III, par le general Salm, *4eme division*
Broeze, Bruijn, Gaastra, *Maritieme geschiedenis der Neder-landen*, Bussum 1977
Jourdan, J.B., *Memoires militaires de la campagne de 1794*, Paris 1796
Jourdan, A., and Leerssen, J., *Republique Batave et Armée francaise*, Amsterdam 1996
Lavisse, E., *Histoire de France contemporaine*, Paris 1920
Lahure, J., *L'echo de la fontiere*, Valenciennes 1846
Legrand, L., *Revolution Francaise en Hollande*, Paris 1895
Lettres sercrets entre Pichegru et Condé 1795, Vienna 1898
Revue du Cercle militaire, Paris 1887
Schama, S., *Patriots and Liberators*, New York 1977

A brave called Tecumseh

Berton, P., *The Invasion of Canada*
Berton, P., *Flames Across the Border*
Coles, H.L., *The War of 1812*, Chicago 1965
Crackel, T., *Queenston Heights, America's First Battles*, Kansas 1986
Eckert, A. W., *A Sorrow in Our Heart: The Life of Tecumseh*
McKenney, T.L., *History of the Indian Tribes in North America*, 1842
Richardson, J., and Casselman A.C., *War of 1812*, Toronto 1913
Tucker, G., *Tecumseh: Vision of Glory*, Indianapolis, 1956

Two bridges to cross

Aubrey, G., *Napeleon*, Paris 1936
Bourgogne, *Memoires de Sergeant Bourgogne*, 1899
Caulaincourt, Comte de, *Memoires*, London 1935
Chambray, Marquis de, *Histoire de l'expedition de Russie*
Chuquet, A., *La Guerre de Russie*, Paris 1912
Clausewitz, K., *Der Russland Feldzug*, Berlin 1843
Fournier, A., *Napoleon I*, London 1914
Markham, F., *Napoleon*, London 1963
Revue Historique, 1939–1946
Archives Nationales, Paris

The Great Potato Famine

Egan, Desmond, *Famine*, Dublin 1997
Edwards & Williams, *The Great Famine*, Dublin 1994
Hayden, Tom, *Irish Hunger*, Dublin 1997
Kee, R., *Ireland*, London 1980
Kinealy, C., *This Great Calamity*, Dublin 1994
O'Grada, Cormac, *Making History*, Dublin 1992
Woodham-Smith, C., *The Great Hunger*, Dublin 1962
Archives of the Irish College, Paris
Special thanks to Robert Kee for his permission to reprint excerpts form his work.

The white death

Bartelo/Fornaro/Rotasso, *Der Grosse Kried der Marmolada*
Italian Army Archives, *Sui campi di battaglia 1915–1918*
Kaiserschützenbund, *Die Marmolata*, Wien 1972
Langes, G., *La guerra fra rocce e gliacci*, Bolzano
Lichem, H. von, *Spielhahnstoss und Edelweiss*, Graz 1977
Mörl, A. von, *Standschützen verteidigen Tirol*, Innsbruck 1958

Österreichischer Generalsstab, *Österreich-Ungarns letzter Krieg*
Österreichischer Heeresmuseum, Archivabteilung Wien
Patera, H. von, *Unter Österreichs Fahnen*, Graz 1960
Pichler, C., *Der Krieg in Tirol*, Innsbruck 1924
Schaumann, W., *Führer zu den Schauplätzen des Gebirgskriegs*
Schemfil, V., *Col di Lana*, Bregenz, 1937
Trenker, L., *Berge in Flammen*, Vienna 1949.
Militärgeschichtliche Forschungsabteilung Wien, Dr W. Etschmann
Tales from the author's father, a participant in the mountain war 1915–1918

The week the panzers froze

Carrell, Paul, *Unternehmen Barbarossa*, Berlin 1963
Dahms, H. G., *Geschichte des 2. Weltkriegs*, Tübingen 1965
Das Kriegstagebuch des OKW, Frankfurt 1960
Dept of Army, *Effects of Climate on Combat in European Russia'*, Washington, DC, 1952
Frankland, N., *Decisive Battles*, London 1976
Goerlitz, W., *Ich stehe hier auf Befehl*, Goettingen 1961
Guillaume, A., *La guerre Germano-Sovietique*, Paris 1949
Hoffmann, J. *Stalins Vernichtungskrieg*, München 1995
Hossbach, F., *Gespraeche im Ostfeldzug*, Osterrode 1951
Hoth, H., *Panzer Operationen*, Heidelberg 1956
Jacobsen/Rohwer, *Entscheidungschlachten*, Frankfurt/Main 1960
Mackensen, E., *Das 3. Panzerkorps im Feldzug 1941/42*, 1959
Mann, M., *Vor Moskaus Toren*, FFM 1961
Orlow, A., *Kreml Geheimnisse*, Wuerzburg 1953
Ropp, T., *War in the Modern World*, 1962
Samsonov, A.S., *The Great Battle for Moscow*, Moscow 1956
Ueberschär, G., and Wette, W., *Unternehmen Barbarossa*, Paderborn 1984
Archives, Institut Historique Allemande, Paris

For those in peril on the sea

Calhoun, C. R., *Typhoon: The Other Enemy*, US Naval Institute, 1981

Costello, J., *The Pacific War*, London 1981

Halsey, W. F., *Admiral Halsey's Story*, New York 1947

Morison, S. E., *History of US Naval Operations*, Vol. 13, Boston 1959

A deluge of fire

Dahms, H. G., *Geschichte des 2. Weltkriegs*, Tübingen 1965

Gilbert, F., *Hitler Directs the War*, Oxford 1950

Hausser, P., *Waffen SS im Einsatz*, Goettingen 1953

Institut Historique Allemande, Paris, archival material

Jacobsen/Rohwer, *Entscheidungsschlachten*, Frankfurt/Main 1960

Kurovski, F., *Von den Ardennen zum Ruhrkessel*, Herford 1965

Landemer, H., *Les Waffen SS*, Paris 1972

Liddel-Hart, B.H., *The Other Side of the Hill*, London 1951

Manteuffel, H., *Die Schlacht in den Ardennen 1944–1945*

Schumann and Groehler, *Deutschland im 2. Weltkrieg*, Köln 1985

Skorzeny, Q., *Der unbekannte Krieg*

Toland, J., *Bastogne*, Paris 1963

Warlimont, *Im HQ der Deutschen Wehrmacht*, Frankfurt/Main 1962

Westphal, S., *Heer in Fesseln*

The author's two interviews with Otto Skorzeny, Madrid and Ireland, 1959

The Wind Factor

Le Monde, 19 June 1975

New York Times, 22 August 1975

Rhodes, R., *The Making of the Atomic Bomb*, London 1986

World Meteorlogical Organization, *Present State of Knowledge and Possible Practical Benefits in Some Fields of Weather Modification*, Washington, DC, 1974

Declassified documents of strategic studies by General Pierre Gallois, father of France's '*force de frappe*', and the author's personal conversations with General Pierre Gallois

Death in the Delta

Durschmied, E., *The Snow Owl* (in preparation)

Personal observations and interviews by the author during his years in Vietnam

'Owning the Weather in 2025'

Begich, Dr N. and Manning, J., *Angels don't Play this HAARP*, 1995

Hess, Wilmot N., *Weather and Climate Modification*, 1974

National Academy of Science, *Weather and Climate Modification*, Washington, DC, 1973

US Army Field Manual (100–5), Dept. of the Army, Washington, DC, 1982

World Meteorlogical Organization, *Present State of Knowledge and Possible Practical Benefits in Some Fields of Weather Modification*, Washington, DC, 1974

The author's interviews with authoritative sources, magazine and newspaper articles.

Index

909
D96